Aging Around the World

Donald O. Cowgill
University of Missouri, Columbia

Wadsworth Publishing Company
Belmont, California
A Division of Wadsworth, Inc.

Sociology Editor: Sheryl Fullerton
Production Editor: Jane Townsend
Managing Designer: Paula Shuhert
Designer: Lois Stanfield
Print Buyer: Barbara Britton
Copy Editor: Russell Fuller
Technical Illustrator: Lois Stanfield

Printed in the United States of America

1 2 3 4 5 6 7 8 9 10—89 88 87 86 85

ISBN 0-534-05166-9

Library of Congress Cataloging in Publication Data

Cowgill, Donald O. (Donald Olen), 1911–
   Aging around the world.

   Bibliography: p.
   Includes index.
   1. Aged—Cross-cultural studies. 2. Aging—Cross—
cultural studies. 3. Social status—Cross-cultural
studies. I. Title.
HV1451.C65 1986   305.2'6   85-7174
ISBN 0-534-05166-9

To Mary
whose love and confidence
have inspired me
for fifty golden years

Contents

Preface

Most of the reports on aging in various societies have appeared in disparate case studies. Although many of these materials have been collected in anthologies, only once (Cowgill and Holmes, 1972) has a serious attempt been made to formulate a theory based upon the cases presented. Fortunately, the cases and anthologies have continued to accumulate, and it now appears possible to pull these materials together, not as disparate cases but as an integrated study of *Aging Around the World*. This should show us both the commonalities and varieties of the aging experience as it has been reported from various parts of the world.

This is not an easy task. The pertinent materials are scattered in many different sources. The physical task of collecting them has been difficult, and the mental task of assimilating them has been formidable. There is no uniformity of definition, method, sample, or range of subject matter. One cannot assume that the term *old* means the same thing in different cultural contexts. In fact, it does not; the criteria for measuring age vary, and even when it is measured in years, there is little agreement as to when old age begins. Some societies consider people old at age 50, while others restrict the term to much later chronological ages. Are reports based upon such divergent definitions really comparable?

Through the years anthropologists have relied primarily upon a participant observer methodology, which has built-in pitfalls for anyone who tries to compare reports from one researcher with those of another. The role of the participant inevitably affects what one is able to observe. For example, the sex of the observer may facilitate access to information in regard to his/her own sex while blocking access to information that is privy only to members of the opposite sex in that society. One reason for the dearth of information about older women in many societies may be that most of the anthropologists studying those societies have been males.

Researchers who rely upon the participant observer method ordinarily give little attention to sampling technique; consequently, others utilizing their reports cannot be sure of the generality of their findings. This becomes increasingly important as populations increase and societies become more complex. No longer can one observer encompass all the variations to be found within a society, and no longer can one community be taken as representative of the whole society.

Only within the last 20 years have anthropologists given much attention to the roles of the elderly in the societies they have studied. Though they have always made extensive use of older informants, they had not previously studied older people per se. Consequently, the information about older people in earlier research is very thin and quite spotty. There is no uniformity in terms of the range of subject matter reported. The samples of societies that provide information about given topics shift with each new topic. Even now there is no standard range of topics covered or questions asked. Therefore, the comparative study of aging in different societies poses risks of misinterpretation. I have done my best to avoid such distortions.

Some readers may think that I have overemphasized the role of modernization in changing the role and status of the aged. I do not think that I have. Though I certainly do not claim to have originated the theory that the status of the aged has declined with modernization, I have been one proponent and expositor of the theory. With the accumulation of historical and comparative evidence, it has become increasingly clear that the theory must be tempered and qualified, but with appropriate qualifications the theory remains the most valid and meaningful framework for the interpretation of the comparative status and role of the elderly in various societies. Holding such a view, I would be dishonest to withhold it or to advocate an alternative. Other theories of aging have been propounded; they are stated in Chapter 1 and are evaluated in the light of the evidence presented in this book in Chapter 8. In general, I find them invalid, irrelevant, or less meaningful for the purposes of comparative gerontology than modernization theory, which remains the basic theoretical perspective of the book.

In Chapter 1 I raise these issues in addition to discussing the problems of definition, methodology, and perspective in greater detail. In Chapter 2 I provide a comparative demography of aging that shows the extent of demographic aging in different parts of the world, the reasons for demographic aging, the probability of its occurrence in developing nations, and some characteristics of older populations.

In Chapter 3 I describe some general value systems pertinent to aging that are found in various cultures around the world. Certain value systems, such as filial piety and familism, are ostensibly favorable to the status and security of older people. But others, such as the work ethic, egalitarianism, individualism, and the cult of youth, are generally inimical to the welfare of the aged. I delineate these in some detail, along with the place of occurrence and description of their consequences for older people.

In Chapter 4 I outline some of the major varieties of kinship systems found in various parts of the world and some different types of household living units associated with specific kinds of kinship systems, and I discuss how these relate to older people. I review four illustrations in some detail and then discuss how families and kinship systems are adapting to industrialization and to the accompanying aging of populations. In the latter part of the chapter the focus shifts to the roles that older people play in relation to their families and kin. In preindustrial societies older people, often widowed, usually live in the same household with some of their children and grandchildren and share in both the tasks and the substance of this haven. In modernized societies they more commonly live in separate dwellings and are maintained by separate incomes, but the roles of parents and grandparents are still significant in terms of mutual aid and affection.

I begin Chapter 5 with an outline of some major types of economic systems and then note how these systems relate to aging persons. In most preindustrial societies people continue as productive workers as long as they are able. However, in industrial societies where much demographic aging has occurred, retirement has become a general practice, and it takes place on the basis of age rather than occupational competence. In preindustrial societies the responsibility for persons unable to care for themselves has partly shifted to a larger corporate unit, which becomes the administering body for pensions or social security. Toward the end of the chapter, I turn to the economic roles that older people themselves play. In some societies, chiefly agricultural or pastoral, males follow an ascending pattern of economic involvement and arrive in old age at the peak of their performance. In others the pattern is one of continuity as long as physical strength and mental competence permit. In modernized societies the policy of arbitrary retirement terminates the major economic role of older people even when they are still fully capable.

Older people play important political roles in many societies. As shown in Chapter 6, these vary with the political structure of the society and range from administrative to judicial to policy making roles and in some include the role of elder statesman. Again, in some societies there is a continuously ascendant pattern, most pronounced in those that are called gerontocracies, but in others retirement from political roles is either required or expected. For whatever reasons, older males are much more in evidence as political leaders than older women.

In Chapter 7 I deal with the religious and educational roles of older people. They have often been magicians, prophets, medicine men, and priests, and age is often an advantage if not a requirement for such a role. Age is also widely associated with experience and wisdom, and, particularly in preliterate societies, the aged are the teachers and repositories of knowledge. One clear effect of modernization has been to destroy this role for elders.

In the final chapter I try to summarize the material of the book and reassess its import. At that point readers will want to ask themselves some questions. How prevalent is the pattern of disengagement among older people in different societies? Is it a necessary and functional aspect of aging everywhere? How extensive is activity as a social norm and social role around the world? Does comparison of different cultures support or refute activity theory? Do all cultures prescribe mutual obligations of successive generations, and are these always viewed as a normative exchange process? Does exchange theory add to our understanding of the meaning of aging in different societies? What effect does general social change have upon the elderly? How do we evaluate modernization theory in the light of comparative gerontology?

I wish to make clear the point of view I bring to this material. I am a retired sociologist with a long-term interest in aging, and I have witnessed the origin and development of social gerontology. I have also been a participant observer in many parts of the world. Though I began my career as a demographer-ecologist, my international experience and lifelong involvement in community affairs led me increasingly in late years to concentrate on the interplay between individuals changing and adapting with the passage of time (aging), families and communities undergoing major structural changes (developing), and whole societies experiencing massive social change (modernization). As a sociologist my major concern has been with the impact of broad societal and cultural changes upon smaller social units, such as families and communities, and upon individuals. Although this is my major perspective, I am aware that some individuals and some small social groups are the ultimate initiators of some of that societal change. It is a matter of perspective.

I do not view aging as a problem; individually it is an achievement.

There may be problems at any age, and some types of problems merely become more probable in old age. Demographic aging is also a social achievement. It is a recent historical development that is a part of the process called modernization. The social problems associated with it are temporary maladjustments that may be quite accurately diagnosed as cultural lags in adapting our social institutions to the new realities of demography. Never before have most married couples had only one or two births; never before have 98 percent of the babies survived infancy; never before could they count on living at least 70 years; never before have children had such a high proportion of grandparents and great-grandparents still alive; never before have one out of six or seven people in the population been 65 or over. Societies are just beginning to readjust to the twin realities of so few children and so many older people. It remains to be seen whether the demographic balance will stabilize long enough for the institutions and culture to catch up.

Certainly no society is static. Even what are or recently were traditional or folk societies are changing, and they are or soon will be aging. This will force further change. Simmons' statement that aging is like riding a bicycle, "if you stop, you fall" (1959:6), is almost as apt for demographic aging as it is for individual aging. Institutions, like individuals, are constantly changing (Amoss and Harrell, 1981:5). Institutions are essentially man's collective habits, and individuals are guided by them but not imprisoned in them. Unfortunately, we never see change per se; we merely see differences between the way people act at one time and the way they act at a subsequent time or, more frequently, the way one group behaves as compared with another that formerly, we think, was culturally akin. We infer that the latter group has changed. Actually both have changed, although they may be changing at different speeds or in slightly different directions. This book is a collection of still pictures of various peoples caught at different stages of their cultural adaptation to a whole host of pressures, one of which may be demographic aging. We will have to infer prior social change, and any judgments as to their current state of development will also rest on inference.

I also assume that in other societies, as in my own, older people are more diverse than any other age group. They differ more from each other and there is greater heterogeneity among them as an aggregate than among younger people in their society. Actually, if this were original research, I would treat this generalization as a hypothesis rather than an assumption, but since this is a reivew of secondary materials that will rarely provide the evidence for such a judgment, the assumption must be acknowledged. It means that I will be wary of statements that imply uniformity among aged individuals within a society, traditional as well as modern. It also means that I will try to be sensitive to variations by region, ethnic group, and gender.

It is impossible to acknowledge or even be aware of all of one's intellectual debts. The references throughout this work signify obligations for particular ideas and facts. But there are debts of a more general nature, debts of philosophy and perspective, debts of personal influence and encouragement. Stuart A. Queen, at 95 years of age, is still my primary professional role model, as he has been throughout my career. Lowell D. Holmes, my erstwhile collaborator, first challenged me to enter the realm of comparative gerontology and continues to challenge me as critic and competitor. Through the years students have provided continual stimulation and challenge; in recent years these have included Barbara Brents, James K. Callihan, Ann Gowans, Ja-soon Koo, Teri Shumate, and Leann Tigges. James K. Callihan assisted with early phases of research for this book and wrote the original draft of the section of Chapter 4 dealing with the classical Chinese family.

Several of my colleagues have read various drafts of this book or parts thereof. I am particularly indebted to Karen Altergott, Bernice T. Halbur, and Deborah Lower. In addition, I would like to thank the manuscript reviewers: Robert Atchley, Miami University; Margaret Clark, University of California, San Francisco; Jose B. Cuellar, Stanford University; Stephen Cutter, University of Vermont; Alice J. Kethley, Benjamin Rose Institute, Cleveland; Harold Orbach, Kansas State University; and Jay Sokolovsky, University of Maryland, Baltimore County. Their comments and suggestions have led to improvements of organization, style, and content, but needless to say, the remaining faults are still my responsibility.

Donald O. Cowgill
Columbia, Missouri
May 1985

Chapter One

Aging and the Aged Around the World

A demographic and social revolution is underway in the world today. As a byproduct of the reduction of the birth rate accompanied by an increased length of life, many populations are experiencing a drastic change in age composition. In broad outline, this change means that while increasing numbers of people are living to advanced years—70, 80, even 90 years of age—relatively fewer children are being born. Of course this combination of demographic trends is resulting in a dramatic and unprecedented increase in the proportions of elderly people in those populations.

This revolution, which has accompanied the Industrial Revolution, began in Europe a century or so ago and is now well advanced in all industrialized and economically advanced countries. The less industrialized and less developed areas are generally not as far advanced in this aging process. Indeed, some may be temporarily abnormally young as a result of recent rapid reductions in infant and child mortality and/or increased birth rates. But these promise to be short-term effects. In the long run, lower mortality, which is now a worldwide reality, will result in more people living to older ages. When less advantaged areas also reduce their birth rates, as some are already doing and as all eventually must, they too will experience demographic aging. Thus, aging is a present reality in the more advanced areas and is the wave of the future in the rest of the world.

Of necessity, such a major demographic change impacts upon the institutions of society. It changes the composition of families and households and alters the relations between generations. It shifts the composition of the productive workforce and modifies the kinds of goods and services needed. It produces different kinds of political demands and gives rise to new governmental functions and services. It diminishes or even abolishes some roles formerly allotted to older people and calls for new functions and new activities for the increasing numbers of elderly persons. It impinges upon the basic values of a culture and raises such issues as the desirability of indefinite extension of life, the quality of life versus length of life, when life should be terminated, the right to die, and so on.

Institutional and societal responses to these alterations vary in relation to local conditions and cultural values. Accordingly, there are hundreds of natural social experiments underway in various parts of the world at any given time, experiments in the adaptation of social institutions to changed proportions of the elderly, and individual and group experiments by older people themselves, as they fashion new roles and evolve new solutions to both old and new problems. In this book I seek to survey and assess the results of some of those experiments.

Some Values of Comparative Study

In a novel situation such as that created by modern demographic aging, all prior cultural adaptations become outmoded. The "ways of our fathers" no longer work. All societies are forced to innovate, and what each is doing may be suggestive for all others. Because all will be aging eventually, albeit at different speeds and therefore at different stages at any given time, the less advanced societies may greatly benefit by knowing what has been tried by the more advanced societies. Such value may be either negative or positive; it may as often be an example of what not to try as of what is worth imitating. In all honesty, we can scarcely claim that the advanced societies have registered signal successes in adapting to their burgeoning populations of elders. Furthermore, given the dynamics of both demographic and social change in such societies, all adaptations must be regarded as tentative and temporary.

There may also be value for more advanced societies in knowing how older people fare and what roles they play in less developed societies. This is particularly true because the elderly appear to have held higher status and played more useful and satisfying roles in some developing societies. Some of their values and practices may be worthy of preserving and/or transplanting. It has been suggested, for example, that Japan has been more successful at maintaining an honorable status for their elderly than other advanced societies (Palmore, 1975a).

Perhaps a primary value of the comparative study of aging, particularly during the present transition, is that it must force us to the conclusion that none has "the solution." All societies are in the process of both aging and adjusting to aging. Each has its own traditional background, and each has its tentative reactions to new conditions. Each may learn from others, but in the end, each must find its own pattern and "do its own thing."

Ultimately, what we do in practice derives from what we believe about the process, and comparative study can provide perspective and insight on the process of individual aging. If we encounter aspects of aging or characteristics of older people that are universal, that is, found in all societies, we may reasonably infer that these are inherent aspects of aging, probably linked with the biological process of aging. However, if we encounter variations in the ways in which people age and variations in the characteristics of older people in different societies or segments of societies, we may be assured that these matters are neither genetically determined nor closely biologically linked. We will probably be inclined to look for social or cultural explanations. Such matters are much more tractable and amenable to human control.

Culture and Aging

The creation, elaboration, and transformation of culture is humankind's most distinctive characteristic (Keith, 1982:111). This capability, more than any other, differentiates humans from other life forms. Of course this capability derives from and is made necessary by the inability of humans to live and adjust on the basis of biologically determined behavior mechanisms, which formerly were called instincts. In the absence of fixed behavior patterns, adequate for mere physical survival but severely limiting in terms of potential for variety of behavior, capacity for esthetic creation and enjoyment, and philosophical reflection and spiritual development, the human infant must learn to be human. The human infant is the most helpless of living beings, and the period of immaturity (infancy and childhood) is quite prolonged. This is not only a period of physiological maturation; most importantly, it is a lengthy period during which the child is learning how to function adequately as an adult in his/her society. Much of what each person learns is the culture of the people.

Culture consists of the learned behaviors, meanings, and interpretations that have become common practice and expectation within a given human society. Such behaviors have previously evolved in a society on the basis of trial and error and have become common practice through imitation and socialization. Each new individual and each new generation must learn the culture of the society, including the meanings, interpretations, and expectations with reference to aging and old age.

How old age is defined, when it begins, what is expected of older people, how they are valued, how other people act toward them, who is responsible for their care, how much care and concern for them is warranted, and how much effort should be expended in prolonging their lives are all aspects of particular cultures. Because many different cultures have evolved through the ages in different geographic settings, we now have great variety in all of these matters. The description and classification of these variations are major concerns of this book. The explanation of their patterns and development constitute my major theoretical interest. Both description and explanation are needed if this knowledge is to be used in the further modification and elaboration of cultures as they relate to aging.

Culture is often thought of in static terms, as though all past experimentation had now stopped and the present behaviors and expectations had somehow become crystallized into a permanent and immutable form. People in modern, highly developed societies are especially prone to this static conception of less developed traditional or folk societies. Such societies may indeed be more resistant to change and they may change more slowly. But all cultures are always in the process of change. It is merely the rate of change that is different.

It is especially important to be aware of this dynamic quality of culture as it relates to aging. All cultural forms arise out of human needs. When new needs arise, cultural changes are sure to follow. As noted earlier, demographic aging is producing new pressures and new needs, and so our cultures are in the process of changing and adapting to these new needs. In a very real sense, we are in the process of inventing new cultures to fit these new conditions.

Theories and Issues

It is not mere idle curiosity that impels us to this task. We are concerned both with theory building and policy. Our theoretical interests include such questions as the following: What is truly universal about the aging experience?

It was asserted some years ago that older people everywhere begin to reduce their roles and activities, that this is a necessary and functional preparation for total withdrawal (death)—necessary and mutually satisfying both to individuals and to the society of which they are a part (Cumming and Henry, 1961). This became known as the disengagement theory of aging. Surely a worldwide review of aging can contribute to an understanding of this issue, and if, as anticipated, we determine that disengagement is not universal, we may still get some measure of the extent to which it happens, in what kinds of societies it occurs, and why.

In the United States, there is widespread commitment to the idea that activity is beneficial and that the aged should therefore maintain a high level of physical, mental, and social activity. How extensive is this notion, and how widely is it practiced?

Some social psychologists maintain that all social behavior is motivated by the efforts of individuals to obtain maximum advantage, reward, or satisfaction for themselves. Individuals, they say, will voluntarily engage in interaction only if there is hope or expectation that they can gain advantage from the exchange. They will use what resources they have to gain or maintain their margin of advantage but will withdraw from the interaction when it is no longer in their interest to continue. Recently there have been attempts to apply this exchange theory to the field of social gerontology (Dowd, 1980). Particular attention is paid to the interrelationship between generations, the relative benefits gained from each other, and the obligations that each generation can enforce upon others. Is this a general human phenomenon? Is this perspective a useful one in comparison of cultures around the world?

Several scholars have found support for the proposition that the status of the aged declines with increasing modernization (Cowgill and Holmes, 1972; Cowgill, 1974; Palmore and Manton, 1974). Others have found exceptional cases and doubt the consistency of the relationship (Palmore, 1975b; Fischer, 1977; Goldstein and Beall, 1981 and 1982; Cherry and Magnuson-Martinson, 1981). Some maintain that the relationship holds only for the transition from agriculture to industrial society, that the generalization does not hold for collective, hunting, or fishing economies, nor for postindustrial society (Sheehan, 1976). Still others would qualify the explanation of the relationship or suggest intervening variables (Maxwell and Silverman, 1970; Silverman and Maxwell, 1983; Dowd, 1980; Cohn, 1982). Perhaps this survey will throw some light upon this important theoretical issue.

Some years ago, on the basis of comparative research in six relatively modern societies, a group of scholars found that there was a prevalent negative stereotype of aging (Arnhoff, Leon, and Lorge, 1964). Is this true of all modernized societies? How general is it? In what kinds of societies do we find other views of aging and old age? Others have suggested that high esteem is correlated with extensive power (Eisenstadt, 1971), but Sanday (1974) disputes this correlation insofar as it applies to females. Does it hold for the aged and is there a difference based on gender?

There are recurring accounts of people with exceedingly long life spans. These are usually located in remote, bucolic settings where records are limited. Do these people really have exceptionally long lives? If so, how are they to be explained? They should provide valuable lessons for the rest of the world.

It has been asserted that people everywhere distinguish between senility and old age. Is this true or is the widespread negative stereotype of old age in modernized societies really a confusion of the two concepts?

Gerontologists today commonly generalize that older people are more heterogeneous than any other age group. Supposedly this is because the discrete forces of the environment have had longer to work upon the malleable substance of human heredity, thus producing greater divergence. But the opposite case could be made for a relatively uniform, slowly changing, traditional society; here we might find that the society has had a longer period for cultural uniformities to operate upon whatever hereditary differences there were at birth to produce more conformity and convergence.

These are a few of the theoretical issues that may animate our intellectual excursion. Each has practical implications. Although there is no assurance that we shall find definitive answers, we can hope that enough information will be forthcoming on enough of the issues to make the effort worthwhile.

Defining Old Age

Whether there is a period in the life cycle that is defined as old age in all cultures is still a moot point. Many have supposed that this was a universal, and Linton (1942:593) stated that old age is one of the elemental categories found in all age-grading systems. But Dowd (1980:73) has recently asserted that there is at least one exception to this proposition: "Among the working class [in industrialized societies] during the late nineteenth century, there was no concept of a distinct period of life called old age."

Glascock and Feinman (1981) undertook a systematic study of definitions of "old age" as reported in 60 societies included in a sample drawn from the Human Relations Area Files (HRAF), compiled at Yale University. They reported that only 62 percent of the reports contained explicit definitions. However, they attributed this low figure to the failure of the original ethnographers to note and report this datum about the societies they were studying rather than to the lack of such a concept or classification by the people themselves. We may still assume that most if not all societies have such an idea.

For those societies in which explicit definitions were reported, Glascock and Feinman classified the criteria used in defining old age, and the resulting tabulation may give us some idea of the prevalence of different concepts. In the first place, it strongly confirms the notion that conceptions of old age vary greatly in different societies around the world. Further, chronology, or the sheer passage of time, was used in only a minority of societies. Much more frequently old people were identified in terms of some change in social role, such as changing work patterns, becoming grandparents, or losing reproductive potential. Senility, invalidism, and change of physical characteristics were rarely used as criteria. About two fifths of the societies were reported to use several criteria, the most frequent combination being change of work patterns plus chronological age. It is significant to note that these authors found that physical debility was rarely used either singly or in combination to define old age and that senility was practically never confused with old age.

Though chronology is used by some societies to define old age, there is certainly no consensus about when it begins. Glascock and Feinman did not supply a classification, but from other sources we know that the onset of old age ranges all the way from 45 to 75. In general, Simmons' statement (1959:6) that the more primitive a society the earlier their people become old appears to be valid. This is equivalent to Cowgill and Holmes' statement (1972:322) that "the concept of old age is relative to the degree of modernization." These same authors continued, "Old age is identified in terms of chronological age chiefly in modern societies; in other societies onset of old age is more commonly linked with events such as succession to eldership or becoming a grandparent."

Age Grading

Though there may be a few societies in which a specific age grade designated as old age is absent, it is inconceivable that there is any without some recognition and observance of categorical age differences. Linton

(1942:593) suggested that the minimal number of age groupings in a society must be four—infancy, childhood, adulthood, and old age. Shakespeare wrote about the "seven ages of man" early in the seventeenth century in England. His rather gruesome list included the infant, the whining schoolboy, the lover, the soldier, the justice, (the man in) "the lean and slippered pantaloon," and second childishness. It is probable that the number of age grades increases with the complexity of society and the rate of social change. In contemporary America there are probably at least 10: infancy, preschool age, kindergarten age, elementary school age, intermediate school age, high school age, young adult, middle aged, young old, and old old. The Inca of Peru also distinguished 10 grades for males (Linton, 1942:593). The Andaman Islanders are said to differentiate 23 grades for men (Tomashevich, 1981:20).

Although the age grades for males and for females usually run roughly parallel, there is a tendency to distinguish more grades for males, and the transitions for females often occur at slightly earlier chronological ages. For example, females are usually permitted to marry earlier and, in fact, usually do so, and in many societies females are also permitted to retire earlier than males.

Attitudes Toward Old Age

Attitudes toward old age vary as widely as definitions of it. American society, as well as most modernized societies, is generally negative toward it (Harris and Associates, 1981:8). We glorify youth and despise old age. We associate old age with loss of usefulness, decrepitude, illness, senility, poverty, loss of sexuality, sterility, and death. As a result people take great pains to preserve a youthful appearance and conceal or understate their actual chronological age.

Furthermore, this negative evaluation applies with extra force to females. Peace (1981:3) aptly describes the difference: "Women 'age,' while men 'mature.' " It is more difficult for women in our society to admit to aging than it is for men, and the cosmetics and advertising industries play upon this aversion.

On the other hand, there are many societies in which old age is "the best part of life" (Simmons, 1959:6). An illustration of this is in Samoa, where, Holmes (1972:76) says,

> The Samoan attitude toward the aged is positive, and much of this is influenced by the attitude which the aged themselves have toward their

stage of life. The fact that Samoan old and young alike view old age as a desirable time of life stems from the fact that advanced years are secure and comfortable ones when less is demanded of the individual but still years of great personal freedom when one can continue to contribute to his group and be valued by his fellow men.

In such societies the trajectory of life is one of rising ascendancy, as we shall note in Chapters 5 and 6. There is a pleasurable anticipation of each new age grade. Among the Ibos, the elderly are believed to be wise and skilled and are revered for these qualities (Shelton, 1972:32). They are esteemed and respected; they have great prestige. Because of their wisdom, they are deferred to by their people. In Bojaca, Colombia, Kagan (1980:70) found that respect for the elderly was based upon the following grounds: (1) their long lives were acknowledged as testimony to their personal strength; (2) this was also a sign of God's grace—God was with them; (3) they had cared for others and deserved loving care in return; and (4) they had experienced much and learned from their experiences—their wisdom should be respected and put to use. In some societies, the elderly wield considerable power, and in those the deference by others is a matter of prudence as well as duty.

Determinants of Status

Many factors play a part in determining the status of the aged in a society. Fundamentally, of course, it must depend upon a mesh of situational factors with the value system. Amoss and Harrell (1981:5) suggested that it depends upon a balance between the costs they represent to the group and the contributions they can make. This might be described as an economist's way of looking at it. They add that a second factor is the degree of control that old people maintain over valued resources; among such resources, land is one of the most coveted and stable. But people also value information, and Maxwell and Silverman (1970; also Silverman and Maxwell, 1983) have strongly argued that a chief determinant of status of the elderly is the degree of their control over valued information. (This issue will be discussed further in Chapter 7.) We also may find that in societies in which belief in animistic spirits abounds, as well as in those given to ancestor worship, the status of the elderly is related to the extent to which they are believed to communicate with and/or control those spirits. (This too will be discussed in Chapter 7.) Of course, in any society idiosyncratic personality factors play an important role, and people who have by their own abilities or charisma achieved important positions in their earlier life may extend that status into their old age.

Cross-Cultural Study of Aging

Cross-cultural study of aging is still in its infancy. Ideally we should have carefully designed parallel research using comparable techniques, covering the same subject matter, and employing comparable concepts in a large, representative sample of discrete cultures around the world. Such research has not yet been done; it would be exceedingly complex, time-consuming, and costly.

From the standpoint of utilization of a wide range of cultures for parallel research, the studies that have made use of the Human Relations Area Files (HRAF) are the nearest approach to this ideal. These include Simmons' (1945) classic study of 71 "primitive" societies; Maxwell and Silverman's (1970) study utilizing a sample of 26 societies from HRAF; their more recent study (Silverman and Maxwell, 1983) employing a sample of 95 societies based on Murdock and White's Standard Cross-Cultural Sample from HRAF; Glascock and Feinman's study (1981) of a probability sample of 60 societies drawn from the same source; and Sheehan's study (1976) of 49 societies. A basic problem with the HRAF is that the units of study are very uneven; some entries are for villages or local groups that are really subunits of other larger entities, such as tribes or nations. The various standardized samples that have been specified and used seek to utilize reasonably discrete and more uniform units. This partially remedies one of the deficiencies in Simmons' early work. These studies, which purport to sample the cultures of the world and therefore permit generalization on a worldwide basis, are now being called holocultural studies (Glascock and Feinman, 1981:13).

However, no research based on secondary analysis can be any better than the original studies, and one of the chief remaining deficiencies, even when utilizing careful samples from HRAF, is shown by Glascock and Feinman's (1981) effort to research definitions of aging. Only 62 percent of their cases included an explicit definition of old age, but we cannot therefore conclude that the other societies had no concept of old age or that if the researchers had been paying attention to the subject of old age they could not have found and specified the definitions employed by the people. The more likely interpretation of the lack of such definitions in 38 percent of the societies in the sample is that the original researchers, not being particularly or primarily concerned with aging or old age, either did not ascertain the definition or did not bother to record it. But if we cannot even find out what old age means in nearly two fifths of the cases and we know that in the other three fifths it means a variety of things, this certainly leads to the conclusion that any research based upon such materials is seriously flawed. The information about old age that is there is obviously so spotty that it does not warrant the sophisticated statistical treatment to which it is sometimes subjected.

In discussing the potential of such sources for cross-cultural research, Frank W. Moore (1968:469–474) asserts that there is no such thing as a random sample of the cultures of the world. This applies with especial force if one is trying to study a topic to which anthropologists have given little attention until recently. This means that in most of the studies covered in HRAF, aging, if treated at all, was covered only incidentally. In this circumstance, even if we could get a representative sample of the cultures of the world, we still could not depend on the coverage to be representative for the subject of aging.

Consequently, the best one who is trying to assess the whole field of aging in worldwide perspective can do is to use what materials are accessible, both in such data banks as HRAF and elsewhere. That has been my strategy in writing this book.

Among the other sources I have utilized are a number of limited cross-cultural studies, restricted to comparison of a few cases, without any pretense of representativeness. Some of these have been very carefully designed to provide comparative results among the few societies included in the research, such as the Shanas et al. (1968) study of old age in three industrial societies—England, Denmark, and the United States; the Bengtson et al. (1975) study of modernity and perceptions of aging in six developing societies—Argentina, Chile, India, Israel, Nigeria, and Bangladesh; and the Arnhoff, Leon, and Lorge (1964) study of stereotypes of aging in six societies—the United States, Great Britain, Sweden, Japan, Greece, and Puerto Rico. As noted, these are usually limited in scope to certain aspects of aging and therefore can be useful only when considering those particular topics.

I make no pretense either to having a representative sample or to having observed all of the niceties of rigorous comparative research. Both are impossible at this state of the art, but as Swanson (1968) says, all research is comparative; it is chiefly the units of observation that differ. The grand theorists who became the fathers of sociology—Durkheim, Simmel, Pareto, Spencer, Ward, Sumner—used the comparative method, comparing whole societies and their institutions. After World War I, with the perfection of some research techniques believed to be more precise and "scientific," surveys of *individuals* became the vogue—applying statistical techniques and making generalizations about *aggregates of individuals,* not institutions or societies. Only such deviants as Parsons and Levi-Strauss continued to dare to compare societies and institutions.

I also dare to follow that tradition. The world of human culture and human relationships as they embody and relate to aging and older people is the universe of study. Except for my own research in Thailand and the United States, the materials employed are all drawn from secondary sources. The units of observation are the units employed by the original observer; they range from individuals to families to senior centers to housing complexes to villages to ethnic groups to regions to nations and total societies. The sample shifts with each topic and is determined by the accident of accessibility.

The subject matter with which we shall be dealing will be the interplay of the institutions of a society and individual elderly people. On the one hand, we will be concerned with the ways in which the major institutions accommodate themselves to older people and how they are responding to changing proportions of the aged. On the other hand, we shall be interested in the roles older people have played in relation to those institutions and how those roles are now being modified as the numbers of potential incumbents increase. However, we must resist the temptation to get involved in a systematic review of programs designed specifically for older people and the details of such programs. Detailed comparison of pension systems, social security programs, and health and social services is beyond the scope of this book, though some published materials are available in these areas.

Brocklehurst (1975) has described and compared geriatric care in the United Kingdom, the United States, and the U.S.S.R.. There are extensive comparisons of pension and social security systems, including Copeland's (1978) overview of worldwide developments and the U.S. Social Security Administration's (1977) statistical comparison. Of special interest may be a description of social security provisions for women in Belgium, France, West Germany, Great Britain, and the United States, published by the International Social Security Association (1973). Social services have been compared in the United States, Canada, France, Israel, Yugoslavia, Poland, the United Kingdom, and Germany by Kahn and Kamerman (1976) and by Kamerman (1976). Hay (1975) has compared a few long-term care facilities in Denmark, Norway, and Sweden, and Kane and Kane (1977) have prepared a comparative description of such facilities in six countries—England, Scotland, Sweden, Norway, the Netherlands, and Israel. The International Federation on Ageing has comparative studies of home help services in a variety of developing and developed countries (1975); has studies on mandatory retirement (1978) in the United Kingdom, Israel, Sweden, France, and the United States; and has published two papers on the role of voluntary agencies (1976). Haanes-Olsen (1974) has prepared a comparative study of housing allowances in the Federal Republic of Germany, Finland, Sweden, and Great Britain. And Noam (1975) has compared legislation, policies, and procedures for licensing, supervising, and inspecting homes for the aged in Europe.

Chapter Two

A Comparative Demography of Aging

The populations of the more highly developed nations of the world are markedly older than those of the less developed nations, but we are probably living at that moment in history when these differences are widest. The differences have increased greatly since World War II, as the more advanced nations have aged rapidly while the newly developing nations have aged very little or in a few instances have become younger. In this chapter, after defining what I mean by demographic aging and identifying some of the most useful measures of it, I shall discuss the process as found in different types of societies. Primitive and premodern societies are quite young in their age composition, and I shall explain why this is true. Then I shall demonstrate and illustrate the aging trend in modern societies and spell out the theory of this modern process. Finally, I shall describe some of the correlated characteristics of elderly populations—sex balance, marital status, living arrangements, and implications for economic dependency.

Measures of Agedness

In the most general sense, the aging of a population is merely an increase in the relative proportion of the older people in it. This may be reflected by a number of indicators: (1) median age, (2) percent of population over some arbitrary age, such as 65, (3) the aging index, or (4) the aged dependency ratio. Each of these has its advantages and disadvantages.

The *median age* is the age that divides a population into two equal segments, with 50 percent younger and 50 percent older. As a measure of central tendency it is usually preferred to other measures of age distribution, such as the mean or average, because the latter methods assume some tendency toward a bell-shaped curve in the distribution of ages, that is, some clustering toward a middle value, and this is seldom true of age distribution of a total population. Rarely is there any semblance of a bell shape in the distribution of a population by age; such a distribution would be most abnormal. Instead, most populations have very skewed age distributions, with the greatest numbers in the younger years, fewer in middle age, tapering off to very small proportions in old age. In such a case an average means little because one very old person will outweigh many infants in the computation of the average. The median avoids this computational limitation, though it too is difficult to interpret because it tells us nothing about the distribution within each half of the range. Quite different kinds of populations can have similar medians. For example, a country with a high rate of emigration and thus a low proportion of young adults may have the same median age as the country receiving those migrants, although the latter would have a high proportion of young adults. This will be true if, as is not unlikely, the median age of the migrants is the same as that of the total populations concerned.

This suggests a measurement that is more specifically attuned to calculating the relative proportion of older people in a population—the *percent 65 and over*. Because it is more specific to the issue, it is much more commonly used than the median age. Of course the age 65 is quite arbitrary; it could with almost as much validity be 55 or 75. The point is that it specifically concentrates on the older population and calculates its proportion of the total. It is a very useful measure of the extent of agedness of a population.

More rarely used and of less defensible logic is the so-called *aging index* (Valaoris, 1950:67–85). This is a ratio between the extremes of age in a population, that is, between the old and the young. One version considers the number of persons age 65 and over per 100 persons under age 15. Because the precipitating factor in the aging of a population is the reduction of the birth rate, this index is perhaps the most sensitive of the indicators considered here; it will react earlier and more visibly than the others. Actually, of course, it is as much an index of the child population as it is of the aged: It measures "younging" as well as "aging." This causes no particular problems as long as both are moving in the expected directions—child population going down while aged population increases—but the index loses much of its meaning and utility if a population is "younging" and "aging" at the same time. This happened in the United States during the "baby boom" following World War II; the child population was increasing rapidly at the same time that the aged population was also increasing. During this time, the percent 65 and over continued to increase, albeit slowly, while the aging index decreased. This incident revealed the measure's weakness; under such abnormal circumstances, it may be misleading.

The fourth measure of agedness to be discussed here is the *aged dependency ratio*. The most common version of this ratio is the number of persons 65 and over per 100 persons 15 to 64. The rationale for it and for its title is that it provides a crude index of the relative dependency load attributable to the older people in a population. It assumes that older people are not in the workforce, are consumers but not producers, and are dependent upon the active producers through transfer payments of some kind. It also assumes that the 15–64 group represents the productive population. As a measure of agedness, it correlates very highly with the percent 65 and over and thus can, if need be, serve as surrogate for that measure, but as a measure of dependency there is little to recommend it. Both numerator and denominator are subject to wide margins of error. Some of the aged are producers, that is, are working, and this proportion varies from society to society as well as from time to time within the same society. By the same token, by no means all of the middle aged are workers, and this too varies. For example, only about 4 out of 5 males age 15 to 64 are in the labor force in the United States, and a little over half of the females are, although the proportion has been increasing rapidly in recent decades. Because neither numerator nor denominator even comes close to representing the groups for which they are supposed to be proxies, there is little excuse for using this as an index of dependency. In advanced societies there are usually much better measures available, such as a ratio between the number of aged who are indeed not working versus the actual labor force.

A visual impression of the age composition of a population is provided by a cartographic device that demographers formerly called a *population pyramid*. Four such pyramids are shown in Figure 2.4, and their significance will be discussed later. Here I wish merely to call attention to the pyramid (a double bar chart) as an alternative means of measuring the age composition of a population. Though it lacks the simplicity of a single statistic, it has the virtue of supplying a visual impression of some of the detail that is compressed into single statistical measures.

The Process of Demographic Aging

Demographic aging is a very recent occurrence in human history. In order to appreciate its recency as well as its extent and novelty, it may be well to sketch a bit of our knowledge of the changes of longevity and population structure from prehistoric societies to the present.

Longevity in Preindustrial Societies

Our knowledge of the length of life and the age composition of prehistoric societies is scanty. No such society had a vital registration system and none took a complete census. Instead we must rely upon indirect evidence and make inferences about both longevity and the composition of population. One approach to these subjects in such populations is through the analysis of skeletal remains. Physical anthropologists can estimate the approximate age of death from these remains, and if there is a sufficiently large and representative sample of skeletons from a specific people of a specific period, it is then possible to estimate the average age at death and the frequency of death by age. From these data in turn it is possible to infer the approximate age distribution of a live population under those conditions and calculate an average expectation of life in those times.

Available evidence of this kind indicates that prehistoric people experienced very high mortality and lived quite short lives. Of the rather small sample of extant Neanderthal skeletons, dating from 150,000 to 100,000 years, only half were adults at the time of death, about 5 percent had reached 40, and only a few lived to be 50 (Howells, 1960:171–172). However, these skeletons were collected from scattered sites in Europe, Northern Africa, and Asia Minor, and the individuals were not contemporaries—they lived as many as 50,000 years apart. Therefore we can only guess at the compositions of specific populations at particular times, but the data would lead us to suppose that most such populations would have consisted chiefly of children. The rest of the population would have been made up of their parents, ranging from the teens to the forties. Old people, by modern standards, would have been exceedingly rare. The average expectation of life in this kind of population must have been less than 20 years, and the usual death rate must have averaged about 50 deaths per 1,000 per year.

Other Stone Age populations of Europe and the Near East reflect similar conditions and distributions; about half lived to maturity, perhaps

10 percent to 40 years of age, and less than 1 percent to 50 (Howells, 1960:169–171). At Indian Knoll, Kentucky, where 1,132 skeletons dating from about 500 B.C. to 500 A.D. were excavated, 57 percent were estimated to have been less than 21 years of age at death. From these remains, Howells constructed a life table indicating that a little less than half survived to age 20, about 3 percent to age 40, and only 0.3 percent to age 50.

Life expectancy increased a little during the Greek and Roman civilizations. Tombstone inscriptions in Greece around 400 B.C. indicate that life expectancy may have been as high as 30, and in the later Greek and Roman periods, while less than half still reached maturity, somewhat greater proportions of those who lived to adulthood survived to middle age and older—18 percent to 40, 9 percent to 60, and a few even to 80 (Angel, 1947:18). However, tombstone inscriptions and epitaphs may exaggerate longevity because it was chiefly the upper classes that left such markers, and even among them there was a tendency to neglect to memorialize infants.

Life expectancy fell back to a near primitive level after the fall of Rome and did not show appreciable improvement until about the seventeenth century in Europe. At this time Halley (1963:596–610), using death records of the city of Breslau, constructed the world's first life table, which gave an average expectation of life of 35.5 years. However, this may have been higher than in most places at the time, because for another hundred years other estimates remained below 30. This means that by the end of the eighteenth century, Europe had been able only to regain the modest level of health and longevity that had been attained by the Greeks and Romans two millenniums earlier. It was certainly not enough to produce any significant change in the age structure of the population, which remained very young indeed.

With high mortality and limited life expectancy, prehistoric populations were composed predominantly of children and young adults. Very few individuals lived beyond middle age, and older people constituted very minor proportions of the populations at any given time.

Modern Prolongation of Life

By the middle of the nineteenth century, the more advanced countries of Europe had achieved an average expectation of life of about 45 years (Stolnitz, 1968:128), and during the ensuing century it increased more than it had during the previous 2,000 years. Table 2.1 shows the gains for five countries since the turn of the twentieth century. For these coun-

Table 2.1. Gains in Expectation of Life at Birth in the Twentieth Century in Five Countries

		Males (years)	Females (years)
United States (whites)	1900–1902	48.23	51.08
	1955	67.30	73.69
	1967	67.80	75.10
Sweden	1901–1910	54.53	56.98
	1951–1958	70.48	73.43
	1967	71.85	76.54
Netherlands	1900–1909	51.00	53.40
	1953–1955	71.00	73.90
	1967	71.00	76.50
France	1898–1903	45.74	49.03
	1950–1951	63.60	69.30
	1966	68.20	75.40
England and Wales	1901–1910	48.53	52.38
	1953–1955	67.52	72.99
	1965–1967	68.70	74.90

Source: Judah Matras, *Populations and Societies* (Englewood Cliffs, N.J.: Prentice-Hall, 1973), p. 241. Original data from United Nations, *Population Bulletin*, No. 6, 1962, and United Nations, *Demographic Yearbook 1969,* No. 21, 1970.

tries, which were already among the highest in the world, the further gains during the first three quarters of the century range from 40 to 50 percent, adding from 20 to 26 years to the average life (Matras, 1973:241).

However, this process did not get underway in most of the rest of the world until the middle of the twentieth century, that is, after World War II. During the past three decades, most developing nations have experienced very extensive and rapid reductions of mortality and consequent increases in longevity. Table 2.2 shows that only a few nations now have an average expectation of life as low as 40, nearly all of which are in Africa. This points up that the Demographic Revolution has begun in even the most remote and technologically underdeveloped parts of the world. Most of the new nations of Africa and Asia have already doubled the average length of life, as compared with primitive levels, and some Asian and Latin American countries are pressing toward the modern standard of 70

Table 2.2. Life Expectancy at Birth, About 1980 (Countries with 10 Million Population and Over)

Less than 50 years		60–69 years	
Afghanistan	40	South Africa	60
Ethiopia	40	Turkey	60
Nepal	43	Philippines	61
Mozambique	46	Thailand	61
Zaire	46	Brazil	62
Bangladesh	46	Colombia	62
Sudan	46	Korea, North	62
Ghana	48	Malaysia	63
Indonesia	48	China	65
India	49	Mexico	65
		Sri Lanka	65
50–59 years		Chile	66
		Korea, South	66
Tanzania	50	Venezuela	66
Pakistan	51	Argentina	69
Uganda	52	Yugoslavia	69
Burma	52		
Saudi Arabia	53	**70 years and over**	
Vietnam	53		
Kenya	54	Romania	70
Egypt	55	Hungary	70
Morocco	55	Poland	71
Iraq	55	Taiwan	71
Algeria	56	Czechoslovakia	71
Peru	57	Germany, West	72
Iran	58	Germany, East	72
		Australia	73
		United Kingdom	73
		Italy	73
		Spain	73
		Canada	74
		France	74
		United States	74
		Netherlands	75
		Japan	76

Source: Population Reference Bureau, "1982 World Population Data Sheet" (Washington, D.C.: Population Reference Bureau, 1982).

Figure 2.1. Percent 65 and over in selected countries, 1880–1980

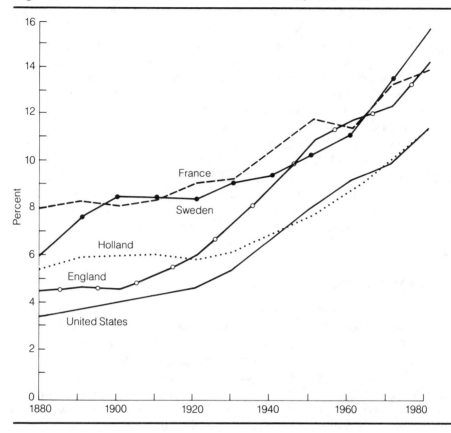

years, which has already been surpassed by most European countries. For example, Taiwan already has an average expectation of life at birth of 71.

The Aging of Modern Populations

The prolongation of life is a necessary precondition for demographic aging, but such demographic aging will not occur to any great extent until fertility declines. This began to happen in many European countries during the last half of the nineteenth century.

Figure 2.1 shows the aging of the populations of five countries from 1880 to 1980. France already had 8 percent of its population 65 and over in 1880, but it continued to age during the subsequent century, reaching

14 percent by 1980. Meanwhile Sweden, which had only 6 percent in 1880, increased more rapidly, surpassed France, and became the oldest population in the world with nearly 16 percent in 1980. England lagged behind these two until the turn of the century, but since then its population has aged rapidly. Holland is following the same trend but at a slower pace, permitting the United States (which was by far the youngest of the group in 1880) to catch up by mid-century; both had about 11 percent 65 and over by 1980. These cases illustrate the prevalent trend toward demographic aging in developed countries.

However, this trend is not yet underway in Africa, Middle America, and much of Asia, as is shown in Figure 2.2. In most of these areas the percent 60 and over has actually been decreasing since 1950. However, according to estimates prepared for the United Nations World Assembly on Aging in Vienna in 1982 (Oriol, 1982), most of these areas will be manifesting appreciable aging by the year 2000, and the trend will become worldwide early in the next century.

The Demographic Transition

The reduction of mortality is only one aspect of what demographers call the demographic transition; the completed process includes a reduction of fertility as well. Both processes of reduction appear to be long term and relatively permanent. The presumed permanence of these changes distinguishes the total process from cyclical fluctuations that may have taken place in primitive populations, especially fluctuations in the death rate. Though no two populations have followed precisely the same pattern through the transition, a general model of the process is presented in Figure 2.3. The curves represent crude death and birth rates that prior to the transition may have varied between 40 and 50 per 1,000 per year. The death rate declines first and is followed after a considerable lag by the birth rate, both eventually stabilizing at levels varying between 10 and 15 per 1,000 per year.

The most obvious and immediate result of this process during the transitional phase is a rapid increase in the total population. In many of the developing nations since World War II, this growth has been so rapid as to justify the term *population explosion*. Less obvious and more subtle is the aging that takes place as the transition draws to its close.

During the early stages of the process, when only the death rate is falling, there will be little aging in the structure of the population because the primary beneficiaries of the improved mortality are infants and children; in fact, if the improvement is very rapid, the population may become younger because of increased numbers of surviving infants and

Figure 2.2. Proportion of the total population that is 60 years and over, by subregion, for 1950, 1975, 2000, and 2025

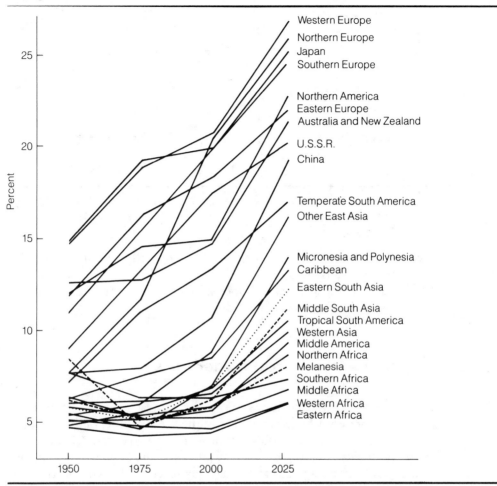

Source: William E. Oriol, *Aging in All Nations: A Special Report on the United Nations World Assembly on Aging,* Vienna, Austria, July 26–August 6, 1982. Washington, D.C.: National Council on Aging, 1982, p. 25. Reprinted with permission.

Figure 2.3. The demographic transition

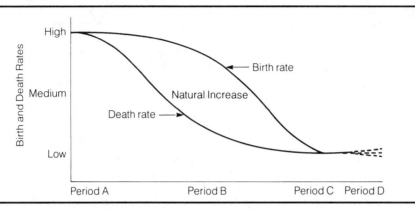

Source: Ralph Thomlinson, *Population Dynamics* (New York, Random House, 1976), p. 23. Reprinted with permission.

children. In time this increased survivorship will begin to increase the *numbers* of adults, middle aged, and eventually even the aged, but the *proportion* of the aged will not increase much until the birth rate drops, decreasing the proportion of children.

Variations in Current Agedness

Because different populations are in different stages of the transition, there are presently wide differences in the age structures of those populations. Indeed there are probably now more marked differences in the age structures of populations than at any previous time in human history, and since we can anticipate that the developing countries will shortly begin to catch up, we may be observing that point in history when the differences are widest; they may begin to converge as more of the developing countries move toward completion of the transition, that is, as they also begin to age.

Certainly there are currently very wide differences in the degree of agedness as measured by the percent 65 and over. Table 2.3 shows that the variation among major nations is from only 2 percent to 17 percent. Utilizing an adaptation of a classification first developed by the United Nations (1956:8–9), we note that most of the "young" populations are in Africa, Asia, and Latin America, and all of the "youthful" populations are to be found in these three continents as well. On the other hand, all

Table 2.3. Percent of Population 65 and Over, 1980 (Countries with 5 Million or More)

Young Populations (Less than 4%)	Mature Aging Populations (7%–9%)
2%—Ivory Coast, Afghanistan	7%—Hong Kong
3%—Morocco, Sudan, Ghana, Guinea, Mali, Niger, Nigeria, Senegal, Upper Volta, Kenya, Madagascar, Malawi, Mozambique, Rwanda, Tanzania, Uganda, Zambia, Zimbabwe, Angola, Zaire, Iraq, Saudi Arabia, Syria, Yemen, Bangladesh, India, Iran, Nepal, Pakistan, Sri Lanka, Kampuchea, Indonesia, Philippines, Thailand, Guatemala, Dominican Republic, Bolivia, Peru, Venezuela	8%—Cuba
	9%—Japan, Canada, Argentina, Yugoslavia
	Aged Populations (10% and Over)
	10%—Poland, Romania, Australia
	11%—United States, Portugal, Spain
	12%—Netherlands, Bulgaria, Czechoslovakia
	13%—France, Hungary, Greece
	14%—Belgium, West Germany, Switzerland, Italy
Youthful Populations (4%–6%)	15%—Denmark, United Kingdom, Austria, East Germany
	17%—Sweden
4%—Algeria, Egypt, Tunisia, Somalia, Cameroon, South Africa, Turkey, Burma, Malaysia, Vietnam, North Korea, South Korea, Mexico, Haiti, Brazil, Colombia, Ecuador	
5%—Ethiopia, Taiwan	
6%—China, Chile	

Source: Population Reference Bureau, "1983 World Population Data Sheet" (Washington, D.C.: Population Reference Bureau, April 1983). (Data are centered on the year 1980.)

but one of the populations of Europe (Albania) are either "mature" or "aged," most of them in the latter category; all but two of the "aged" populations are in Europe, the exceptions being the United States and Australia.

Figure 2.4 provides a visual impression of the four types of populations. The youngest, Mali, illustrates why this device is sometimes called a pyramid. Mali has a very high birth rate and as a result has by far the greatest proportion of its total population in the youngest age category. This gives it a broad base, and in general the child population is a high proportion of the total. The proportions in older age brackets shrink rapidly and in the oldest ages are very small indeed—only 3 percent are

Figure 2.4. Population pyramids of young, youthful, maturing, and old populations

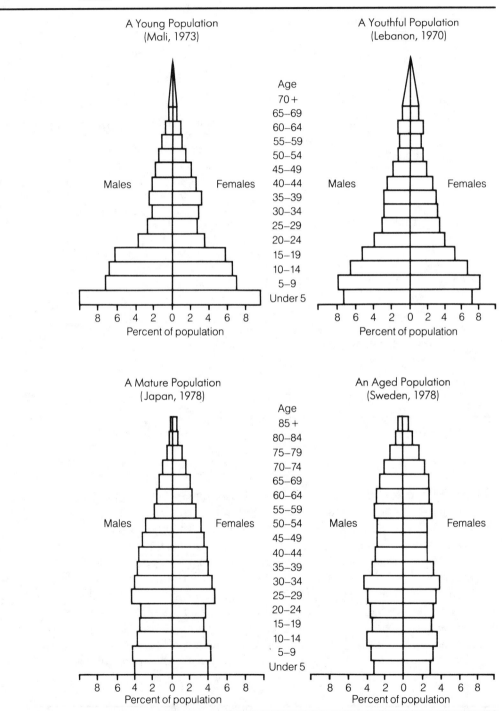

65 and over. Lebanon has begun to age but is still youthful in composition. The youngest age group is no longer the largest; instead the largest group is now 5 to 9 years of age. Above this level the figure is still a concave pyramid, but there are obviously greater proportions at nearly all higher age groups than in the case of Mali. Lebanon is a population with 5 percent of its people age 65 and over.

Japan is a rapidly maturing population. As the result of legalization of abortion shortly after World War II and the subsequent promotion of contraception, Japan's birth rate fell rapidly and has remained low ever since. Therefore the population under 25 years of age in 1980 was a much smaller proportion of the total than in Mali or Lebanon, but the population over 25 is swelling out into a convex pyramid. The proportion 65 and over has already reached 9 percent in Japan and is increasing rapidly. Sweden is the oldest population in the world, with 17 percent age 65 and over. She was among the first to experience the demographic transition, and her death and birth rates have been among the lowest in the world for decades. Other developed countries are approaching the type of aged population that is now represented by Sweden.

As suggested above, the chief reason for these differences in agedness is that different populations are in different stages of the demographic transition. However, this is somewhat modified in some cases by migration. Israel and New Zealand are somewhat younger than they would be without continuing immigration. On the other hand, many of the European countries are slightly older because of the loss of emigrants, most of whom are young adults.

Some Demographic Correlates of Age

As the age structure of population varies, so too do some other demographic characteristics. *Sex ratios* (males per 100 females) tend to be low in aged populations; in other words, older populations are predominantly female in composition. This is the consequence of the shorter life expectancy of males. In any given population the sex ratio decreases with increasing age; therefore, if older age groups make up a high proportion of the total population, the sex ratio of the whole will tend to be lower. A counterpart of this generalization, then, is that the populations of developed nations have lower sex ratios than those of underdeveloped or developing nations. India is an almost unique case in which the total sex ratio is relatively high and the sex ratio of the elderly population itself (60 and over) is high and rising; it has risen from 81.4 years in 1881 to 106.6 in 1971 (Vatuk, 1982:74).

In the world as a whole there are only about 75 males age 65 and over per 100 females of that age (United Nations, 1982). However, these sex ratios vary from a high of 136 in Senegal to a low of 42 in Russia. The high sex ratios of the aged, as of total populations, are found in Africa, Asia, and Latin America, that is, in the less developed areas. In Europe there are only 66 older males per 100 older females, and in the parts most decimated by World Wars I and II, the ratios are even lower.

Data on *marital status* of the aged in different countries are limited and sketchy. We must rely on data from only a few countries. The U.S. Bureau of the Census in March 1982 surveyed marital status of the population age 65 and over, as shown in Table 2.4. This indicates that very little, only 5 or 6 percent, of this older population consists of persons who have remained unmarried throughout their lives, that there is little difference between the sexes in the proportions (slightly fewer males than females), and that the percentages have decreased in recent years. Even smaller proportions are reported to be divorced, again with little difference between the sexes, but the percentages have increased since 1970. However, here the similarities end; there are major differences between the sexes in the proportions of older people who are married or widowed. Four out of five males are married, while less than two out of five females are. On the other hand, whereas about one in eight of the males is currently a widower, more than half of the females are widows.

These differences by sex in the marital status of older people are due to three factors. First, the death rate for males is higher than that for females at all ages. Therefore, female life expectancy is almost eight years longer than that of males. Second, because of differences in age at the time of marriage, most husbands are older than their wives. Therefore, even if age-specific death rates were the same, husbands would tend to die before their wives. Third, there is a greater tendency for males to remarry if they do experience widowhood, and often their new wives are considerably younger than they. We may also note that the proportions of both sexes who are currently married have been increasing, while the proportions widowed have been decreasing.

The same structural tendencies are also evident in other developed countries. For example, Shanas et al. (1968:230) found from two thirds to three fourths of the older men in Denmark and Great Britain married and from half to two thirds of the older females widowed, separated, or divorced. The most striking difference between these countries and the United States appears to be in the greater proportion of women remaining single for life. No doubt this is chiefly a legacy of World War I, during which many of the potential husbands of today's generation of older women were killed.

Table 2.4. Marital Status of Persons 65 and Over, United States, 1970 and 1982 (percent)

	Males		Females	
	1970	1982	1970	1982
Total	100.0	100.0	100.0	100.0
Single	7.5	4.4	7.7	5.7
Married	73.1	80.0	35.6	39.4
Spouse present	69.9	77.6	33.9	37.8
Spouse absent	3.2	2.4	1.7	1.6
Widowed	17.1	12.4	54.4	51.3
Divorced	2.3	3.2	2.3	3.6

Sources: For 1970, Jacob S. Siegel, "Demographic Aspects of Aging and the Older Population in the United States," U.S. Bureau of the Census, *Current Population Reports,* Series P-23, No. 59, May 1976, Table 6.1, p. 46.
For 1982, U.S. Bureau of the Census, "Marital Status and Living Arrangements: March 1982," *Current Population Reports,* Series P-20, No. 380, May 1983, Table 1, p. 8.

In the urban community of Tel-Aviv-Yafo in Israel, a city of about 400,000, the elder population probably reflects some of the recency of its settlement and growth (Har-Paz, 1978:17). It has higher proportions married (86 percent for males 65 and over and 53 percent for females) and lower proportions widowed (6 and 39 percent, respectively). We may presume that relatively few widowed persons have been included in the migrant population that has settled there and that even the older population is still skewed toward the lower end of the age group, 65 to 70, where most are still married.

Thailand may provide us with some insights as to how the situation in a developing country compares with that in the above-mentioned developed countries. The census of 1970 showed the pattern of marital status for persons 65 and over as set forth in Table 2.5. Here we see that very few of these men and women never married, 2 percent or less. Apparently marriage has been nearly universal for adults in that society. When we take into account that the statuses of the divorced and separated are combined in this table, whereas Table 2.4 shows them as separate categories, the total divorced and separated in Thailand is about the same as the total divorced only in the United States. Interestingly, the proportions of older people of both sexes who are currently married are slightly lower in Thailand than in the United States. The counterpart of this is that the proportions widowed are quite high. Almost two

Table 2.5. Marital Status of Persons 65 and Over in Thailand, 1970 (percent)

	Males*	Females*
Total	100.0	100.0
Single	1.7	2.0
Married	75.1	34.7
Widowed	20.7	60.6
Divorced and Separated	2.5	2.7

Source: National Statistical Office, *Population and Housing Census,* 1970.
*Priests and unknown not included.

thirds of the older women of Thailand (60.6 percent) are widowed, in contrast with only slightly over half (51.3 percent) in the United States. The percentage of widowed older males is much lower than females in both countries, but again the percentage in Thailand is higher than in the United States, 20.7 percent versus 12.4 percent. No doubt this condition reflects the fact that until quite recently the death rate has been higher in Thailand and life expectancy for both sexes has been lower. This higher mortality has led to earlier widowhood of both males and females, and thus a higher proportion of older persons are widows or widowers at any given time. These proportions will undoubtedly decline in the future as death rates decline further.

The same pattern is evident in India. Vatuk (1982:73) reports that, of the population age 60 and over in 1971, only 2.4 percent of the males and 0.4 percent of the females had never married. Almost insignificant proportions were divorced or separated, 0.5 and 0.4 percent, respectively. On the other hand, nearly three fourths of the males were currently married (74.7 percent), as compared to only 30.0 percent of the females. The proportions widowed were 22.4 and 69.2 percent, respectively. Remarriage of widows was formerly forbidden and is still relatively rare, varying from 19 percent in rural Mathura to 45 percent in rural Madhya Pradesh. In contrast, 61 percent of the widowers in six northern villages had remarried (Vatuk, 1982:78–79). However, most of those who remarried were young; only 10 percent of the widowers over 40 remarried.

Marital status is important; it impacts on other social roles and modifies one's feeling about life in general. In American society widows have lower morale than married women (Morgan, 1976), but this varies with age. Widowhood is especially damaging for younger women who are

Table 2.6. Living Arrangements of the Noninstitutional Population of the United States, 65 and Over, 1970 and 1982 (percent)

	Males		Females	
	1970*	1982[†]	1970*	1982[†]
Living alone	14.8	14.5	35.5	41.4
Married, spouse present	73.2	77.6	35.7	38.5
Living with someone else	12.0	7.9	28.8	20.1

*Recomputed for noninstitutional population from Jacob S. Siegel, "Demographic Aspects of Aging and the Older Population in the United States," *Current Population Reports,* Series P-23, No. 59, May 1976, Table 6.2, p. 48.
[†]Computed from U.S. Bureau of the Census, "Marital Status and Living Arrangements: March 1982," *Current Population Reports,* Series P-20, No. 380, May 1983, Table 6, p. 36.

still rearing children and who have few age peers in the same circumstances (Blau, 1973:83). Morale is especially low for widows with limited incomes and poor health; in fact, for older women, poverty and poor health are more harmful to morale than widowhood per se (Morgan, 1976). In general, older people who are still married are more socially active, and this appears to bolster morale, but there are also variations in relation to cultural expectations. For example, isolation from family members is more damaging to the morale of older Mexican-Americans, whose culture continues to stress close contacts with extended family members, than it is to Anglo-Americans, who are more attuned to less frequent association (Morgan, 1976).

Living arrangements have much to do with the roles older people play, especially familial roles. In the United States most older people live in private households; only about 5 percent live in institutions or other types of group quarters. Details of living arrangements of the noninstitutional population for 1970 and 1982 are shown in Table 2.6. Whereas about three fourths of the males are living with a spouse, only about one third of the females are living with husbands. In contrast, much higher proportions of the females are living alone or with persons other than husbands; more than a third are living alone and almost one fourth are living with other persons. Of course most of these females are widows.

Significant changes appear to be taking place in these living arrangements, as shown by the differences between the percentages in 1970 and 1982. The increased proportions of both sexes living with spouses are probably due to increased longevity and to a greater readiness for and frequency of remarriage after widowhood. Both males and females

Table 2.7. Family Status of Persons 65 and Over in the United States, March 1982 (percent)

	Males	Females
In Families	83.6	56.7
Householder	76.8	10.0
Married, spouse present	73.9	1.7
Spouse of householder	3.1	36.4
In related subfamilies	.6	.3
Other, not in related subfamily	3.0	9.9
Not in families	16.3	43.2
Nonfamily householder	15.4	42.4

Source: U.S. Bureau of the Census, "Marital Status and Living Arrangements: March 1982," *Current Population Reports,* Series P-20, No. 380, Table 2, May 1983, p. 14.

manifest a reluctance to live with other persons, particularly children, and as a result the proportions living with someone else (other than spouse) are declining. The counterpart of this is that more older couples continue to live independently, and, in particular, more widows choose to live by themselves.

A decade ago the living arrangements of older people in Denmark and Britain were quite similar to those in the United States (Shanas et al., 1968:184–189), but we do not have data to indicate whether the same trends are underway in Europe since then. However, they clearly have the same strong preferences for independent living. When they reside with children or persons other than their spouses, it usually represents a compromise dictated by poor health or economic circumstances.

If we pay attention only to households headed by elderly people (65 and older) in the United States, as shown in Table 2.7, some further patterns are revealed. First, only a little more than half of such households are made up of families, that is, two or more persons related by blood or marriage living together. The basic reason for this is the high proportion of widowed persons. Of those who are living in families, five out of six are headed by married couples. Second, the households that do not include a married couple, both family and nonfamily, are usually headed by a female—four out of five. Of course, as we saw in Table 2.6, many of the nonfamily households consist of widowed women living alone.

The families headed by persons 65 and over are usually quite small; the average is only 2.3 persons. Again, a very high proportion of these consist of an elderly married couple. However, there are ethnic variations in this. The families headed by elderly blacks are larger, averaging 3.0 persons, and include more younger persons. A smaller proportion of such families include a married couple.

We find a sharply contrasting pattern of living arrangements in Japan. Most observers agree that in recent years about 75 percent of the elderly are still living with children (Kii, 1976:28; Palmore, 1975b:37). Not only is this a much higher percentage than in the West, the pattern also differs. Whereas most older people in the Western countries live with daughters, in Japan about four out of five are living with sons. Of course this is a survival of the traditional patriarchal system buttressed by Confucian teaching of filial piety, which placed the burden of parental support squarely on the shoulders of the oldest son. There is less than perfect agreement as to current trends. Palmore (1975b:37–44) notes that the proportion living with children has declined only 6 percent in 20 years and that more than three fourths say they prefer to live with children. He feels that Japan is maintaining the traditional pattern to a remarkable degree. However, Kii (1976:32) suggests that the downward trend is significant, even if slow. He asserts that joint living arrangements are maintained largely out of economic necessity rather than mutual preference.

Although no comparable statistics are available for Korea, the same Confucian ethic has been traditional there, and, if anything, current practice adheres more closely to it than in Japan. Though there appears to have been a slight decrease in the prevalence of extended family households in the country as a whole (Koo, 1977:2), it is not clear that this represents a decline in the proportion of older people living with their children and grandchildren. Koo's sample was purposely limited to three-generation households, which were assumed to be the typical arrangement, but within these, both children and grandchildren expressed strong approval and support for grandparents living with them. They thought the grandparents also approved of the arrangement. It is worth noting that oldest sons, those who must bear the burden, are most supportive of the custom of older persons living with their children and grandchildren.

Seventy percent of older people in Bombay live with children or other relatives, and if children live elsewhere it is considered abandonment (Borders, 1976). Vatuk (1982:88) finds that 54–78 percent of the elderly live with married sons. Very few live alone.

The situation is more varied and less predictable in Thailand. While older people usually live in the same compound with one or more married children, those children may be either sons or daughters. In northern Thailand daughters are more likely to stay with their parents (de Young, 1955:23; Cowgill, 1968:159–160), whereas in central Thailand and Bangkok there is about an equal chance of it being a son (Kaufman, 1960:24).

Goldstein and Beall (1982:745) found 73 percent of elderly Sherpas in a rural area of northeastern Nepal living alone or in households consisting of elderly couples only. However, this was a new situation brought about by the intrusion of modernization into this remote area. The youngest sons, with whom they were supposed to be living, by cultural norms, had migrated to Katmandu or India. The older people were not economically deprived and they were generally in good health, but they were unhappy because, by cultural definition, their youngest sons had deserted them, and to live with any other children would connote dependency.

In Israel we see sharply contrasting patterns depending on place of origin prior to migration to Israel. Older people who lived in other parts of Asia or Africa before coming to Israel usually live with their children in old age, whereas most of those of European origin reflect the Western preference for independent living by maintaining households separate from their children (Weihl, 1972:201). In fact there is a trend away from joint living arrangements with their children (Har-Paz, 1978:31).

Russia appears to follow the Eastern pattern. Grandparents are traditionally included as members of the household (McKain, 1972:151). This pattern persists in modern Russia in such strength that young couples lacking natural parents to fill the role are said to adopt them. Not only is the *babushka* important as a homemaker and substitute mother while both parents are away at work, the extra income from the pensions of the older people is a welcome addition to the family budget. Furthermore, the shortage of housing often makes such doubling up necessary.

Thus we see a considerable range in the living arrangements of older people in different parts of the world. In Japan and Korea there is evidence of extensive survival of the patriarchal stem family in which the elder male is still the dominant member. In Thailand the dominant member is as likely to be female as male, and the younger members, whether male or female, tend to have great autonomy vis-à-vis the older generation. In Russia older men and women are valued members of the household, but in secondary rather than in dominant roles. This contrasts with the prevailing nuclear family household in the United States and Western Europe, where the older members usually live in separate households, either as couples or as single individuals.

Age structure is also related to *economic dependency* but not in the way that is popularly believed. Demographers sometimes use a measure called the total dependency ratio as a crude indicator of economic dependency. This measure is the ratio of the young (under 15) and the old (65 and over) to the population of working ages (15 to 64). The rationale for such a measure is that both the young and the old tend to depend economically upon the working population, represented by the middle age group. If we accept this rationale for the moment and compare total dependency ratios with percentages 65 and over, we find that contrary to general belief, older populations have lower dependency ratios than young populations. In a study of 87 nations and territories as of about 1970, a correlation of -0.560 was found between the percent 65 and over and the total dependency ratio. The reason for this unexpected result is that the child population is a much larger component of the dependency ratio than the aged, and the dependency ratio is therefore largely determined by what happens to the child population. As shown earlier, the aging of a population largely reflects a decrease in the proportion of the population that is young, so this inverse correlation should be no surprise.

However, there are much better measures of economic dependency than these age ratios. Probably the best of these is the percentage of the population not in the labor force or, to use United Nations terminology, not "economically active." But again the correlation is negative, -0.455. This should provide conclusive evidence that the aging of a population does not increase dependency loads; instead the increase in the aged population is far outweighed by a much greater relative decrease in the child population. This means that the average worker is required to support fewer dependents in a modern (aged) population than in a premodern (young) population.

It should not be surprising therefore, as Selby and Schechter (1982:185) point out, that declines in the birth rates of developing countries have been accompanied by increased security in old age. After all, the countries with the highest proportions of older people are the ones that can best afford them (see Figure 2.5).

Do They Really Live That Long?

In 1513 Ponce de Leon sailed from Spain in search of the Fountain of Youth, which was believed to be on an Island called Bimini in the Caribbean, off the shores of the New World. He never found the Fountain of Youth, but perhaps it is symbolically appropriate that he landed in Florida, which later became a haven for elderly retirees in America. His quest represents a persistent desire and search for means of prolonging

Figure 2.5. Percentage of population age 60 and over/per capita GDP

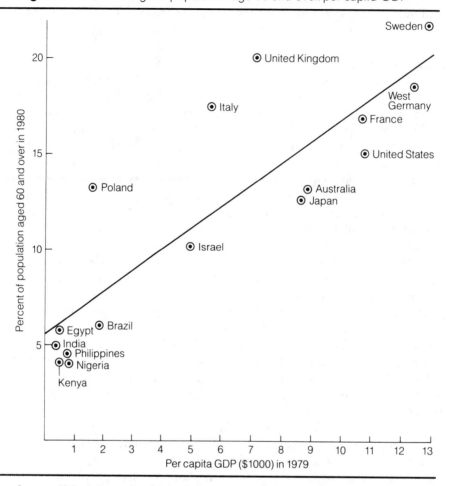

Sources: Philip Selby and Mal Schechter, *Aging 2000: A Challenge for Society* (Lancaster, England: MTP Press, 1982), p. 210. Original data from Provisional Projections of the United Nations Population Division, 1982 (percentage of populations aged 60+). Figures supplied by the United Nations Statistical Office (per capita GDP). Reprinted with permission.

Note: For Nigeria, the per capita GDP in 1978 is given. For Poland, the per capita net material product is given.

life. That desire has given rise to extensive and persistent myths about places where this ideal is supposed to have been achieved. James Hilton exploited the theme in his novel *Lost Horizon* (1934) and contributed the term *Shangri La* to our vocabulary.

In his study of this type of prolongevity literature, Gruman (1966) found that some people projected such utopias to a prehistoric past; these follow what he called an "antediluvian" theme. Others, like Hilton and Ponce de Leon, placed their demographic utopias in some distant, isolated place; these represent an "hyperborean" theme. We still hear of such places, and their demographic wonders are sufficient to impress some serious scientists and to justify a brief discussion here.

Perhaps the best-known contemporary Shangri La is a region in the Caucasus inhabited by people called Abkhasians. This is the area from which Stalin came; he repeatedly bragged about the longevity of the people there, and not many dared dispute him. The chief claim is that there are an unusual number of exceedingly long-lived people in the area, some far beyond what is currently thought to be the biological limits of human life. Sula Benet's (1974) prime informant, for example, was supposed to be 140 years old, and the ratio of centenarians is reported to be 50 per 100,000, compared to only 3 per 100,000 in the United States (Aiken, 1978:8). There are supposedly about 500 people in the Caucasus who are more than 120 years old (Holmes, 1983:71). The problem is that there is no documentary proof of such longevity—no birth, census, or church records—and even some Russian scientists suspect that these people have exaggerated their ages (Medvedev, 1974:381).

Another place that had a short-lived reputation for long life is the village of Vilcabamba high in the Ecuadorian Andes. In 1969 a Peruvian doctor took a medical team to Vilcabamba to investigate its claims to good health and longevity. The team found 9 centenarians among the more than 300 elderly people whom they examined. Since the total population of the town was only about 800, this would have been a very high ratio of centenarians. However, when a team of social scientists returned to the village to verify the ages of the persons concerned from such records as existed, they found that the oldest person in the village was actually only 96 (Mazess and Forman, 1979) and that there was a systematic pattern of age exaggeration. It began at about age 70 and accelerated with the years; by age 84 they were claiming to be 100. The people who had claimed to be centenarians were actually in their eighties and nineties.

The Hunza people of Pakistan have also gained a reputation for longevity, although the claims are much less extravagant; they seem to rest on a very few cases and rather vague impressions. When Leaf visited there in 1971, the oldest resident was alleged to be 110 and was supposed to have sons who were 70 and 74. Leaf gained the "impression of an unusual number of very vigorous old folk" (1973:96). He was more impressed with the robust health of people in their eighties and nineties than he was with any unusual number of exceedingly old people. Again there were no birth, census, or church records to document actual ages, but there was also less need of them because no extravagant claims were being made.

The latest addition to the list of Shangri Las is Paros, Greece. This is a small island with a total population of 2,703 and good records reaching back for a century, so there is no problem of identification of people and verification of age. In the early 1970s there were 5 authentic centenarians, which is a very high ratio in such a small population (Beaubier, 1976). However, five cases scarcely warrant any broad demographic conclusions (the ratio has probably declined by now anyway); in fact, a life table constructed on the basis of the age-specific death rates of the total population indicates an average life expectancy of 77, which is only one year more than Japan and Iceland.

Much attention has been devoted to finding the unique characteristics of these Shangri Las (climate, heredity, diet, habits, lifestyles) that would explain the long life alleged, but until it is established that people really do live as long as they claim, that such claims are actually extraordinary, or that the samples on which they are based are large enough to warrant any conclusions at all, such efforts seem to beg the question.

Summary

Many nations have experienced a marked increase in the proportion of their population that is old. We call this process demographic aging and have noted that it is a byproduct of a broader demographic process known as the demographic transition. This transition includes a long-term, presumably permanent decline in mortality, resulting in increased expectation of life. If there is a subsequent secular decline in fertility, as has happened in all modernized societies, the result will be an upward shift in the age structure of that population—demographic aging. Different societies are presently in different stages of this process; therefore there are some very "young" populations and some very "old" populations. The young populations are for the most part very poor, with the most primitive technological development, while the "aged" populations are to be found in the richest and most advanced societies (Rosset,

1964:201–203; United Nations, 1956). These more advanced societies, with their older populations, have higher ratios of workers to consumers and lower total dependency ratios because, while the numbers and proportions of the aged have increased, the proportions of children have decreased sufficiently to completely offset the increase in the aged.

Older populations have low sex ratios; that is, they have low proportions of males and high proportions of females. Most older males are living with wives, but high proportions of older females are widows. The living arrangements of the elderly are partly determined by demographic factors, particularly the sex ratio, but cultural factors are also important. In many societies, particularly in the Orient, older people are expected to live in the same household with adult children who can care for them if they need it. In contrast, the cultures of the United States and Europe emphasize individualism, self-reliance, and independence. This is reflected in their living arrangements; much higher proportions of the elderly live alone or as couples only, separate from their children. Prolongevity is still an intriguing theme, and people still create and take seriously myths about Shangri Las, where people supposedly live to extraordinary old age. However, no such utopia has been authenticated. We shall take a closer look at some of the cultural values that impinge upon the lives of the elderly in the next chapter.

Chapter Three

Value Systems and Aging

$\mathcal{N}$early 50 years ago, Ruth Benedict, in her classic book *Patterns of Culture*, made a strong argument for a holistic view of man and his culture (1934:53): "A culture, like an individual, is a more or less consistent pattern of thought and action. Within each culture there come into being characteristic purposes not necessarily shared by other types of society." The whole is not merely the sum of its parts. Those parts are meaningfully structured in relation to each other and cannot be understood, indeed may be misinterpreted, if considered apart from the total cultural context. The central unifying theme in such a culture pattern, or what is sometimes called the *ethos* of a people, is likely to be found in its dominant cultural values. Walter Goldschmidt (1954:64) stated it this way:

> A society is a group of people organized as a unit and sharing a common cultural heritage. The central organizing principle in any society is the values that its people have acquired as a part of their cultural heritage. For values give direction to the lives of the people, make meaningful their acts, and serve as a bond among them.
>
> Values are sometimes defined as those broad principles which each culture assumes, and which underlie the specific acts of the people. In such a view, democracy and individualism are values of our society—just as "having a good heart" and self-effacement are values in Hopi society. Each culture has broad values of this type that govern conduct.

Clearly, the meaning of aging and the import of the behavior of others toward the elderly within a society cannot be accurately assessed without attention to the ethos of the people and the cultural value system within which these items are embedded. This is the rationale of the present chapter.

However, we obviously cannot survey in Benedict's holistic sense all the relevant cultures of the world; after all, she covered only three in her classic study. Furthermore, this is not an encyclopedia of cultural anthropology; it is an attempt to illustrate the various ways in which aging and old age are viewed within different societies. Instead of an encyclopedic approach, which would be patently impossible, I shall describe certain value systems that are particularly salient for the topic of aging and note the implications of those systems for the roles available to older people within them.

I will not be describing different cultures but dominant cultural themes that inhere in various cultures and cut across several cultures. The value systems I have chosen for this type of treatment are: the work ethic, filial piety, familism, egalitarianism, individualism, and the cult of youth.

The Work Ethic

The first section of Max Weber's three-volume work, *Religionssoziologie* (1920) bore the title "Die protestantische Ethik und der Geist des Kapitalismus." It was later translated and published as a separate volume as *The Protestant Ethic and the Spirit of Capitalism* (1958). The thesis of the work is that the value system advocated by the Protestant reformers of sixteenth-century Europe furnished the ethical basis for the subsequent development of Western capitalism. In its early form the Protestant ethic included the following ideas: (1) each individual is responsible for his or her own salvation; this is a matter between the individual and God—the intercession of the church is not required; (2) hard work is strong testimony that one is predestined for salvation; (3) frugality and wise investment of one's savings are further signs of God's favor; (4) hard work will be rewarded, and worldly riches are symbols of moral character; and (5) success in this life signifies salvation in the next.

Many have questioned various aspects of Weber's thesis. One criticism is that it attributes too much to the Protestant reformers; the notion of the efficacy and necessity of work did not originate with the Reformation, nor have the Protestants ever had a monopoly on the idea. At a more abstract philosophical level, there is also the debate over whether ideas really become causal agents in history, as this particular work by

Weber maintains, or whether ideas, such as these, are in reality rationalizations after the fact. For example, the causative sequence ascribed in this publication by Weber appears to be diametrically opposed to the Marxian view that economic events are the determinants of the course of history.

Regardless of the source of the ideas and the historical debates about them, the elements of what I prefer to call the work ethic have doubtless been very prevalent and important in Western society in recent centuries. Stripped of the theological trappings and supernatural sanctions with which the reformers had invested it, the essential elements of the work ethic are: (1) work is the central business of life; (2) what one does for a living is the chief basis for his or her identity and status; (3) work is good for one's character; (4) the individual who does not work is not a worthy citizen. Two hundred and fifty years after the Reformation, the American sage, Benjamin Franklin, expressed it succinctly in his epigram "Idle hands are the Devil's workshop."

Numerous kinds of evidence may be adduced to demonstrate the presence of this ethic in American social life. Studies of social stratification have repeatedly shown that occupation is the primary and most heavily weighted factor in determining social status (Warner, Meeker, and Eells, 1960). After one's name, occupation or work position is the most common way by which a person is identified. A very frequent plaint (really a boast) is how hard one is working or how many hours one puts in at the job. Unemployment is not respectable, and one who is intentionally unemployed is a "bum." The Elizabethan Poor Law in England more than three centuries ago decreed that in order to receive public support, able-bodied poor should be put to work at the "work house," which very shortly became identified as a penal institution. Proposals of the same order—providing work as the test of worthiness—continually crop up in America today.

This ethic has particular relevance to aging in those modernized societies where occupational retirement has become almost universal. Under the terms of the work ethic, retirement deprives a person of his or her central role in life, status, and basic identity. Even though we may try to rationalize the exception in terms of one's having earned the right to retire, lifelong habits and attention to the imperatives of the ethic are not easily sloughed off. No doubt this is why so many of our retired people feel impelled to keep busy. About a third of a national sample of retired Americans 65 and over said they would rather be working (Harris and Associates, 1975:89). About 22 percent were doing volunteer work, and another 10 percent said they would like to. Many Americans have become "workaholics," and when retirement deprives them of paid employment, they seek substitute activities. Some are never satisfied with the "roleless role" into which they are thrust.

In the areas of the world where the work ethic has been prevalent and retirement has become customary, and these tend to be the same areas, aging has become problematic. This may be only a transition period, and eventually the elderly may find alternative roles, but it is probably the work ethic itself that dictates that they must have a role.

Filial Piety

A second value system that has obvious and profound implications for the condition and status of the elderly in a society is the institution known as filial piety. It was most clearly enunciated and most extensively enforced in those parts of the world that were influenced by the philosophy and teachings of Confucius. (This subject will be treated further in Chapter 4 as part of the description of the traditional Chinese family.)

The ethic of filial piety imposed heavy obligations upon children concerning their behavior and responsibility toward their parents. First, children owed their parents absolute obedience; disobedience, or a show of disrespect for parents, was one of the most heinous offenses known in classical Chinese society (Dawson, 1915:159). Beyond respectful obedience, devotion in the nature of a religious commitment was expected. After all, one owed one's very life to one's parents. They were the most immediate ancestors, and ancestors, particularly in the patrilineal line, were to be revered. Third, children owed their parents support in their old age. This was a sacred duty. Moreover, the obligations did not end with the death of the parents. An appropriate funeral was required along with continued obeisance, and memorial rituals were to be performed regularly at their graves.

Of course, given the principle of primogeniture, these burdens rested most heavily and most particularly upon the eldest male heir, but this was only because he was the official lineage representative; other sons were also held responsible, as were the sons' wives. The latter, for all intents and purposes, became members of their husbands' lineage upon marriage. They too owed absolute obedience and homage to their elders.

I have noted how the ethic of filial piety operated within the classical Chinese family; it applied equally to Korea, to pre–World War II Japan, and to Taiwan. The ethic was not only a part of the mores of these societies, it was embodied in the laws of the lands. For example, the Meiji Civil Code in Japan specifically provided that support of one's parents took precedence over support of one's own children (Kii, 1976:24–25).

Under these conditions, it is obvious that the principle of filial piety not only favored high status and material support for the elderly, it was legally guaranteed to the limit of family resources. Of course the legal requirements have been changed in the direction of equality of rights and obligations and mutual responsibility between generations. In Japan the Constitution of 1948 removed the priorities favoring the aged, making generations mutually responsible for each other, and left it to the courts to decide if it was necessary to assign priorities in specific cases. Likewise, in the People's Republic of China, the Marriage Law of 1950 provided that "Parents have the duty to rear and to educate their children; the children have the duty to support and to assist their parents. Neither the parents nor the children shall maltreat or desert one another."

But these legal changes have certainly not erased all vestiges of filial piety. Though in China the aged can no longer "tyrannize" the young, and though it is possible to view the Revolution of 1949 in part as a revolution against such tyranny (Tien, 1977), it has by no means abolished the relatively privileged position of and high regard for the elderly. Nearly all of China's elderly continue to live in family settings. Those who have no families to turn to are usually cared for in small, beneficently operated institutions known as "Homes of Respect." Within the family households, the elderly appear to be loved, respected, and influential. In Japan the ethic of filial piety has doubtless retarded the erosion of the elderly's status by modernization forces. Three fourths of them still live in the traditional household setting with one of their children, usually the eldest son. Four fifths feel that their lives and circumstances are satisfactory (Maeda, 1978:67). However, these formal vestiges mask subtle changes that are in progress, such as the emancipation of the Japanese women from subordination to their mothers-in-law (Masuda, 1975) and the general disregard for the "silver seat" reserved for the elderly on trains and subways, as observed by me and by Palmore's students in a formal study of the phenomenon (1975b:102).

Harrell (1981:196–197) reports that veneration of the elderly is still very much in evidence in Taiwan, and he attributes it fundamentally to the Confucian ethic of filial piety. Furthermore, Chinese and Japanese people carry the culture pattern with them when they migrate to other parts of the world, although the circumstances of the migration and the treatment in the host country obviously condition the duration and strength of its persistence. For example, third-generation Japanese-Americans still manifest a strong sense of filial responsibility (Kalish and Yuen, 1971:42; Kiefer, 1974a), certainly stronger than most other

Americans. On the other hand, the Chinese-Americans—who generally came earlier, more often without their families, and who suffered the indignities of coolie labor and persistent poverty—show a greater decrement in the ethic of filial piety (Kalish and Yuen, 1971:40–41).

Familism

Bearing many similarities to the ethic of filial piety in its implications for the elderly but flourishing far beyond the confines of Confucian influence is the value system that clearly and strongly assigns first priority to the family. Of course the extent of emphasis is a matter of degree. After all, most societies either really or verbally favor the family over other groups. But in some the emphasis is much stronger, and any conflicting loyalties are quickly and categorically overruled.

A classic case of familism in this sense is provided by the culture of southern Italy, which has provided a large proportion of the Italian migrants to the United States. These immigrants have of course brought their culture, including the emphasis on familism, with them. As Colleen Leahy Johnson (1983) shows in her excellent study of Italians of Syracuse, New York, this value system has remarkable staying power in competition with the American ethic of individualism. This is such a good example of familism and its implications for the elderly that I shall draw from it in some detail.

Johnson studied 76 families in which both spouses were Italian and 98 families in which an Italian had married-out, and she compared these with an unspecified number of non-Italian Protestant families in Syracuse. She describes the cultural tradition out of which these Italian families came as one in which "the family is depicted as the core of the social structure and the source of an all-pervading influence over its members." Comparisons between the Italians and the non-Italians in Syracuse revealed that the older Italians were accorded decidedly higher status within their families, as shown by marks of respect and esteem, frequency of contact with children and other relatives, and concrete assistance given to them. When Johnson sought explanations for this elevated status of the elderly through both statistical procedures and content analysis, the significant factors appeared to be (1) interdependence, (2) authority and power, and (3) affect and emotions. By interdependence she meant a continuous interchange of mutual services, accompanied by intimacy, need satisfaction, and a deep sense of group allegiance. At the same time, the "godfather" image was there as a dominant authority who enforced conformity to family goals and did not countenance divided allegiance. Emotions were effusively and expansively expressed, which tended to both give expression to family cohesion and provide a safety valve to release the pressure when internal family authority confronted deviations resulting from outside influences.

The honor of the family was crucial, and individual members were expected to support the male authority, sacrifice for the family, respect parents, and avoid bringing shame on the family name. Within this framework, there was only limited leeway for individual self-expression, which in any case was to be subordinated to the family interest. The cohesiveness of the family was shown by the limited patterns of migration; they did not move far from home. Two thirds of the middle-aged Italians still lived in the old neighborhood or in adjacent suburbs. They had continual contact with elderly parents and other family members. Twenty-one percent of the elderly lived in the same household as one of their children, and another 34 percent had a child within walking distance. Three fourths had daily contact with children, and nearly all had contact at least once a week. Grandchildren were almost as important as children. Nine out of ten saw their grandchildren at least once a week.

Middle-aged children included elderly parents in the activities of their nuclear families, and a majority rejected outright the notion of ever permitting their parents to be placed in a nursing home. The Italian families were twice as likely to extend frequent aid to their elderly parents as were the families of the control group.

For both males and females the family continued to be the center of attention and social contact in old age. Men retired from work appeared to intensify family involvement, and women moved easily and naturally from the role of mother into that of grandmother, with continued nurturing activities.

A most interesting finding of this study was that the older people who were more acculturated in the American setting, those who had been born here and who could speak English, had greater solidarity and higher status with their children than those who had been born abroad and could not speak the language that had become the favored tongue of their children and grandchildren. Apparently some adaptability to the changing scene was necessary to maintain family integration, but by "bending a little" these older people could maintain to a higher degree a central value of the traditional culture—familism.

A study of middle-aged Italians in Baltimore paralleled the above findings from Syracuse in most respects (Fandetti and Gelfand, 1976). These too strongly favored intergenerational living arrangements for their elderly parents and showed marked reluctance to sanction institutional living unless the institutions were under church or ethnic-group management. However, the insistence upon family living and the resistance to institutional arrangements were both weaker in second and third generations.

A comparable emphasis upon familism appears to characterize Mexican culture and is also carried by Mexican migrants to the United States (Adams, 1972; Clark and Mendelson, 1969). In a study of 214 elderly Latinos in San Diego, most of whom were Mexicans, 55 percent were living in households containing relatives, usually children and/or grandchildren (Valle and Mendoza, 1978:52). Nine out of 10 had relatives within the immediate neighborhood, and 7 out of 10 said they would turn first to a family member in case of emergency.

Wherever the ethic of familism prevails, the elderly are included within the boundaries. They are not only accorded full membership, they are honored and respected. They are therefore relatively secure in their old age, both financially and emotionally.

Individualism and Independence

The value systems of individualism and independence are theoretically separable, but if by independence we mean independence of the individual, they are practically inseparable. In many respects they are the antithesis of familism, and as individualism has been given progressively more play in the modern world, familism has declined.

Andrei Simic (1977:56) has contrasted the prevailing familism of Yugoslavia with the general individualism of the United States. Of the dominant American value system, he says

> American children are socialized from their earliest years toward the goal of independence. A key element in this process is the concept of *privacy* (one notably lacking in many other cultures) with its connotation of the *right* and *pleasure* of being alone as expressed in the exclusive control of space and material objects, and the freedom from the intrusion of others. Ideally, each child, even a baby in the crib, is provided with a room separate from that of his parents so as to respect the mutual need for privacy. In the same way, wherever possible, siblings are similarly isolated from each other, both because of the presumed requirement for individual private space, and the belief that each child's principal interests will lie not with his older or younger brothers and sisters, but rather with his extrafamilial age-mates.

This insistence upon private space continues into adult life. Children leave the parental home when they reach adulthood. When they marry they establish separate neolocal residences. Thus individualism and its associated values of privacy and independence continue to put distance between family members throughout their lives. Nuclear family households become the norm, and as adult children depart from the parental homes, the parents are eventually left in an "empty nest." The insistence upon independent residences continues even after the death of one's spouse. Those who can physically and financially maintain separate residences generally do so, and the proportion of those who do continues to increase. In fact the proportion of elderly Americans in nonfamilial living arrangements increased faster from 1960 to 1970 than could be explained by increased incomes alone (Pampel, 1981:170–171). The increase in separate living quarters has continued to the present time. Apparently the value placed upon independent residence is growing.

Socialized in such a value system, Americans of any age find it difficult to accept a dependent role. The consequences for the aged are hinted at by Simic as he continues (1977:58):

> It seems inevitable that the aged, caught up in a system stressing individual psychological and socio-economic independence and in which excellence is judged in terms of dedication and virtuosity in the performance of occupational tasks, deprived of their work statuses, and lacking a system of intense interdependence with children and kin, are left in a state of cultural and social semi-isolation in their declining years. It is not coincidental that the rallying cries of the retired echo the values of the society as a whole: "Be independent" and "Stay active."

Small wonder that the elderly of this society have a phobia about being a burden on their families or, equally horrible, having to live in an institution and depend on its services.

Francis Hsu (1961:216–219) contrasts the American attitude toward independence with that of the Chinese:

> The American core value . . . is self-reliance, the most persistent psychological expression of which is the fear of dependence. . . . Under this ideal [of self-reliance] every individual is his own master, in control of his own destiny, and will advance and regress in society only according to his own efforts. . . . A man in traditional China with no self-reliance as an ideal may not have been successful in his life. But suppose in his old age his sons are able to provide for him generously. Such a person not only will be happy and content about it, but is likely also to beat the drums before all and sundry to let the world know that he has good children who are supporting

him in a style to which he has never been accustomed. On the other hand, an American parent who has not been successful in life may derive some benefit from the prosperity of his children, but he certainly will not want anybody to know about it. In fact, he will resent any reference to it. . . . In American society the fear of dependence is so great that an individual who is not self-reliant is an object of hostility. . . . "Dependent character" is a highly derogatory term, and a person so described is thought to be in need of psychiatric help.

So strong is this phobia against dependence that some have found it to be at the base of some mental illness in America (Clark and Anderson, 1967). Clark (1972a:273) states the case as follows:

> In American culture, as I have described, morality is intimately bound to self-reliance, and self-reliance in turn, is tied to work and productivity, as well as to social and economic independence. From our research in San Francisco, it would appear that there can rarely be any happy prolonged dependence between the generations—neither of parent upon child, nor of adult child upon aging parent. The values do not sanction it, and both players resent it. The parent must remain—or, at least, appear to remain—strong and independent. This independence is sustained at the price of ever-increasing social distance, and in many American families social relationships between generations are formal and dispassionate. Those who can sustain the semblance of complete self-reliance in this way have higher morale and self-esteem than those who cannot. They may be lonely and in need, but they are at least remaining true to their most cherished ideals. This social mechanism, I believe, has often been confused with an inevitable characteristic of aging which some people call disengagement. A continued engagement with the young, moreover, is often confused with neurotic dependency.

An extreme extension of this prescribed way of life is perhaps to be found in the single-room occupancy (SRO) hotels in which many impoverished elderly males live. In one such establishment in Detroit, Stephens (1976) found 100 tenants living in a "society of the alone," characterized by "atomism" and norms of freedom, privacy, and utilitarianism. They were "loners" who had "broken all ties to family, friends and for the most part do not attempt to replenish what was already an impoverished repertoire of social relations." Others hold that this is an exaggeration of the extent of atomization and isolation and that these residents usually do have a network of regular social contacts on whom they can rely in emergency (Sokolovsky and Cohen, 1981). Even with this possible amendment, however, the residents of these institutions nonetheless represent a rather extreme extension of the norm of individualism and independence.

Of course Americans have no monopoly upon this value system. It is even found to some degree in some less developed societies. For example, Nahemow (1979) finds that the Baganda people of Africa emphasize "independence and individual achievement above familism," which may explain why their culture has been less disrupted by contact with Western civilization than many other traditional cultures. It is probably significant that Bagandan society does not ascribe any special position or role to its older people. Though they pay lip service to the ideal of respect for their elderly, this does not seem to have any particular meaning to the young people of the society.

In contrast, dependency is a virtue among the Ibo (Shelton, 1968). Children are socialized early to the inevitable dependence, including the dependence of old age. Consequently, there is no trauma about growing old, and there is minimal mental disorder of any kind. Another society in which individualism is disapproved of is that of the Zuni Indians of the American Southwest (Benedict, 1934). Here a man who seeks distinction is likely to be persecuted for sorcery. Instead, the ideal person is one who cooperates in the affairs of the society, including its many rituals, and who is self-effacing and generous.

Individualistic societies force individuals into a kind of precarious existence. They do not have the protective umbrella of the group to shelter them from life's exigencies. The strong may prosper and revel in the freedom to enjoy the advantages supplied by their strength—as long as it lasts. But when that strength fails, they are vulnerable and unprotected. So as some modern societies have opted for individualism, they have abandoned the protective shield of familism and have subjected their more vulnerable members, including the elderly, to risks of isolation and insecurity not found in familistic societies.

Egalitarianism

In *Growing Old in America*, Fischer (1977) contends that the decline in the status of the elderly since colonial times was due not to industrialization and urbanization, which came later, but to the egalitarian ethic that found expression in the American and French revolutions. Following Fischer, Williamson, Evans, and Powell (1982:44) draw a parallel between the effect of democratization in America and that in the time of Solon in Greece:

By the late eighteenth and early nineteenth centuries, Aristotle's claim that the young are better equipped to lead than the old was restated in very similar terms. As Americans fought for independence and news of French assaults on inequality drifted across the ocean, age—a major basis for inequality—came under fire. Just as elderly Greeks suffered a major loss of power with Solon's implementation of a democracy, so did colonial septuagenarians take it on the chin with cries of "liberty."

Whether these are accurate interpretations of history or not, it is true that a really democratic ethic is incompatible with any system of stratification based upon ascribed statuses, be they caste, race, sex, or age. You cannot have gerontocracy and democracy at the same time. "The autocrat of the breakfast table" does not listen comfortably to lectures on children's rights.

Democratic movements in societies that have been characterized by age stratification are bound to produce some strains. Young people all over Africa have been concerned about what to do with their elders as their countries have become self-governing and have shown some aspirations toward democracy. Tien (1977) maintains that the Chinese Revolution of 1949 was largely a revolt against the "tyranny of the aged."

Wherever there is a monopoly or near monopoly of power by the elderly, their interests obviously will take precedence over those of the young or middle aged, but with the revolt of youth the pendulum may swing to the opposite extreme, and the values and interests of the young may take priority over the elderly.

The Cult of Youth

The United States has often been described as a youth-centered society. No doubt this is in part an adaptation to rapid change. High value is placed upon efficiency, speed, and adaptability, and the young may have an advantage within this kind of value system. Greater physical strength and agility may have practical value. More recent socialization and education make the young more up-to-date and attuned to the current conditions and needs of the society. All these qualities are aspects of what Parsons (1960:163–164) calls instrumental activism. Emphasis is upon achievement and success, and therefore upon keeping doors of opportunity open. This is interrelated with the "accent on youth" and the assumption that the older generation has responsibility for providing these opportunities. Once youth has achieved its independence, there is little concern with the older generation who made it possible.

But the system is circular; once the values are established, it is discriminatory in favor of youth. The young are then given more opportunities in terms of health care, education, employment, recreation, and social services. This enhances their advantages still further.

Other qualities of the young, which may or may not carry inherent advantage, may nevertheless, by association, come to be included in the favored stereotype. Supple, unwrinkled skin comes to be defined as an attribute of beauty. Quick reflexes, physical activity, and endurance are given preference. Youth is not only utilitarian, it is beautiful.

Within such a value system, of course, old age becomes a disadvantage. The inevitable counterpart of the cult of youth is prejudice and discrimination against the elderly. This is what has been termed *ageism* by Robert Butler (1975:11–16). It is "a deep and profound prejudice against the elderly." It is manifested in "stereotypes and myths, outright disdain and dislike, or simply subtle avoidance of contact; discriminatory practices in housing, employment and services of all kinds; epithets, cartoons and jokes."

One irony of ageism is that it comes to be internalized by the aged themselves. In nationwide surveys in 1974 and 1981, Louis Harris and Associates (1975; 1981) found that the American people were indeed afflicted by ageism—they believed that the elderly were sick, lonely, poor, dependent, neglected, isolated, bored, inactive, morbidly afraid of death, and lived in constant fear of crime. Most significantly, the older people in the sample held these beliefs to almost the same degree as the younger respondents. However, although the older people who were interviewed were selected as a representative sample of the older people of the country, when asked to describe themselves, very few thought they fitted the stereotype. They apparently believed that older people in general were like that but that they themselves were exceptions.

Thus one consequence of the cult of youth is that older people themselves come to define old age negatively, leading them to deny that they are old, to dread becoming old, and to take frenetic measures to avoid appearing old. But there is also real discriminatory treatment of them in the form of differential medical and psychiatric treatment, denial of opportunity for jobs, preferential treatment of the young in housing, recreation, and various services. Further, if services for the elderly are provided, they may be offered with a patronizing attitude that older people schooled to the ethic of independence find demeaning.

Summary

In this chapter I have called attention to six general value systems, each of which has important implications for the status of elderly members of the societies subscribing to those values. Perhaps the reader will have noted some tendency among these systems to aggregate into mutually incompatible clusters at opposite extremes of favorability to the aged:

Cluster A (High Value and Extensive Involvement of Elderly)	Cluster B (Low Value and Minimal Involvement of Elderly)
filial piety	work ethic
familism	individualism
	egalitarianism
	cult of youth

At one pole are filial piety and familism, which are favorable to high status and full involvement of the elderly in society. At the opposite pole are the work ethic, egalitarianism, individualism, and the cult of youth, all of which militate in the direction of a relatively low status and minimal social involvement of the elderly. Egalitarianism tends to topple them from their previously favored positions, and the cult of youth pushes them into an unfavored one. The work ethic, because it results in a retirement system that extrudes them from their most significant role in society, tends also to lower their status, and the system of individualism tends to alienate them from society and leave them in a vulnerable condition in their later years. When all the values in cluster B are found in the same society, as they are in American society, they tend to reinforce each other and produce an exaggerated effect. This helps explain the markedly low status of the elderly in our society. Escape from that status may motivate some older people to migrate to retirement communities, and the higher morale found among residents of such communities (Bultena, 1974) may be a measure of the extent to which they have escaped the denigrating norms of the larger society. Within their own age-segregated communities, they can develop alternative value systems (Keith 1982:11).

Filial piety and familism are not only mutually compatible, they tend to support each other and to some degree tend to be found together empirically. Likewise, the four systems in cluster B are generally compatible with each other and tend to exert a positive valence toward each other. But the two clusters are antithetical to each other. Individualism runs counter to familism, and egalitarianism is incompatible with filial piety. Perhaps I should have included a cult of age as the opposite of the cult of youth and located examples of it in the gerontocracies and patriarchies of the world. (For a discussion and illustration of gerontocracy, the reader is referred to Chapter 6.) It is also pertinent to point out that cluster A appears to be most extensively represented in premodern, preindustrial societies and that cluster B is generally associated with highly modernized societies.

Chapter Four

Kinship Systems and Family Roles

$\mathbf{A}$ging in both a demographic and a personal sense takes place within a sociological context, and in both senses the most significant sociological context is the family. More than thirty years ago, Leo Simmons (1945:177) stated, "Throughout human history the family has been the safest haven for the aged; it is just here, in the home and the circle of kinship, that the old have always found their greatest security during the closing years of life." Yet there are wide variations in the forms of family life, and the relations among kin and these variations inevitably require different kinds of relationships between other family members and their old folk. In this chapter I shall analyze some of the varieties of families and kinship groupings and note how they seem to impinge upon their older members. I shall illustrate the principles drawn from this analysis with a number of cultural case studies. Then I shall call attention to some modern changes and experiments that are in process in the Western world, modifying both family life and the lives of older people. I shall note some of the familial roles played by other persons and how these relate to the structure of the family. And finally I shall attempt to formulate a theory of the relationship between form of the family and the family's response to its older members.

Varieties of Kinship Systems

Kinship systems can be classified according to many different criteria. In this chapter, I shall limit the discussion to four criteria: power relationships, lines of descent, forms of marriage, and patterns of residence. These appear to be the aspects of kinship that have greatest salience for older persons.

Power Relationships

When kinship groupings are viewed in terms of who has the most authority within the family, most cases can be subsumed under two headings: patriarchal and egalitarian. The patriarchal form is quite common, being found in the classical Chinese family, as well as among the ancient Romans, the biblical Hebrews, and so on. In this form the primary authority rests with males, and the central authority is usually focused in the oldest living male of the family. Simmons (1945:212) notes that old men have more secure status and economic prerogatives in patriarchal societies.

The egalitarian or democratic form of the family is one in which males and females wield approximately equal influence. It is most commonly associated with neolocal residence and bilateral tracing of descent. It is the normative standard for white middle-class Americans, but as we shall see, it is often associated with lower status of the aged.

Anthropologists have speculated about a matriarchal form of the family, but while there are individual cases in which females have become dominant personalities within families, there is no authenticated case of a society in which the norm is female dominance. In view of the predominance of women in aged populations, such a family system would have profound implications for the status and welfare of the elderly.

Lines of Descent

There are three pure forms for the tracing of descent—matrilineal, patrilineal, and bilateral. To be sure, there are some permutations and subtypes, but we need not be concerned with them here. Under the matrilineal system, descent is traced through the female line, and property is usually inherited accordingly. The patrilineal system is just the opposite, descent being traced through the male line and property normally passing from father to son. Such unilineal systems have the advantages of simplicity, avoidance of conflict of loyalties, and less dissipation of inheritable properties. But in many societies descent through both lines is acknowledged, and inheritance may pass to sons and daughters alike; this is the bilateral system.

In a tabulation of 560 societies in the World Ethnographic Sample (Nimkoff, 1965:25), only 80 were classified as matrilineal, compared with 239 that were patrilineal and 241 that were bilateral. Lineage per se does not determine other patterns of family life, including the treatment of elderly persons, but lineage is strongly correlated with residence patterns, which do have a bearing on where older people live and who looks after them if they become dependent. There is also some relation between descent patterns and the type of economy. Most pastoral societies, in which the main form of property is herds of animals, are patrilineal, and patriliny is also the most frequent form in agricultural societies, in which land is the most valued form of property. However, fishing and hunting societies lean more toward bilateral descent patterns and matriliny (Nimkoff, 1965:41). In general, older people have more power and prestige under conditions of unilateral kinship, but Simmons (1945:214) found that both older men and older women fared better under patriliny. This may mean merely that they are more secure in agricultural and pastoral societies.

Forms of Marriage

The form of marriage is obviously intimately linked with any discussion of family and kinship systems. In nearly all societies husbands and wives live together in a common household, and in all societies marriage identifies the group within which sanctioned reproduction may take place. But here, as in other aspects of human culture, we find variation encompassing almost all logical and biological possibilities.

Marriage is a socially sanctioned, sexual/reproductive relationship between one or more females and one or more males. The number of each sex included in the relationship defines the different forms of marriage with which we are concerned. There are only four: monogamy, polygyny, polyandry, and group marriage. Monogamy includes only one person of each sex. Polygamy is a generic term for any form of plural marriage, of which there are three subtypes. Polygyny refers to marriage of one man to two or more women concurrently. Polyandry is just the opposite, the marriage of one woman to two or more men. Group marriage links more than one male to more than one female. It is very rare, and in those few instances where it has been reported, it appears to be a transitional phenomenon or an aberrant combination of the other two types of polygamy.

Though monogamy is undoubtedly the most frequent form in actual practice, it is not universally the most preferred form. Societies are usually classified as polygamous if plural marriage is permitted or encouraged, even though a majority of the marriages are actually monogamous (Murdock, 1949:28). Polygyny is permissible or preferred in most societies—415 out of 554 societies included in the World Ethnographic Sample (Murdock, 1957:686). Only 135 societies required monogamous unions, and only 4 practiced polyandry. In none was group marriage a dominant or approved form. In some polygynous societies older men may add to their wealth, prestige, and household labor supply by marrying additional young and healthy wives (Simmons, 1945:175–182). In view of the excess of females in older populations, some people have suggested that were it permitted, polygyny might provide both more efficient living arrangements and more congenial lives for older people.

Patterns of Residence

Most other aspects of family life are conditioned by and interrelated with the customs governing place of residence of the young couple at the time of marriage. There are many varieties of such customs, but the most important and most frequent are designated as patrilocal, matrilocal, bilocal, neolocal, and avunculocal.

Patrilocal marriage refers to the practice whereby a newly married couple goes to live with the family of the parents of the groom. This may be in the same household or merely in the same village or vicinity, but it has the effect of separating the bride from her kin while binding her to the kin of her husband. Matrilocal residence is the opposite pattern, under which the newlyweds live with the parents of the bride, and it tends to unite the husband with the family of the bride. In most cases the prevailing rules of exogamy, requiring marriage outside of one's own kin group, mean that such rules of residence force a choice and require one or the other member of a new marriage to move to a new locality. Matrilocal residence is strongly but by no means invariably associated with matriliny, and the same association is found between patrilocality and patriliny. Avunculocal marriage is an alternative to matrilocality and is nearly always found in connection with matriliny; this is the pattern whereby the newlyweds reside with the maternal uncle of the bride. A bilocal system permits the couple to reside with either set of parents. The prevalent and preferred form in the United States is known as neolocal. Under it the young couple sets up a new household apart from both sets of parents. This tends to produce a nuclear family as the household unit. In its early stages it is devoid of older members, while in its late stages it may consist entirely of older persons living apart from their children.

The patrilocal form is by far the most frequent pattern of residence; it characterized more than half (313) of the 560 societies included in the World Ethnographic Sample (Nimkoff, 1965:25). Only 85 were matrilocal, and an additional 13, avunculocal. Twenty-seven were neolocal, and another 30, bilocal. The rest consisted of a wide range of rare varieties.

When an extended kin network is concentrated in a household, compound, or village, older people tend to remain as members with full rights and acknowledged status, but neolocal marriage tends to separate the generations, making the status and care of older people more problematic.

Household Groups

Though all of the above aspects of kinship bear on the issue of which people live together in a common household, they do not clearly define such a unit; nor is the term *family* adequate for that purpose. The concept of family has no standard, unambiguous meaning as applied in different cultures. For Americans it commonly connotes a household group consisting of husband, wife, and children, but when children leave home they do not necessarily cease to be members of the family. And in other contexts the term may include other relatives, such as grandparents or even in-laws who are not and never have been members of the specific household. Furthermore, Firth, Hubert, and Forge (1970:289–291) note that the "extended family" in London did not incorporate all relatives within designated degrees of kinship; instead there was always selectivity. Some first cousins might be included but others not; some aunts and uncles were considered part of the family, but others were not. Because of this ambiguity, these authors preferred the term *intimate kin set* to refer to the particular cluster of individuals designated as family by any specific individual.

If there is lack of agreement on the meaning of family within given cultures, small wonder that differing concepts in different cultures can cause misunderstanding. In her study of the Indo-Chinese migrants to the United States in the wake of the Vietnam War, Garkovich (1976:224–228) found that arbitrary application of the prevailing American definition of the term *family* to these Vietnamese and Cambodian refugees created heartache and serious problems for both the refugees and their American sponsors. In this case the American bureaucrats assumed that a family (for residential and economic purposes) included only husband, wife, and children, and they deployed these to various American communities, but the Indo-Chinese families who were arriving were not so restrictive in their definition of family membership. For them the family was a more inclusive concept, including consanguinal relations within at least three generations. In many cases they arrived as fragments of three or four generations of a family, as conceived in their societies, only to find that American bureaucrats recognized only the nuclear unit as a family and physically tore the Indo-Chinese family apart, dispersing the various fragments to different geographic destinations within the United States. A predictable sequel to such a policy was that the various segments of those Indo-Chinese families, as they conceived of family, would try to get back together. Consequently, there has been much remigration and reuniting of families at various points in the country.

Three intermingled and overlapping relationships are commonly used to designate those individuals who belong to a family: consanguinity, marriage, and common residence (Nimkoff, 1965:14–20). Various degrees of blood relationship may be included within the cultural definition of family, ranging from the narrowest conception—encompassing only siblings of common parents, a prevalent view of the family in American society—to the widest, consisting of all people supposedly related through an actual or mythical common ancestor, as in traditional China, where those with a common surname or patronymic were considered related and therefore subject to the rule of exogamy prohibiting marriage among them.

However, it should be noted that in the latter case the concept of relationship is applied unilaterally, applying only to those of common descent through the male line; relationship through the female line is lost sight of beyond the mother's generation. In many societies, including traditional Chinese society, the consanguinal bond is more important than the marriage bond in determining family membership, and in such societies marriage is controlled by and is subservient to the clan or lineage; a person may have more regard for and obligation to his or her brothers and/or sisters than to his or her spouse. For example, a man may have more obligations to his sister and her children than to his own wife and children.

Nevertheless, marriage is a second bond defining who is to be included within the definition of the family in most societies, and in nearly all societies people who are married to each other live together in a common household or compound and therefore belong to the household group, whether or not that is the same as or included within the group considered to be the family. The Nayars of southern India are an exception in their exclusion of husbands from the conventional residential group; after the fourth day of marriage, husbands are only occasional nocturnal visitors in the households of their wives (Mencher, 1965:163). But this exceptional case illustrates the importance of the distinction made by Murdock (1949:42) between the "residential kin group" and the "consanguinal kin group."

The consanguinal bond is probably more widely used and most often takes precedence over the residential group commonly connoted by the term *family*. But as Murdock points out, the residential kin group may include all forms of the family, from those based on the marriage bond, the *conjugal* family, to those based on the several varieties of blood relationship, the *consanguinal* family.

Households Based on Marriage

Households based primarily on marriage incorporate all the various types of marriage outlined earlier. When monogamous marriage is combined with neolocal residence, the resulting residential unit, assuming that the marriage is fertile, is the nuclear family. It is important to note that the nuclear family, as a sociological group consisting of husband, wife, and their children, is a nearly universal phenomenon that occurs in various contexts as a separate and distinct residential unit produced by monogamous, neolocal marriage, and as a subunit within households based on polygamous marriages as well as in households based on various conceptions of consanguinity.

Because the nuclear family is so prevalent as a free-standing residential unit in Western industrial societies, there is a strong ethnocentric tendency to assume that this form is dominant everywhere, which has led to a tendency to understate the extent of change caused by modernization. (I will discuss this issue more fully later.)

Of course most households in the United States and other Western industrialized countries are nuclear family units. Sussman (1976:230) has estimated that 48 percent of American families consist of husband, wife, and children (37 percent intact nuclear families and 11 percent remarried couples). Eleven percent consist of couples only—newly married, childless, and "empty nest"—and another 12 percent have only one parent present. Because the latter two types may be considered merely incomplete forms of nuclear families, this indicates that at least 71 percent of American families are basically nuclear in form and constitute distinct household units. But even this understates the case because the largest portion of the remainder (19 percent) consists of unrelated individuals who also may represent incomplete nuclear units—not yet married, widowed, separated, or divorced. Only 4 percent are clearly extended families, some of which include three generations. The remainder are called "emerging experimental forms"; these include communes and families in which the parents are not married. These demographic data agree with information about attitudes of people of all ages, indicating a very strong preference for independent households for conjugal units and even for unrelated individuals (Streib and Thompson, 1960:477–481).

However, extended forms of the family constitute households with greater frequency in other societies and are the preferred or normative arrangement in many. Murdock (1949:23) found that 140 out of 187 societies in his World Ethnographic Sample sanctioned some form of compound families as household units. These included both families extended by polygamous marriages and those extended through inclusion of consanguinal kin.

In polygamous societies households commonly consist of all the married spouses and their children. For example, among the African Bagandas the household consists of a man, his several wives, and their children. However, to this conjugal unit is often attached some additional consanguines, such as unmarried or widowed sisters of the husband and perhaps his aged parents (Queen and Habenstein, 1974:74). A Baganda man may make old age more secure by acquiring more wives, who not only add to his wealth and prestige but also provide more hands to care for him. He is never without a home; should he have to dissolve his own, he is free to join that of a son. The Tiwi of Australia also count wives as wealth, and older men have often acquired several wives along with other forms of wealth to provide them with a measure of security in old age (Boyd, 1973:36).

Much more rare is the polyandrous family household, including one woman, her several husbands, and their children. This type of household is found among the Todas of southern India (Queen and Habenstein, 1974:25). In this case the husbands are usually brothers, and sometimes the households include the parents of the husbands.

Households Based on Consanguinity

The other dimension along which the household is extended is consanguinity, but the extension may be vertical, including more than two generations of blood relatives, or it may be lateral, involving the families of several married siblings. Occasionally we may find both types of extension combined.

Residence is usually congruous with lineage; that is, patrilocal societies are likely to be patrilineal, and matrilocal societies are matrilineal. Out of 560 societies, Nimkoff (1965:25) found that 313 were patrilocal and 85 were matrilocal. Only 27 were specifically neolocal.

Nearly always, vertical extension involving three or more generations in the same household follows a unilineal pattern; that is, it is either patrilineal or matrilineal. In patrilineally extended households we commonly find the oldest patriarch, his sons, their wives and children, plus any unmarried daughters of the patriarch. Such households, compounds, or villages may be very large, but they operate as a single household with a common treasury and integrated daily activities. In such cases the older male wields the power, controls the property, and demands respect of the subordinate kinsmen. This appears to have been the condition among the ancient Hebrews, where such patriarchs as Abraham and Jacob in their old age ruled extensive households, including their sons and their wives, plus all unmarried daughters of any generation (Queen and Habenstein, 1974:165). The elders in such families, being very powerful and in control of the property of the lineage, were generally revered and cherished.

On the other hand, the household in a matrilineal society may include an elderly female, her female descendants, their husbands, and all of their unmarried children. This type of household is characteristic of the Hopi Indians of southwestern United States (Queen and Habenstein, 1974:50). A variation of this is the avunculocal household, with the matriarch's brother as the head of the household, as among the Haida Indians of the Northwest (Murdock, 1949:34–35). In such situations older women may be very influential.

A limited form of extended family is the so-called *stem family* or *la famille-souche*. The term was first used by Frederic Le Play (1874) in reference to the type of family found rather extensively in rural France and Spain during the nineteenth century. The stem family may be either matrilineal or patrilineal in structure; the key feature distinguishing it from other vertically extended families is that only one of the adult children remains in the parental household, assuming primary responsibility for the care of the parents in their old age and inheriting the family homestead. The patrilineal form of the stem family is the traditional pattern in Japan and is still widely observed (Palmore, 1975b). Similar patterns occur in both Ireland (Streib, 1972:167–181) and French Canada (Queen and Habenstein, 1974:415–416). In northern Thailand it is usually the youngest daughter who remains in the parental compound to look after her parents and to inherit the property (de Young, 1958:23; Cowgill, 1972:94), but in other parts of the country it appears that either sons or daughters may assume the responsibility (Kaufman, 1960:24).

On the other hand, the joint family involves lateral extension of the family and household, with married siblings remaining in a common household. Such is the pattern among the Mapuche Indians of Chile, where brothers are expected to remain together in the same household or compound throughout their lives (Boyd, 1973:36). Thus, they continue the family heritage and maintain security for themselves and their families.

So we see that households vary widely in terms of who is included, but in general, the vertically extended family household provides a more secure and honorific status for the elderly members, while the neolocal nuclear family tends to separate older members from younger generations. Such families provide less intimate and continuous contacts within the family, and in such societies primary responsibility for the economic security of the aged tends to be delegated to the state rather than to the family.

Some Illustrations

Perhaps some case studies of family and kinship systems and their relations to older members will help clarify concepts and principles. For this purpose I shall describe the classical patriarchal extended family of pre-revolutionary China, the stem family of nineteenth-century France, the stem family of contemporary Thailand, and the nuclear family household of the United States.

The Classical Patriarchal Extended Family of China

In its prime the extended family of imperial China functioned as a well-organized and unified household that provided direction and security for all its members, especially for the aged.* The patrilineal structure of the family vested authority in the eldest male member—the patriarch—who was responsible for the continued prosperity of the family. His authority extended over the entire family, and refusal to abide by his decisions was considered an intolerable offense. His position as family head, buttressed by the younger generations' fidelity to the prescriptions of filial piety, was as much the seat of honor as it was that of authority. "He was," writes sinologist C. K. Yang, "at the pinnacle of the age hierarchy."

---

*Much of the material on the classical Chinese family was gathered and written by James K. Callihan.

For the eldest female the situation was somewhat different, although she too was highly respected by the junior members of the family. As the patriarch was the object of his family's esteem, his wife was the object of its affection. Her authority, although quite genuine, was restricted to the female members of the family, as she was responsible for ensuring their proper assimiliation of the family's traditional rules and regulations. Even in old age, however, she was obliged to respect the authority of the male members: "A woman should obey her father before marriage, her husband after marriage, and her son when her husband has deceased" (Lee, 1953:275). Nonetheless, old age for the female family member signaled a period in her life when the bonds of servitude to the male members of the family were loosened and a modicum of authority became available. By and large, the aged Chinese couple occupied a dependable status, received formal deference, and were the objects of unbounded respect. To suggest that they were central to the family is but to recognize that it was largely upon their shoulders and by their command that the extended family was constructed and did endure.

Although the extended family provided its members with a veritable security, it would be erroneous to assume that this classical form of the family was enjoyed by even the majority of Chinese. It would be more correct to regard the extended family as a cultural ideal, sought after by the majority of Chinese but available only to a few. For those Chinese among the gentry and officialdom who could amass the wealth necessary to sustain the large, extended family, the cultural ideal became reality; but for those without the financial wherewithal, the extended family remained but an object of admiration and a sign of prosperity. "It is significant," writes Yang (1959:9), "that this form of family organization was intimately associated with the classes having social, economic and political dominance." Family structure among the large peasant population, rather than assuming the extended family form, was usually small and more likely of a nuclear or stem family nature.

In discussing the patrilineal organization of this exalted form of the family, it will become apparent that propagation of the male line was considered vastly more important than cultivation of the female line, that the father-son (consanguine) relationship was of far greater significance than the husband-wife (conjugal) relationship, and that maintenance of the family as a cooperative unit was more essential than that of any specific individual within the family. In its accomplished form the extended family consisted of parents belonging to the senior generation, their sons (natural or adopted), and their sons' wives and children sharing a common household and engaged in a communal effort to increase the family's wealth and social position. The family extended vertically to encompass three and preferably more generations, often resulting in a household unit in excess of twenty members. The extended family household, situated in the broader organizational context of a patrilineal sib, might have consisted of literally hundreds of individuals owing allegiance to the same patrimony.

The patrilineal organization of the family focused primary concern upon the maintenance of the male descent group and, in contrast, afforded little consideration of the female group. When a daughter married, the exogamous marriage rules and the patrilocal residence rules signaled her inevitable departure from her natural family. A Chinese proverb states that "a boy is born looking in; a girl looking out" (Freedman, 1958:31). Accordingly, her youth was spent largely in service to the male members of the family as well as in preparation for the eventful day when she would marry and leave her own family to join that of her husband. So complete was her severance from her natural family that a married woman was considered to have only one family, that of her husband, and she could return to visit her parents only with the permission of her husband. The emphasis upon the male descent group had similar connotations for the daughter-in-law. Expected to steadfastly adhere to the traditional rules of her husband's family, her place was one of dutiful obedience not only to the male members of the family but to the eldest female as well. Whereas giving birth to a son strengthened her relationship with the male-dominated family, failure to bear sons was considered sufficient grounds for her expulsion from it. Occupying an inferior position within the family, the woman's only hope for increased status was in the birth of sons and the onset of old age.

For the male members of the family, the situation was radically different. Authority, name, and property were the possessions of the male descent group, and inheritance passed only from father to son. In the case of more than one son (which undoubtedly was preferred), each possessed an equal share in the family's holdings, but the patriarchal authority was transferred only to the eldest. While the father was alive, he directed his sons' collective efforts to maintain and increase the family's holdings. His age, which signified a technical expertise, allowed him to remain actively engaged in productive efforts until about age 60, when it dictated his retirement from physical labor and movement into the role of advisor or supervisor. It was to their father, rather than to their wives, that the sons owed their complete loyalty and respect. And in a similar fashion, it was toward his sons that the father's life was directed. The sons' duty to their father and the father's duty to his sons bound a relationship so tightly that any sign of its deterioration brought dishonor to both father and son. This glorification of the father-son relationship, and of the male descent group in general, provided the foundation upon which the classical extended family was sturdily constructed. Upon the father's death, should the sons agree to divide the family's holdings, each son received an equal share save the eldest, who received a slightly larger share in order that he might finance his added responsibility of maintaining the family's genealogy and the ancestral shrine.

The father-son relationship, pivotal to the patrilineal organization of the extended family, was strengthened even further by the doctrines of filial piety that permeated the whole of China's social fabric. Primarily of Confucian origin, filial piety prescribed the proper relation between members of the junior and senior generations and placed extreme emphasis on the son's recognition of the supreme importance of his parents. Filial piety prescribed unmitigated obedience and devotion to the parents and, in cases of unfilial behavior, empowered the parents with the authority to call for the death of their recalcitrant son. "Under traditional social order," writes Yang (1959:87), "it took exceptional courage and imagination to be an unfilial son." And the *Hsiao King*, the Confucian book of filial piety, states that "there are 3,000 offenses against which the five punishments are directed; there is none of them greater than to be unfilial" (Dawson, 1915:159). Beyond obedience and devotion, filial piety commanded that the son should not only provide his parents with ample material security but also honor them by the proper organization and development of his own personality. The filial son, inculcated with a belief that his life was a gift made to him by his parents, was careful not to bring dishonor upon them by inappropriate behavior. As the good name of the father provided a good name for the son, so did the son's development of a good name for himself bequeath honor upon that of his father: "During the first thirty years of a man's life, people look at the father and respect his son; thirty years later people look at the son and respect his father" (Hsu, 1949:76). Any deviation from the expectations of filial piety meant disgrace for both father and son. Such was the importance of filial piety that the *Hsiao King* states, "Filial piety is the way of Heaven, the principle of Earth, and the practical duty of man" (Fung, 1952:366).

This type of family has obvious advantages for its older members. Because they have power and authority, they can, within limits, control their own destiny as well as that of others. Authority usually carries with it the prerogatives of respect and honor, and these are reinforced by the values of the society. Thus the status of the elders is high and secure. And to the extent that the family commands economic resources, the elderly share in them. This type of family is the social security for its elders.

The Stem Family of Nineteenth-Century France

The term *stem family* originated with a brilliant nineteenth-century French social scientist named Frederic Le Play (1874); of course the French term he used was *la famille-souche*. This was a compromise between the large patriarchal family, which he thought was conservative and restrictive, and the "unstable" family that seemed to be developing in the modern cities. The latter was the small, neolocal, nuclear family, which he thought incapable of transmitting the values necessary for societal survival and too fragile to protect its members against the various hazards of life, particularly the hazards of urban life.

The stem family is a family in which only one married child stays in the parental home and inherits the homestead. The other children move elsewhere upon marriage, but they are usually provided with assistance out of the estate toward a start in their chosen vocation. The oldest male is the supreme authority and trustee as long as he chooses to bear the responsibility, but he often passes the mantle to his heir upon marriage of the latter. If the head of the family dies without children, his widow usually inherits his role and carries on in the interest of the welfare of other members, who may include unmarried persons of any generation.

The primary concerns of the family as a whole are the raising of children and the protection of dependent members, including the aged and widowed. Le Play notes that this type of family is best adapted to the needs of sedentary agricultural people among whom land is the main form of property. He asserts that in addition to southern France and northern Spain, it is found in rural areas all the way from Scandinavia to northern Italy. In essence the father, the surviving grandparents, and the heir apparent are the trustees of the land and the homestead, and they allocate the produce in the interest of the family as a whole or for the special needs of particular members. The general family interests include such things as memorials to ancestors, religious ceremonies, home repairs, taxes, and so on. In addition to the provision of daily sustenance, personal needs to be paid for by the family exchequer include educational expenses and dowries. Inheritance succession appears to be at intervals of about 25 years (Le Play, 1874:28–39).

Le Play provides detailed descriptions of several such families. One of these includes 18 persons: the heir and his wife, 25 and 20 years of age; his father and mother, 52 and 47, married 27 years; the grandfather, 80; an aunt and uncle, sister and brother of the father, both unmarried; 9 children of various ages; and 2 servants (1874:33). Another family of 15 is composed of the following: the *maitre de maison*, a widower, aged 74; his daughter and her husband, aged 45 and 60, married 19 years and she pregnant with her eighth child; 7 children, including one son; a brother and sister of the *maitre*, both unmarried; two unmarried sons; and an unmarried servant, 59 (1874:123). It will be noted from these illustrations that inheritance is not strictly patrilineal; property may be passed to daughters as well as to sons.

Le Play may have idealized this form of the family, but by his account it provided a secure, dignified status for older people and incapacitated members. They not only shared fully in the produce of the family enterprises, but the older persons in particular remained influential members of the primary decision-making group. They had a share of power and they were honored members. Perhaps more importantly, they were anchored emotionally at the heart of an intimate family group and thus were secure not only economically and physically but also emotionally. Le Play does not tell us what happened to the children who married out of this parental nest or how they fared in old age, but for those who remained in *la famille-souche*, it appeared to provide a safe and potentially happy haven in old age.

Le Play's theories as to the types of families extant in nineteenth-century France and the trends therein were confirmed by an ingenious study of census information (Parish and Schwartz, 1972). The patriarchal extended family had practically disappeared, and in its place the stem family was common in rural France; but as Le Play predicted, the nuclear family was becoming more prevalent in the cities.

The Residual Stem Family of Thailand

In contemporary Thailand there is a variable and flexible type of family that usually eventuates in a stem form during the later years of the parental couple. This comes about as a result of a sequence of stages of family life. During the early years of marriage, a couple conventionally lives with one or the other set of parents. There is no hard and fast rule as to which set of parents, so it is impossible to say whether Thai marriage is patrilocal or matrilocal. Kamnuansilpa (1975:33) suggests that this is less a matter of custom than of economics; the couple tends to reside with the set of parents that is better able to accommodate them. However, it is crucial to recognize that for most couples this is merely a temporary place of residence. The length of stay appears to be contingent primarily upon two factors: marriage of other siblings in the family and birth of their own children. If there are other siblings in the parental home who are unmarried, their decision (or that of the parents) to wed may precipitate a housing crisis, forcing someone to seek new quarters. In Thailand it is usually the older siblings and spouses who move out to make room for the newlyweds. Phillips (1965:23) found that the average stay of the young married couple in the parental home was four years.

This cyclical rotation of newly married couples out of the parental home continues until the last child, who usually stays on indefinitely. Because it is basically the last child to be married that determines who will continue to live in the parental home, there is no set pattern by sex; in northern Thailand this was most commonly a daughter (de Young, 1958), but in other parts of Thailand it appears quite variable. For most Thais this pattern of rotation of residence produces cyclical shifts in the composition of the households in which they are residing. Early in marriage they are living in a stem family, and then most of them move out and live for a time as a nuclear family. This stage lasts until the first child is married, when it again becomes a stem family; and with a sequence of married children rotating through the household, it remains a stem family until the old folks die.

In Thailand, however, the term *household* is somewhat elusive and ambiguous. The climate is semitropical, and a great portion of one's life is spent out-of-doors. To a very great extent this includes cooking, eating, and visiting. Thus the physical structure of the home is often little more than a bedroom situated within a compound, while the cooking, eating, bathing, visiting, and even much of the working takes place in the compound rather than in the physical structure of the home. Hence when we say that the young married couple lives with the parents of one of them, the young couple usually sleeps in a separate structure within the parental compound. This usually involves common cooking and eating facilities, but this too is flexible, especially since eating is more of an individual matter and less often a scheduled group activity. Western definitions of household membership are not easily applied in this type of society.

Nevertheless, older people usually live within a stem family context—in the same compound, if not the same house, as at least one of their married children. They easily and naturally transfer authority and responsibility to the younger generations and in return are monitored and cared for by the younger members, who have been taught early to honor their elders. The Buddhist religion sanctions and supports a mild version of filial piety, and much merit making consists of doing favors for and showing honor to one's elders. Other forms of merit making, such as serving in the priesthood, are thought to benefit one's parents as well as oneself. It brings them honor in this life and accumulates spiritual assets that will benefit them in the next life.

The Nuclear Family Household in the United States

The American family is predominantly nuclear and neolocal in form, and because children generally leave the parental family residence at marriage and establish their own homes elsewhere, when all the children have gone, the parents are left in an "empty nest."* Only two generations ago one or the other of the parents frequently died before the last child left home (Glick, 1977:6), but with the increase in life expectancy and the early cessation of childbearing, today most parents survive this event by many years. This has extended the empty nest period from an average of less than 2 years for those born in the 1880s to almost 13 years for those born in the 1950s.

In the early part of this period at least, the older couple maintains its economic and residential independence, and for the most part the father remains as head of an independent household. He is in the late stages of his occupational career, his children are in the early stages of theirs, and they are usually also in the process of family formation. During this period, roughly from 50 to 65 years of age, the older parents commonly offer considerable financial assistance to their children, helping them to buy homes, purchase furniture, and so on (Hill, 1970:68).

Only with the death or disability of one of the older parents is there any question of "disengagement" or sacrifice of independence. American mores thoroughly support the independence of both parents and children as far as residence is concerned (Streib and Thompson, 1960:477–481). Only widowhood or disability, not age per se, interrupts this pattern.

Most of the older people living with their children are older women living in the homes of their daughters. Surviving widowers show a marked reluctance to live with their children, of either sex, but older widows are much more amenable to living with their daughters, and the daughters are more prone to accept this arrangement.

By "living with" I mean living in the same structure, in the same household, and as a member of the family. There are now emerging many other arrangements that provide approximations to the same mutual services and interrelationships. Many older parents do not actually live "with," in the above sense, but live "near." These arrangements include all of the following varieties: living in adjacent apartments, the older person having a separate apartment within the home of the child (usually

---

* The material in this section is mainly taken from D. O. Cowgill, "Aging in American Society," in D. O. Cowgill and L. D. Holmes, *Aging and Modernization* (New York: Appleton-Century-Crofts, 1972), pp. 243–261.

a daughter) and her children, separate or unattached quarters for the older person (or couple) on the same lot, a residential trailer for the older person (or couple) parked on the property of the child, or a house or apartment within a short distance from the child. Of course there are varying degrees of the latter case, from those who live next door to those who may be several miles away but close enough that the children can look in on the older couple daily or more often.

Partly because of the development of these many residential arrangements, which are difficult for an organization such as a national Bureau of the Census to detect, it appeared for several decades that the nuclear family had completely supplanted the extended family in the United States. More recently, special local research projects have revealed, even in urban areas, a high degree of interaction between older parents and their children (Axelrod, 1956; Bell and Boat, 1958). This has forced a reappraisal of the residential and ecological relationships.

However, it should be stated that whatever the residential arrangements, most older people in the United States are not sociologically isolated. On the average, even in metropolitan areas, they have contact with relatives at least once a week, and three fourths of them have such contacts at least once each month.

Furthermore, it should be pointed out that in an affluent, highly mechanized society, the term *contact* takes on a different meaning. If a daughter, though thousands of miles removed, calls her mother every week or writes to her every day, the relationship may be more intimate than if she lived in the same town but stopped by only once a month.

There is certainly much mutual aid between adult children and their aged parents, but it should be emphasized that this is mutual. It is not merely a matter of the children caring for aged parents; parents also assist their children. As far as financial assistance is concerned, the flow is definitely from parents to children (Sussman, 1953), although of course this varies with social class. Parents also serve as babysitters and occasionally as nurses or homemakers, especially during the illness or confinement of a daughter or daughter-in-law. On the other hand, children provide companionship and sociability through visits, letters, and telephone calls; they also provide transportation (for parents who no longer can drive or take the bus), nursing service, and sometimes housing. It is estimated that family members provide 80 percent of all personal care and medically related services to older people in America and that most of it is provided by women, especially by daughters (Archbold, 1982:12–13; Brody and Lang, 1982:20).

There is of course some conflict and misunderstanding between generations, but folk humor has exaggerated the extent of this; mothers-in-law are not usually meddling dictators who are resented by their sons-in-law, and daughters-in-law are not usually at odds with their husbands' mothers.

The United States is a mobile society; about 20 percent of the population changes residence each year. Spread over a lifetime, this expands into rather extensive and gross migration patterns. These statistics obscure the impact on families; internally they mean a tendency for children to move away, not merely from the parental home but also from geographic proximity to the parents. Usually the children move and the parents stay. With the massive movement from rural to urban areas that was characteristic of American society for several generations, this means that many older people were left in the rural areas while their children moved to the cities. More precisely it means that many of the towns and villages of the Midwest have high proportions of older people, whose children are to be found in urban and metropolitan areas. One consequence of this type of movement is that some of the older people in the villages of the Midwest are geographically more separated from their children than are older people in metropolitan areas (Cowgill, 1965). Because of their expanse and inclusiveness, metropolitan areas, for all their reputed impersonality, tend to include within their vast confines a greater proportion of the children of a given couple than does an isolated rural hamlet. Hence within the metropolitan areas, most older people have one or more of their children within commuting distance, and thus we find that three fourths of such older people are visited by their children at least once a month. Recently the migration patterns have shifted, and now the net flow for both generations is toward nonmetropolitan areas. The effect of this upon intergenerational contacts has not yet been assessed.

Thus in the United States, where the nuclear family is the predominant household group, most older people are found in their own separate households; this includes not only older couples but older widows and widowers as well. These people live within a culture that since pioneer days has emphasized individualism and personal independence. These values are hazardous for older people. But this has not resulted in the extent of isolation of the elderly that had been predicted. Though most older people in this society are living in households apart from their children and other generations, they are not isolated socially. Most of them still have regular and frequent contacts with their children.

Modern Adaptations of Family Structure

Throughout the preceding discussion there have been hints of systematic differences in family structure between developing societies and modern industrialized societies. Furthermore, these differences suggest that there may have been long-term trends resulting from adaptations in response to the multifaceted forces of modernization. Therefore it seems appropriate to review some of the classical statements on this subject and the recent revisions based upon new evidence.

Classical Theory of Family Trends

More than a century ago Le Play thought he observed a trend away from the patriarchal family toward what he called an "unstable" form of the family (1874:9–11). By the latter he meant the nuclear family household that resulted from neolocal marriage, which separated the conjugal pair from the large family network, provided an insufficient base for the transmission of familial and societal values, and which was incapable of protecting its members from the hazards of life. He noted that the trend toward this unstable family form was most evident in the cities.

This theme has been repeated in various forms many times. In the 1930s Ogburn and Tibbitts (1933:661–708), writing about the family in the context of a broad study of recent social trends, found that the family was decreasing in size and was in the process of diminishing or sloughing off many of its traditional functions, including economic production, education of the young, religious instruction and practice, recreation, and protection of incapacitated members. A decade later Burgess and Locke (1945) had reformulated the theory to a trend from the family as an institution to the family as merely a unity of interacting personalities. Meanwhile Folsom (1943:187) asserted that grandparents, aunts, and uncles were living within extended family households less frequently and that neolocal marriage and the nuclear family household were becoming standard; this was thought to be associated with increasing dependence of the aged upon the community rather than the family. But the theory was given its most prestigious endorsement when Talcott Parsons (1942:615; 1954:89–93) stated that not only was there a trend toward the "isolated nuclear family" but that this was the only form of the family that was compatible with modern industrial society. At about the same time, in a textbook on the family, Kirkpatrick (1955:138) was asserting that a transition was underway in the form of the family, which included a trend from the extended form to the nuclear, from consanguinal relationships to conjugal relationships, from lineage-local marriage to neolocal marriage, and from unilateral descent to bilateral descent. A cautious but succinct version of the theory was that of Goode (1963:6):

> Wherever the economic system expands through industrialization, family patterns change. Extended kinship ties weaken, lineage patterns dissolve and a trend toward some form of the conjugal system generally begins to appear—that is, the nuclear family becomes a more independent kinship unit.

The Modified Extended Family

However, evidence began to accumulate during the 1950s and early 1960s that the nuclear family, while living as a separate residential unit, was not sociologically isolated. Sussman (1959:333–340) challenged the notion of isolation in 1959. And evidence continued to accumulate that the nuclear family and remnants thereof were not as widely separated in space as the theory had projected, did in fact maintain close and frequent contacts, and did continue to operate as instruments of mutual aid (Troll, 1971:263–290). This evidence came not only from the United States (Litwak, 1960; Sussman and Burchinal, 1964:231–240) but from England (Townsend, 1957) and Denmark (Stehouwer, 1970). In order to emphasize the continuity of familial responsibility and interdependence in spite of attenuated spatial relationships, these critics proposed that the new type of family that was being observed be called the "modified extended family." Meanwhile Rosenmayr and Köckeis (1965) were observing the same types of relationships in Austria but chose to emphasize the spatial separation in their description of the resulting pattern; they called it "intimacy at a distance." By this phrase they meant to connote that the older people preferred to live in separate dwellings from their children but still close enough to maintain intimate relations with them.

It is evident that the modified extended family is not limited to the dominant white population in the United States. Schweitzer (1983:174) tells of an Indian family in Oklahoma that exhibits the same tendencies. An elderly couple lives in one house, while two daughters and their children, as well as a nephew and his family, occupy separate houses within the same block. Two sons take turns living in the house with the old folks. Schweitzer suggests that such a living arrangement has a historical, cultural base in that in traditional culture, it was common for a man's married children to occupy adjacent tipis during the bison hunt.

Morgan and Hirosima (1983:279) note that the persistence of the extended family household in Japan—about 30 percent of all—results not so much from tradition and personal preference as from economic necessity, because housing costs are so high, and from the strategic advantage of having grandparents to supply affordable homemaking and child-rearing assistance while both father and mother are working away from home. The parents would prefer separate housing, but it is usually not affordable in close proximity to the grandparents.

Qualifications and Additions

Adams (1968:169), studying kin relations in an American urban area, concluded that most urban residents did indeed maintain intimate contact with their immediate relatives and that distance was a qualifier of that relationship, not a deterrent. However, he noted that in comparison with other societies, adult kin relations appeared to be peripheral to the mainstream activities. Firth, Hubert, and Forge (1970) found modest support for the "modified extended family" hypothesis in the English kinship system but distinguished between "kin sets"—those kin who were known about—and "kin groups"—those with whom one interacted. They also found that beyond the range of the family of orientation, the relationships were very shallow, very selective, and certainly permissive. There were no set rules determining with which kin one maintained intimate relations; usually the kin group did not extend beyond first cousins; selectivity was never symmetrical and tended a bit toward the maternal side. In other words, while Londoners maintained intimate relations with *some* kin, they definitely did not maintain such relations with *all* kin, and there was no tightly knit corporate body corresponding with lineages or sibs in other societies; each kin group in this society was idiosyncratic, based largely on personal preference.

Meanwhile Taietz (1970) found support for the classical theory in the decline of the extended family in eastern Holland. And Blumberg and Winch (1972), using Murdock's Ethnographic Atlas to correlate family forms with other societal characteristics, found that extended forms of the family were most closely related with extensive forms of agriculture and intensive agriculture without irrigation; the nuclear household, however, was most characteristic of simple hunting and gathering societies and of those with highly developed hydraulic agriculture. Thus, according to their findings, the trend line as far as the nuclear family was concerned was a U-curve, high in the most primitive societies, low in less developed agricultural societies, and rising again in the more intensively developed agricultural societies.

Current Knowledge and Family Trends

The choice of the term *modified extended family* to typify the current situation in modern industrialized societies was unfortunate because it tended to imply that little had changed under the impact of industrialization and urbanization. This is definitely not the case; the family has been undergoing a major transition. The classical theorists may have appeared to claim too much, but the revisionists are equally guilty of appearing to minimize the real trends. Part of the problem stems from ambiguity in the use of the term *family*; it is not always clear whether the authors are talking about a residential unit or a sociological unit based upon interaction. When this ambiguity is clarified, the differences of perspectives are greatly narrowed, and it appears that our current knowledge about the adaptations of the family to modernization may be stated approximately as follows:

1. The extended family as a corporate unilineal body is rarely maintained as a household residential unit in modern society. Instead the nuclear family is the standard residential unit.

2. With the change in structure, the household has also diminished in size. On the one hand, there are fewer peripheral relatives from outside the range of the immediate nuclear family living as members of the household; on the other hand, there has been a drastic reduction in the number of children born within the nuclear unit.

3. Within the range of the family of orientation, that is, father, mother, brother, and sister, kinship continues to be very important throughout adult life. These kin maintain contact, intimate relations, and some mutual assistance. However, the parent-child bond is much closer than the sibling bond. Furthermore, the mother-daughter bond is closer than the other parent-child relations.

4. Though relations within these groups are intimate and contacts are frequent, they should not be equated with the daily, continuous interaction of people living within the same household. Weekly visits are not the same as living together. That difference is illustrated by the tension caused when elderly parents try to reestablish the more intense relationship with children after living apart for many years (Hornum, 1983:215).

5. Relations with kin beyond the range of the nuclear family of orientation are tenuous and selective. Aunts, uncles, and cousins are usually

not within the intimate circle; these are relatives who are usually encountered only at weddings, funerals, and family reunions.

6. Grandparents are within the intimate group, but relations with grandchildren tend to be less frequent and more formal than the relations between adjacent generations. Furthermore, grandparent roles are not well institutionalized. Links between grandparents and grandchildren of the same sex tend to be closer (Wood, 1982:23).

Institutions for the Aged

In preindustrial societies most older people lived out their lives as heads of their own households, within the confines of a family group. Only in modern societies has it become a common practice to develop specialized institutions for the housing and care of infirm older members. Though monasteries and convents were sometimes used as places of asylum by all kinds of distressed and dependent persons, the first public old folks home is thought to have been established by Maria Theresa in Austria in 1740 (Doberauer, 1981:46). The reasons for the development of separate institutions for the elderly are complex, but among them are the following: (1) There are many more old people in modern societies (this is an aspect of the Demographic Revolution discussed in Chapter 2). In addition to the sheer increase in the older population, there has been a concomitant increase in the old-old, that is, those over 75, who are more likely to suffer from infirmities or handicaps and thus are less able to care for themselves. (2) The elderly are less likely to be included in an extended family household, as was more commonly the case in many preindustrial societies. They will have been living in their own nuclear family households during their adult years, apart from the households of their children. In preindustrial societies, fewer people lived to become grandparents, and a sizable proportion of the babies born did not grow up; thus the net size of the households was not as great as the popular stereotype. But the important point is that if people lived to become grandparents, they often did live with one of their children. Because one set of grandparents could not live with all of their children, a large proportion of the households did not contain grandparents. And though many children did die, the number who grew to maturity was still greater than today. Laslett's finding (1976) that most seventeenth-century English households were nuclear is beside the point; more relevant are the data showing that widows and widowers usually lived with a married child. This was also true of France, Germany, Estonia, Latvia, and Hungary during the same era. (3) There are fewer adult children today to share the burden of caring for aged parents. (4) Families are more mobile than in most preindustrial agricultural societies (colonial and frontier America was probably more mobile than most agricultural societies). (5) In many modern urban families, all adults are employed outside the home, and thus during much of the day there is no one available within the home to care for older members not able to care for themselves.

Within Western societies several types of institutions have developed for the housing and/or physical care of older persons (Kane and Kane, 1977). Of course there are variations from country to country, and there are changes through time, but some of the main types are boarding homes (or rest homes), nursing homes, geriatric hospitals, and hospices. Boarding homes are designed for ambulatory persons who are competent to care for themselves in most of their daily activities but are in need of or desirous of a minimally protective environment. In such establishments the common services provided by management may include, in addition to gardener service and building maintenance, maid service, congregate meals, and social or recreational facilities. Such institutions do not provide medical supervision or nursing care. These services are provided in nursing homes, which are designed for more severely restricted persons with daily need of nursing service. Therefore the regular staff includes nurses and physicians available on call. Geriatric hospitals have physicians in residence. The hospice is a relatively new type of institution that is most extensively developed in the United Kingdom. It is designed for the terminally ill, and the objective of treatment is not to cure an illness but to prepare for death. The patient is made as comfortable as possible, and both he or she and the relatives are assisted in coming to terms with the inevitable. At any given time, 4–5 percent of the elderly people of England, the United States, and Denmark live in institutions (Shanas et al., 1968:21).

Aged Communities and Communes

There are still other types of residential facilities for the aged. The extensive retirement communities, including conventional single-family detached structures, mobile homes, trailer parks, and apartment complexes, serve mainly elderly couples in the empty nest stage of family life. But some apartments and retirement hotels cater more to unattached older persons, most of whom of course are widowed. From one perspective these may be viewed as alternatives to living with children in an extended family household, but it should be recognized that this is the preferred alternative, which increases as the older people find that they can afford to live independently.

The single-room occupancy (SRO) hotels and rooming houses that have emerged in the older sections of our central cities tend to attract unattached older men who have limited means but are fiercely jealous of their independence. Alienated from their families, they forge networks of social contacts among themselves to provide minimum essential security (Sokolovsky and Cohen, 1981).

A recent development that provides alternative housing and some of the services commonly available to older people living within families is the establishment of some communes for older people. These are most extensive in Florida, but the idea appears to be catching on elsewhere. The prototype of this movement appears to have developed in Orlando upon the initiative of an Orlando businessman and was labeled Share-A-Home (Kellogg and Jaffe, 1976). Each commune operates as a nonprofit organization, with members sharing expenses and hiring staff to provide such services as they decide they need. New members are admitted only upon vote of the group. In addition to the services that are provided by hired help, the members provide much mutual aid among themselves. In fact they act very much like a family, with mutual concern and much sociability.

Familial Roles of Older People

Thus far in this chapter I have concentrated upon the structure and varieties of family and kinship groups and the ways in which they adapt to older members. Now I want to examine the behavior of those older members as they live within those structures. What roles do they play, and how do those roles vary in different settings? Some continue to be husbands and wives. How do married partners behave toward each other in advanced years? Most are parents. How do elderly parents relate to middle-aged children? Many become grandparents, and increasing numbers become great-grandparents. What is the nature of these roles in different societies? Many have brothers and sisters who are their peers in age. What is the sibling role in old age and how does it vary?

Older Spouses

Very little scholarly attention has been devoted to the roles of older people as husbands and wives. There is considerable literature on other roles of older people—their roles as parents and grandparents, or as citizens, and so on—but very little on their relationships to each other as spouses. Furthermore, most of the extant literature pertains to the aged in Western society and for the most part assumes that the older couple is living in an empty nest after the departure of children.

Older couples are as likely as young ones to express satisfaction with their marriages, and they give about the same reasons (Riley and Foner, 1968:539). They are less likely to report problems with their marriages. Frequently reported is a tendency in old age for male and female roles to converge. How much of this is generational difference as distinct from aging change is not yet clear, but older husbands are said to become more domestic, doing some of the shopping, washing dishes, and so on (Lipman, 1961; Reichard, Livson, and Peterson, 1962:42), while older women may become more aggressive and egocentric. Each is often required to take on responsibility for caring for the other in times of sickness, a combination of nursing and homemaking (Shanas, 1962:111; Stehouwer, 1965:155).

Many have remarked on the greater continuity of the woman's role, assuming that her primary role has always been homemaking, and. Townsend (1957) states that there is great reluctance in giving up the role, since it symbolizes her identity and purpose in life.

Another myth of Western society is that sexual interest and capacity for sexual performance decline rapidly with age and disappear entirely beyond middle age. This is manifestly not so, as shown by in-depth interviewing in this taboo area. Kinsey, Pomeroy, and Martin (1948:235–237) found that in their total male sample, only 5 percent were sexually inactive at age 60 and less than one third (30 percent) by age 70. Among married males 60–65 years of age, 83 percent were still having intercourse with their wives and 70 percent of those 66–70 years old were doing so. In their study of females, Kinsey and his associates (1953:528) found confirming evidence; 82 percent were still sexually active at age 60. Both researchers and marriage counselors testify that not only do many older people continue to have satisfying sexual relations in their seventies and even eighties, others could do so if they were not inhibited by guilt feelings or convinced of incapacity by cultural myths (Butler and Lewis, 1976:1–9).

Many societies have taboos on sexual relations under certain conditions that are applicable to young adults but tend to be relaxed in later life. Sex is often forbidden for warriors preparing for battle and for hunters readying for the hunt. Such behavior is thought to be either debilitating or unlucky, but such taboos obviously become inoperative when the men cease to be active as warriors and hunters. Pregnant or menstruating women must avoid hunters and their equipment among the Coast Salish. They also must stay away from fishing sites and clam beds (Amoss and Harrell, 1981:16). Of course such taboos no longer apply after the woman passes through menopause. Many societies require people to avoid social contact with certain categories of persons of the opposite sex; for example, a man must avoid his mother-in-law or his own sisters after they reach puberty. But again these taboos are usually relaxed in old age. The widespread practice of seclusion of women in Moslem societies, known as *purdah,* is commonly abandoned at menopause (Flint, 1976).

Though in most societies sexual intercourse is expected to decrease in frequency with increasing age, there are a few in which an opposite tendency may occur. In the upper Skagit of western Washington, old age is a time for carefree love and sexual dalliance (Collins, 1974:232; Tomashevich, 1981:30). Elderly lovers are not considered disgusting, and sexual relations between aged and youthful partners are especially romantic (Amoss, 1981a:231). In several polygynous cultures of Africa, older men may marry additional young wives and thus gain additional helping hands and increase their wealth and status at the same time. Although sexual intercourse is expected in such cases, no one knows the extent or frequency of such contact. The Abkhasians of the Caucasus region, who are alleged to have high proportions of very old people who maintain good health and physical vigor, are also said to continue their active sex life into late old age (Benet, 1974:85–86).

For the most part it appears that the roles of older spouses are extensions of the roles that were developed in younger years, and in the main these follow the cultural prescriptions of the particular societies. There is probably more continuity in such roles for those who become old in less developed societies and greater discontinuity in the more developed societies. One of the discontinuities in such societies is introduced by the departure of children to set up neolocal households, but the extent of disruption occasioned by this departure has been exaggerated. Marriage is the normative status for all adults in all societies, and this is true of old as well as young, but in all societies this is eventually terminated by the death of one spouse. However, widowhood takes place at later ages in the more developed societies; consequently, there are many older couples still actively involved in the roles of husband and wife in these societies.

In most societies remarriage is an option for widowed persons, an action that can reestablish for the survivor the role of spouse, albeit with a new partner. In only a few societies, such as traditional Hindu society, is such an option foreclosed by legal or cultural prohibitions of remarriage of widows. In Western societies, including the United States, not only is remarriage a possibility, it is evidently becoming more frequent (Vinick, 1977). Of course in most societies the opportunity for remarriage is more viable for older males than for older females. There are several reasons why this is true. Foremost among them is the sex ratio; there are many more women than men available. Secondly, in many societies males are expected to take the initiative in courting relationships, and comparable aggressiveness on the part of the females, particularly older females, may be frowned upon. Furthermore, even at younger ages, men customarily marry women who are younger than they. In the case of remarriage in later life, this difference in the ages of spouses may be considerably greater, and in Western society older men often do marry women much younger than they. In some polygynous societies older men with several wives might marry additional women who are probably younger than their previous wives. This may be motivated somewhat by a wish for greater security in old age, the younger women being presumably in good health and better able to care for others. Such motivation may apply not only to the husband involved but also to his older wives. Simmons cites a number of societies in which the marriage is instigated by the older wife as a means of securing help with the housework (1945:176–182).

Older Parents

The status of older parents vis-à-vis their grown children varies widely around the world. This ranges all the way from an authoritarian or domineering relationship toward their children to a complete reversal of roles, resulting in abject dependence of the parents on their children.

Among the most authoritarian elder patriarchs known to us were the ancient Romans, the Hebrews of Old Testament times, and the classical Greeks, but some contemporary African tribes rival those ancients in the retention of patriarchal power. In many tribal areas of southern and eastern Africa, older people as heads of families or lineages are very powerful and for the most part are highly respected. Young people defer to them in the knowledge that eventually they will succeed to those positions of honor and power. This is true of the Samburu (Spencer, 1965), the Sidamo of southeast Ethiopia (Hamer, 1972), the Chaggas of northern Tanzania (Moore, 1978), the Zulus of South Africa (Krige, 1950), and the Swazi (Kuper, 1947). Such respect is not necessarily coupled with love; in fact there is often much ambivalence in the feelings of children, and in some cases they appear to bide their time, waiting their turn to tyrannize their successors. In rural Ireland the elder male retains firm control until a late age, but when he finally decides to step down, the transfer of power—and ownership—is a formal and legal one, with the older one retaining only specified limited rights and prerogatives (Streib, 1972:172).

Nowhere do we see elder females exercising formal power over adult children, but that is not to say that they do not often domineer. There is an element of truth in the stereotype of the Jewish mother presented by Philip Roth in *Portnoy's Complaint*. Barbara Myerhoff notes the extension of this nurturing role on the part of older Jewish women who have been isolated from their children to other people and causes (Myerhoff and Simic, 1978:239). Some Latin American women assume a similar domineering stance in relation to their adult children. Velez (1978:127) provides an example in the person of a Mexican matriarch who not only manages her own life and that of her alcoholic husband but is called *una torre* (a tower) by her children because of her wide-ranging influence on and support of all of them.

Myerhoff (1978) reports on a 95-year-old eastern European Jew living in California who maintains a respectful relationship with his sons living in the same area but whose meaningful reference group is the clientele of a senior citizens center. He is financially independent but maintains affectionate familial bonds with his children.

Contrasting slightly with this independent relationship is that of the elderly Serbian couple visiting their son and his family in the United States after ten years' separation. Here the elderly were somewhat dependent upon the younger generation because the elders were not only visiting at the expense of the son, they had been the recipients of the son's financial contributions throughout his employed career. But both generations easily accepted this degree of dependence because it was in accord with the value system of their native ethnic culture, under which each member of the extended family was expected to contribute to the whole according to his or her ability. Family ties and cultural traditions remained strong despite geographic separation.

Simic also presents a contrasting case, whom he describes as a "loser." This is an elderly Serb who because of his mean and improvident behavior was completely alienated from his wife and children, living as a charity case in an old folks home in southern Yugoslavia. This case is probably the epitome of "desolation," a concept that Shanas and her associates (1968:258–287) present in contrast with mere "isolation," which need not entail any trauma, alienation, or loneliness.

It is safe to say that most older people in all parts of the world live close to their children. In traditional China nearly all older people lived with their sons and their families. Apparently this is still true in modern China, as I found only 10 older people living apart from their own families in a commune of 40,000. Although this pattern has weakened somewhat in modern Japan, three fourths are still living with children (Kii, 1976:28; Palmore, 1975a:37). The same pattern was inherent in the old *zadruga*, the patrilineal extended family that operated as a work group in Serbia, but now a more common pattern is for the elders to alternate their residence among their sons (Simic, 1978:102). Certainly most aged Africans live in the same compound or the same village as some of their children (Moore, 1978), and the same is true of Thailand (Kaufman, 1960:24).

In the Western world few older people actually live with their children, but most of them live near. In his London sample Townsend (1957) reported an average of 13 relatives within one mile. More of these were daughters than sons, reflecting a quasi-matrilocal tendency for young couples to live close to the wife's parents' residence. Young and Geertz (1961:128) found that 45 percent of the old people in Woodford, England, had children within five miles; this is in addition to the 14 percent living in the same household. There was a very similar pattern, with a little greater scatter, in Menlo Park, California, where 28 percent had children within five miles and 15 percent lived in the same house.

In any society there are always a few older people who are childless and a few who are estranged from their children, but these are extremely rare in traditional societies, and they remain a small minority even in urban industrial societies.

In general, the frequency of contact between elder parents and adult children is inversely proportional to the distance between their places of residence (Youmans, 1962:14; Adams 1968:43). That is, those living at the same place have the most frequent contacts, while those living at greater distances from each other have few or infrequent contacts. This appears to be a principle with worldwide application.

Of course in those traditional societies in which nearly all older people live with or in the same village as their children, this means that very frequent contact is maintained. But in societies that have developed patterns of neolocal residence, especially urban industrial societies with relatively high rates of mobility, there is the potential for decreasing and variable rates of contact. However, as already noted, even in these modernized societies there are strong patterns of propinquity in residence, resulting in relatively high frequency of contact. In fact one unexpected application of the principle is that in advanced societies, the older people who are living in cities have more frequent contact with their children than rural elderly have with their children (Youmans, 1962:17). No doubt this is because there is less distance between them in the urban centers than in the more sparsely settled rural areas.

In national samples in Denmark, Britain, and the United States, remarkably similar patterns of contact were found. About two thirds had seen at least one child during the 24 hours prior to the interview (Shanas et al., 1968:195), and another one fifth had had such a contact during the previous week. This means that about five out of six older people in these highly developed societies have at least weekly contact with one or more of their children. That there is some selectivity and perhaps some sharing of responsibility on the part of several children is indicated by the fact that when adult children in England were asked how frequently they had seen their mothers, the proportions were a bit lower. Half of the daughters had seen their mothers within 24 hours, and four fifths, within the week (Young and Willmott, 1957:30). One third of the men had seen their mothers on the previous day, and two thirds, during the previous week. Significantly, the men saw their mothers-in-law more frequently than they saw their own mothers (Young and Willmott, 1957:49), doubtless because they often accompanied their wives when the latter visited their mothers. Furthermore, in England, as throughout Western societies, the mother-daughter bond is clearly the strongest lineal relationship. In another study comparing British and American communities, it was found that the proportion of older people who had daily contact with daughters was about twice the proportion having daily contact with sons (Young and Geertz, 1961:131–133). But this is in part just another application of the principle of propinquity, because we also know that older people in these societies live closer to their daughters than to their sons.

Adams (1968:47) points out this propinquity principle should be qualified in modern societies because of the availability of the improved means of long-distance communication. Frequent contact via telephone or mail is maintained between elderly parents and their children even if they are so far apart that they cannot see each other often in person. Half to two thirds of the adults whose parents lived out of town telephoned them at least monthly, and up to three fourths corresponded once a month or more often. This type of frequent contact is in sharp contrast to the situation in some parts of Africa, where Moore (1978:36) reports that people are always surprised at the arrival of out-of-town guests because, without telephone or postal service, they never know ahead of time that they are coming. The presence of grandchildren also appears to make a difference in the frequency of contact with children. Rosenmayr and Köckeis (1965:216) found that those elderly in Vienna with grandchildren saw the parents of those grandchildren much more frequently than they saw children without progeny.

When older people continue to live in their own homes along with unmarried adult children, they tend to prolong the parental role, with only very gradual and sometimes reluctant cession of authority and responsibility. In rural Ireland the elder male relinquishes his authority over the patrimony very reluctantly, and because the sons commonly delay their marriages until they have gained control of their inheritance, their marriages take place at a very late age (Streib, 1972). But in other societies, too, parental responsibility and authority tend to be attenuated as long as the children remain under the parental roof.

Even if the children marry and bring their spouses to live with parents, this may enlarge the parental role rather than diminish it. In Western society, with its strong traditions of neolocal marriage, an important motivation undergirding such marriage is the younger couple's desire to establish their independence from parental control. They believe that as long as they remain in the parental home, the parents will continue to treat them as immature children. No doubt there is some justification for this belief, whether the behavior is based on custom or merely on personal habit.

In traditional Oriental societies, there was a strong custom, if not a moral imperative, toward this prolongation of the parental role. In traditional China, for example, marriage of a son meant the addition of another person, the son's bride, to the authority and responsibility of the patriarch, and because the patriarch's wife was granted control over most domestic matters of the household itself, the new bride was subjected to the authority of her mother-in-law in these matters. If the mother-in-law were temperamentally inclined to be authoritarian, the daughter-in-law could be reduced to a veritable slave in this new household. That such things happened is not questioned, but whether it was the rule or the exception, we cannot say. It is probably much less frequent in modern China, because the new Marriage Law of 1950 explicitly forbids the exploitation or coercion of one generation by another. And in Japan, where the same Confucian ethic was formerly prevalent, Masuda (1975:57) finds that the former authority of the mother-in-law has been completely abolished, and currently it is more likely that the daughter-in-law will dominate the management of the household.

But in both of these societies, as well as in Thailand, the older mother retains many aspects of the motherly role, even if she no longer has legal or moral authority to dominate the household. Because in all these Oriental societies young and middle-aged women are as likely as their husbands to be employed outside the home, the role of major homemaker still devolves to the older woman. She controls the domestic budget, manages the daily marketing, plans the meals, and oversees the cleaning and other household activities. Indeed it is often she more than the daughter-in-law who supervises the daily activities and guides the education of the grandchildren. It is notable that when in these developing countries, as often happens, it is necessary or advantageous for young people to go overseas for extended periods to study, their children are left very naturally and comfortably with grandparents. This can happen easily because the grandchildren are often already living with their grandparents, and they merely continue in the same arrangement during the absence of their parents.

In working-class families in England, the older woman, who is often called "Mum" by her children, plays a central role in the extended family relations (Young and Willmott, 1957:49). Her home is the family meeting place. Her husband, if he is still alive, plays a subordinate role (Townsend, 1957). He has always left the housework to his wife, and this continues in retirement; his interests and activities remain outside of the home. His wife continues to dominate the home and play "Mum" to her children and grandchildren. Mum's role includes substitution as homemaker during childbirth or illness of her daughter, shopping, laundry, advice, and babysitting (Young and Willmott, 1957:50–56). Similarly, Oscar Lewis notes that older Mexican women tend to dominate their households (Boyd, 1973:40). Velez (1978:127–128) depicts such a dominant matriarch, who despite a separate residence was known as *una torre* by her children. She visited her son's home daily, usually arriving before noon, criticized the daughter-in-law's housekeeping, rearranged furniture, supervised grandchildren, berated her son for his infidelity to his wife, and gave advice liberally.

However, most older mothers in Europe and the United States are not so domineering. They tend to live apart from their children, have less frequent contact with them, and play a supplemental role—providing assistance in time of emergency, helping with housekeeping and home repairs, and entertaining children and grandchildren as visitors and weekend guests (Shanas et al., 1968:254). Streib (1965:472) reports that common elements of the elder parenting role in the United States are visiting, corresponding, providing care during illness, giving financial help, giving advice, and occasionally providing domicile.

Older women are much more active and involved than older men in the parenting role. This appears to be true in most societies. It is generally true in Western industrialized societies, where women continue their homemaking and nurturing activities into old age. But women who have been active occupationally apart from the home and away from the family have recently become less involved in parenting activities after retirement. They play major roles in gift giving and financial aid but are less active in child care, babysitting, and homemaking chores than are older women who have not been employed. This is true also in Russia, where the *babushka* (grandmother) is a household institution, carrying much of the responsibility for homemaking—cooking, mending, washing, and the very time-consuming shopping. The grandfathers are much less involved, sharing only limited responsibilities for shopping and babysitting. My limited observation in modern China suggests that older Chinese men may be more active than those in Russia. One 73-year-old stated that he had retired the previous year to take care of his grandson while his son and daughter-in-law worked. And certainly one sees many grandfathers walking or wheeling young children in the streets and parks of China's cities. This role may be a recent response to the new social system based upon egalitarian principles and incorporating an explicit system of retirement.

If elderly parents around the world are involved in some aspects of a continuing parenting role, so middle-aged children generally are laden with some responsibilities toward their parents, and whether through obligation or affection, most adult children continue to interact with and perform services for their parents. I have noted how the Confucian ethic of filial piety emphasized the duty of sons to care for their parents and honor them in their old age. This principle was widely influential in China, Japan, and Korea.

In Europe and the United States normative expectations are less clear cut. Though requirements for housing and support of parents have largely disappeared, in a few places parents may still be denied public assistance if the children are adjudged able to support them, and legal suits may be brought against the children for their support. But the main bonds are attitudinal and affectional rather than legal. From half to two thirds of the older people in the United States and Britain report receiving help from children, but the proportion is much lower in Denmark (Shanas et al., 1968:214). Much of such assistance is in the form of services—shopping, cleaning, nursing, and providing transportation; relatively little of it is financial. Furthermore, these services are usually rendered willingly and lovingly. They are rarely coerced, and the children often provide more assistance than is expected by the parents (Streib and Thompson, 1960:483).

In addition to these aid patterns being much less prescriptive in the Western world than in Asia or Africa, there is also a contrast in terms of the sex of the provider. In the Western world the daughter is usually most involved in helping her parents. As noted earlier, daughters live nearer and have more frequent contact with elderly parents than do sons; many of those contacts entail services. But part of this difference may result from a shift in the kinds of services involved. Children are much less involved in providing either housing or financial support in Western society. Housing is more commonly provided by the older people themselves, and the basic means of financial support in modernized societies have been institutionalized in the forms of social security and pension systems. When children do provide substantial financial support to elderly parents, the sons more frequently shoulder this responsibility than the daughters. But this form of filial assistance has diminished to relatively small proportions in the Western societies, and both housing and financial assistance have become differentiated from other kinds of assistance, which therefore loom large, and these are the kinds of assistance usually rendered by women. Because women are no longer restricted to patrilineal confines and because residence patterns have shifted in the direction of matrilocality, most filial services to elderly parents in Western society are provided by daughters.

There is a widespread belief in the United States that the "generation gap," that is, conflicting beliefs and values between adjacent generations, results from the rapid pace of social change. Contemporary research in Africa indicates that such conflicts may have been endogenous to relatively stable societies (LeVine, 1965). The points of intergenerational conflict most common in Africa are inheritance of property, usufruct, and privileges. These may be between father and son, as among the Gisu of Uganda, where delay in accommodating a son's ambitions sometimes leads to patricide, or as among the Korongo and the Mesakin of the Sudan, where the elder is often suspected or accused of witchcraft, practiced to rid him of a rival. Among the Tallensi of Ghana, although the sons deny it, the eldest son is often suspected of wanting to hasten the father's demise (LeVine, 1965:190).

Surrogate Parents

In some societies special relationships are established between people who are not necessarily related by blood that simulate the parent-child relationship. The English terms *godfather* and *godmother* carry some suggestion of this relationship, but for the most part these terms denote only a ceremonial relationship in which the older persons serve as ceremonial sponsors at baptism; no strong or binding obligations are entailed on the part of either generation. In contrast, the *compadre* system in the Philippines includes much more serious and long-term obligations, as does a similar surrogate parent relationship in Japan (Bennett and Despres, 1960). The gerontological implications of this type of simulated kinship have not been analyzed.

Grandparents

Most people, if they live long enough, become grandparents, and in consequence most older people in any given society have grandchildren.

The relative frequency of this attribute from society to society varies with fertility levels and the state of public health. But historically these two factors have tended in opposite directions: as death rates decline, life expectancy increases and greater proportions of the population survive long enough to become grandparents; but when subsequently birth rates also decline, as has happened in modernized parts of the world, the number of potential grandchildren declines. At the same time there has been some tendency to delay marriage, to avoid it altogether, or to remain childless, so the proportion of older people who are devoid of grandchildren is probably greater in advanced societies than in traditional societies. Special studies in the United States (Havighurst and Albrecht, 1953), England (Townsend, 1957), and West Germany (Burgess, 1960:286) report about 70 percent of older people with grandchildren. Comparable figures are not available elsewhere.

In cross-cultural research Apple (1956) found confirmation for the theory that when grandparents possessed authority over their grandchildren, the relationship with them tended to be reserved and formal, but when there was no such authoritative implication, there was often an informal, intimate relationship. Many people have noted the tendency for relationships between grandparents and grandchildren to be more relaxed and intimate than those between parents and children, and they have theorized in the same vein that because the grandparents are not responsible for the upbringing and discipline of the grandchildren, they can afford to be indulgent. Certainly such informality and indulgence are widespread (Radcliffe-Brown, 1950:28; Keesing, 1958:250). Nadel (1951:235) found a "joking relationship" between grandparents and grandchildren among the Nubas in Africa, and Beattie (Boyd, 1973:41) reports that among the Bunyoro it is customary for grandparents to "spoil grandchildren who enjoy informality with the grandparent in distinction to the more formal relationship to their parents especially to their fathers." Similarly, Dozier states that among the Kalinga of northern Luzon in the Philippines, grandparents are very permissive and maintain a very close relationship with their grandchildren (Boyd, 1973:41). Occasionally the relationship takes on some of the coloration of a conspiracy, with grandparents and grandchildren forming a coalition against the middle generation.

Simmons (1945:102–103) remarks that babysitting is not a new or unique role for grandparents in Western society, and Turnbull (1983:140) says it occurs in every society. Andamanese grandparents remained in camp with the grandchildren, while the able-bodied parents went off to hunt or to collect firewood. Old Bontoc Igorot women cared for their grandchildren and often took the babies to the riverbanks to bathe them.

Caring for grandchildren is a traditional function of grandparents in Samoa. Holmes (1980) asserts that the usual reason for migration of elderly Samoans to the United States is to babysit, that is, to care for grandchildren while the parents of those children are at work. Townsend (1957) also found that grandmothers in London often took care of their grandchildren, gave them baths, and walked them to and from school. And Laslett (1976:95) suggests that this type of substituting for parents is not new; seventeenth-century orphans in England were often sent to live with grandparents. This is a very common role for grandparents throughout the Orient.

Another function of the eldest generation is that of linking the descendants together. In Western society the role of "kinkeeper" usually devolves to women, only in part because they are the usual survivors. Grandmothers and great-grandmothers serve to keep children and grandchildren in touch with each other. After the deaths of these key people, the various secondary kin—aunts, uncles, and cousins—tend to lose contact with each other (Adams, 1968:167).

In Western society, despite the fact that grandparents have generally been relieved of any authoritative responsibility for the discipline and upbringing of grandchildren, the relationship is usually rather formal and distant. Grandparents are interested in and take pride in the accomplishments of grandchildren, but they are not usually intimate with them, and there is relatively little affect in the relationship. But in this case, the distance results not from any interference based on authority but from physical separation and conflicting social involvement (Cowgill, 1977:12). The general pattern of neolocal residence results in grandparents living in separate households from their grandchildren. Frequent mobility tends to increase the probability of spatial separation. Improved health, increased employment on the part of women, and shortening of generations generally results in grandparents being still physically active and socially involved while their grandchildren are young. Furthermore, the grandchildren in turn are extensively engrossed in activities arranged for their entertainment or socialization by the various institutions of modern society—nursery schools, kindergartens, schools, churches, scouting organizations, and so on. Thus both grandparents and grandchildren tend to be preoccupied with interests and activities with their age peers, and all of this tends to minimize contacts, reduce interaction, and attenuate the relationship.

About 40 percent of the older people in the United States are great-grandparents, as compared with only 22 percent in Great Britain and Denmark (Townsend, 1968:141). Naturally this percentage varies by age, and the older people are, the greater the probability that they will have achieved great-grandparenthood. In the United States 57 percent of the men over age 80 and 68 percent of the women of that age are great-grandparents, as compared with 46 percent of the men and 64 percent of the women over 80 in Denmark and 43 percent of the men and 52 percent of the women of that age in Great Britain (Townsend, 1968:151). Because of increasing life expectancy and shortening of generations, more people are achieving great-grandparenthood (Peace, 1981:36), but the quality of the relationship is still more attenuated than grandparenthood. The strains imposed by mobility, distance, and competing interests are compounded by an additional intervening generation and a greater disparity of age. Great-grandparents usually yield the active role of organizing family reunions to their children, the grandparent generation. They attend the reunions and other rites of passage, but these may mark the rare occasions on which they have contact with their great-grandchildren (Cowgill, 1977:12).

In some societies certain children, usually grandchildren, are selected to become companions and aides to older people, especially those who have become frail. Moore (1978:36) reports the distress of an elderly Chagga woman when her 17-year-old granddaughter left to go to school. The girl had been her constant companion for seven years, including sleeping in the same room. This was such a common custom among the Chaggas that this woman and her husband felt that she had a right to a grandchild, and they lamented the fact that there were no other grandchildren available. This practice is not confined to primitive people. Eaton (1964:97–98) reports that elderly Hutterites are nursed and cared for as a community responsibility and that the solicitude includes arranging for a child to sleep with the older person so that he or she will not "be alone at night."

Older Siblings

Another quite significant familial relationship maintained throughout life is that of brothers and sisters. There is little information on the sibling relationship in late life in a comparative context. The richest body of data comes from Shanas and her associates in their comparative study of aging in Denmark, Great Britain, and the United States (1968). In all three of these countries about four out of five elderly persons (65 and over) had living siblings (Townsend, 1968:142), and there was a wide range in the numbers of brothers and sisters. In Denmark as many older people had five or more siblings as had none at all or had only one. But obviously time takes its toll, and the oldest people have fewer living brothers and sisters than the not so old. For example, 85 percent of those age 65–69 in the sample of three countries had living siblings, compared with only about two thirds of those who were 75 and over.

In all three countries close relationships with siblings were evidently maintained to a much greater extent by those who had never married or had children of their own. Single persons were much more likely to be living with siblings than were married or widowed persons. If people had been married at some time in their lives, they were much less likely than people who never married to reestablish close relations with brothers and sisters (Townsend, 1968:154). Townsend calls this a principle of compensation; in the absence of spouse, children, and grandchildren, relationships established in childhood are perpetuated into old age. Compensation is also somewhat evident in the fact that widowed persons without children tend to resume closer ties with siblings upon the death of the spouse, but the relationship is not as close or as frequent as in the case of single persons (Townsend, 1968:166).

In Denmark and Britain, but not in the United States, childless men are more apt to live with siblings than are childless women. In Denmark this amounted to 19 percent of the childless men, as compared with the only 14 percent of the childless women; in England the percentages were 33 and 29, respectively; but in the United States only 19 percent of the childless men lived with siblings, as compared with 32 percent of the childless women (Stehouwer, 1968:189).

Sibling ties are described as close much less often than the parent-child relationship (Streib, 1965:471). In the cross-national survey, contacts of older people with their brothers or sisters were less frequent than with children. About one third of the respondents had had contact with a sibling during the previous week, and about one-half, during the previous month (Stehouwer, 1968:198). Such contacts are still important in the lives of these people, but they are less frequent and less significant than the contact with children. Of course the frequency of contacts with siblings declines with increasing age (Stehouwer, 1968:213). In part this results from decreasing availability because of the deaths of many of the siblings.

However, at all ages and in all three countries, women have more contacts with siblings than do men (Stehouwer, 1968:199). This is in contrast with the residential pattern noted earlier, in which higher proportions of the men in Denmark and Britain were living with siblings. But again it is the never-married who are in most frequent contact with their siblings, about two thirds having such contact within a week prior to the survey.

These data, though they do not describe the roles played by siblings, indicate that such relationships are important in the lives of older people in these industrialized countries. They are probably also important in other types of societies, although they are probably not as prevalent because higher death rates will have depleted the numbers of siblings available in old age.

Summary

We have seen that there are many varieties of kinship groups and families around the world and that these have differing meaning for and impact upon their older members. The most salient ways in which kinship patterns vary relate to authority patterns, lines of descent, marriage, and residence. When authority traditionally inheres in senior members, as in patriarchal forms, older people obviously have an advantage. It would be surprising if they did not look after their own interests. Hence in such societies older people not only wield power but obtain economic privileges for themselves, claim prior rights in social affairs, and are usually accorded honor and prestige. Similarly, when a culture stresses lineal descent and the inheritance of both property and prerogatives through bloodlines, older generations tend to be favored. They frequently have strong influence if not absolute control over the inheritance, and this gives them a measure of power. Furthermore, as transmitters of the lineage, they are repositories if not monopolists of important knowledge and lore. If this is combined with a reverence for or fear of ancestors, the elder members of the lineage are in a strategic position, entitling them to honor, respect, fear, and deference if not admiration and love.

The implications of marriage patterns for the elderly are not as clear-cut; their effects appear to be mediated by residence patterns and composition of households. Plural marriages, simply by enlarging the household, provide a margin of security for old age, and if honor is accorded in proportion to the number of spouses, some advantage accrues to the elderly who have many mates. More important is the pattern of residence. Living with or near one's kin not only provides a strong measure of economic and physical security, it may also provide increasing honor, prestige, and usefulness with increasing age. Neolocal marriage, however, by separating the generations, imposes some risks for older people. The resulting nuclear family household is a fragile, vulnerable unit, and unless it is buttressed by extrafamilial supports, old age can be a lonely and desolate condition.

Because modernization, including industrialization and urbanization, tends to impinge upon kinship systems and family forms, generally precipitating what has often been called the "family transition"—diluting the authority of family elders, diminishing the significance of blood descent and social bonds related to it, decreasing plural forms of marriage, and strongly encouraging neolocal marriage, with the resultant nuclear family households—early sociological theory was pessimistic about the survival of the social forms necessary to the security and happiness of older people. However, recent evidence indicates that our social institutions have been adapting to these social changes and that the nuclear family has not been left isolated and unassisted. Not only has the state progressively assumed responsibility for ensuring financial security for older people through social security, but various facilities have been developed for their housing and health care. But most important of all, the kin group has not deserted the nuclear family. Despite distance between the households, close kin maintain contact and provide needed attention and concern for their elders.

A high proportion of older people in any society are widowed, and in most societies the majority of these are females. In traditional and underdeveloped societies, most of these older people, widows or widowers, live in the same households as one or more of their children. But in Western and most industrialized societies, there is an increasing tendency for older people to maintain separate households.

With increased longevity and improved health in modernized societies, widowhood occurs later, and therefore a greater proportion of older people continue to live independently as married couples. The period of the "empty nest," after all the children have left to establish their own households, is a new phenomenon, peculiar to modern societies with aged populations. Under these circumstances the older couple, while retiring from employment, remains active and engaged in familial roles. Many remain sexually active, but in other respects the roles of husbands and wives show some tendency to converge; men engage in more domestic activities, while women become more aggressive and self-sufficient.

In patriarchal societies in which extended family households are customary, older men tend to retain their authoritarian role, and older women tend to continue to manage their households. However, in Western society, with prevailing patterns of independent residence of nuclear family units, older people have no such customary authority, and when patterns of dominance by older persons are present—as with the Jewish mother or the Spanish *duenna*—it is more a matter of idiosyncratic personality traits than of cultural prescription. Nevertheless, the parenting role is still very important in modernized and Western societies. Though elderly parents do not live with their children, they live close to one or more. There is in consequence frequent contact and mutual service.

Older parents perform many supplemental functions for their children and serve as resources in time of crisis, including becoming substitute or surrogate parents at times. Filial responsibility for care of aged parents is still a strong tradition in many parts of the world, although its form and extent vary considerably. In modernized societies, where social security and/or pensions have become the prevalent means of providing financial support, children have been relieved to a great extent of this responsibility. But they are still very extensively involved in performing other services for their older parents, and it is significant to note that these services are performed willingly and lovingly.

When grandparents live close by and do not have authority over or responsibility for grandchildren, the relationship is often intimate and informal, but in modernized societies the relationship tends to be attenuated by distance and competing activities. Still, grandparents are important resources as surrogate parents, and grandchildren are sometimes companions and aides to elderly people.

Older people who have no children or grandchildren tend to maintain close relationships with brothers and sisters. A significant minority of these live together, and many continue regular and close contact.

These familial roles are central to the lives of most older people, occupying a large proportion of their time, giving a major degree of satisfaction, and providing essential services and security.

Chapter Five

Economic Systems and Economic Roles of the Aged

*T*he economic system of a society impinges deeply upon all aspects of life, and the lives of older people are certainly not immune. Whether they are active workers in the system or merely consumers, there are institutional adjustments to their presence and to their roles in the system; conversely, their customary roles and activities imprint upon the system. In this chapter I shall discuss how various kinds of economic systems accommodate themselves to the presence of older people and to the phenomenon of aging. Then I shall reverse the coin and examine the economic roles of older people within the various systems.

Among the questions to be examined are: Do different kinds of economic systems foster different degrees of continued integration and participation on the part of older members? Do some encourage reduction or discontinuance of productive activity by older persons? What kinds of societies can afford the luxury of retirement of a significant portion of their older potential workers? Are such retired workers always penalized for their nonparticipation? Does retirement always entail some loss of status as well as reduction of income? Is the loss of income systematically related to the affluence of the society? How do the dominant values of a society, as mediated through the economic institutions, affect both the security and status of older members? Do some types of societies promote individual achievement and personal independence at the expense of security in old age? Is it easier for older people to accept a dependent status in some types of societies than in others? How does economic change affect older people? Is it true that rapid change, especially economic change, is always detrimental to older people? Certainly we shall not expect to obtain definitive answers to these questions, but perhaps our explorations may at least provide helpful perspectives on some of them.

Types of Economic Systems

There are many ways of classifying economic systems. Among the criteria sometimes employed for such classifications are (1) source of food supply (McConnell, 1960), (2) level of technology, (3) structure of productive units, (4) extent of division of labor, (5) level of energy consumption (Cottrell, 1960), (6) systems of media of exchange, (7) control of wealth and capital (Nash, 1968:360–363), and (8) rationality of organization (Goodfellow, 1968:55–65; Moore, 1979). Of course these are not mutually exclusive, and there is no need in this context to carry on an extended discussion of their relative merits. Because no one of the above criteria yields a completely satisfactory classification for the purposes at hand, we shall be interested in examining variations in the fortunes of the aged in several of these dimensions.

Of course we shall want to know how older people fare in hunting and fishing economies as compared with agricultural and, in turn, the differences between these and industrial societies. These involve differences not only in source of food supply but also in technology, structure of productive units, division of labor, and level of energy consumption. A separate issue is that of communal versus individual and public versus private ownership and control of wealth and the means of production. These obviously can and do vary with considerable independence from the other dimensions mentioned above. As for the comparative rationality of different systems, I hold that it is impossible successfully to maintain that one type of enterprise is more rational than another. Though some (Moore, 1979) have argued that modern economic organization is distinguishable from primitive economics in terms of the greater rationality of the former, such an argument always appears to rest on ethnocentric myopia. When one understands the values of the particular society, economic activity that may appear quite irrational to the outsider usually turns out to be quite understandable and rational (Herskovits, 1968:41–55).

Economic Support Systems

In all human societies the major economic resource for the elderly, as well as for all other age groups, is the family. In some societies the family, in the sense of mutually supportive kin, may be almost the sole resource, but many societies have evolved other supplemental systems to backstop the family when it alone is inadequate to the task. In Western society there has been a gradual enlargement of the social unit deemed responsible for the economic support of dependent and destitute persons. Initially they were forced to rely upon family and kin, but when family resources were not available or were inadequate, individuals in need resorted to begging alms from strangers. Later the Christian church became the collecting and dispensing agency for such alms. Then when itinerant beggars began to overwhelm the resources of local parishes, the state began to take a hand, requiring local parishes to take care of their own, but only their own, residents. The alms began to resemble taxes, and help given verged on public relief. The English Poor Law of 1601 sought to channel the services provided by alms by placing dependent children in foster families under arrangements known as indenture, requiring able-bodied adults to perform labor in institutions labeled workhouses, and caring for disabled persons, many of whom were elderly, in almshouses. In time the pressures of urbanization and industrialization led to the supplemental growth of many philanthropic charities, providing still more specialized assistance to such groups as orphans, widows of soldiers and sailors, disabled veterans, and so on. Cyclical depressions, with hordes of unemployed, overwhelmed both the almshouses and private philanthropy, creating more pressures for governmentally financed outdoor relief (relief provided to people in their own homes). Ultimately, in order to systematize the process and build reserves for its support, governments applied the principle of social insurance to particularly pressing and widespread risks.

Remnants of all these systems are still present in all modern societies, but highly modernized societies are the only ones that have developed elaborate systems of social insurance, including old age insurance, commonly called social security.

Family Support Systems

Because they are present to some extent in all societies, we all have some familiarity with family support systems for the elderly. Surprisingly, Simmons (1945:214) found that among the 71 primitive societies that he studied, there was much less variation in the extent and type of family support for the elderly than might have been expected. Aged men and women fared about equally in matrilineal and patrilineal societies, although both were better off in the latter. This was because the patrilineal societies tended to be agricultural, and in such economies, where residence was settled and grain was the staple food, the supply was more ample and more predictable. This benefited the populace in general, including the elderly.

Perhaps we may infer that another reason for the slight advantage for the aged of living in agricultural economies was the more clean-cut differentiation of the family as the basic economic unit. Because there was usually no question of either family membership, including the elderly, or family responsibility for all its members, when the family had ample land for its private use, all its members could be more secure than in collective, hunting and fishing economies in which the vagaries of the hunt or catch militated in the direction of communal sharing of a very uncertain and vacillating food supply. (I will have more to say about communal sharing later.)

In Chapter 4, I described at some length several forms of the family and how these operated in relation to the elder members. Here we may simply recall the economic aspects of that operation. We saw how the classical Chinese family provided an extended social group, with the eldest male as the patriarch in power and authority and, in theory at least, the manager of the family enterprise. The elders reaped from this system an economically secure old age, with sons strongly obligated to guarantee that security and made to suffer disgrace if they failed to do so. The rules were not as clearly formalized and the lines of descent and responsibility not as rigidly patrilineal in the stem family of nineteenth-century rural France, but this family offered some of the same security in numbers to its dependent members. Able-bodied members of whatever age contributed to the common family budget from which all members received necessary food, clothing, and shelter, plus allowance for special personal expenditures they could justify to the person controlling the purse strings.

I also noted a similar stem family arrangement in contemporary Thailand. However, in this case there appeared to be more regular rotation of older married sons and daughters out of the parental household, as younger children married and replaced them in the line of succession both to inheritance and primary responsibility. Still, all the children, whether living in the parental household or not, shared the responsibility for the economic support of elderly parents.

Finally, I described the nuclear family household that has become so characteristic of the United States and other Western modernized societies, though I noted that separation of residence does not signify cessation of responsibility. In fact the term *modified extended family* is currently used to emphasize continuity of social contact and mutual assistance despite separate residence. However, such modified extended families seldom operate on the basis of a common budget. They reside in separate households because of a strong preference for independence in living arrangements and "intimacy at a distance" (Rosenmayr and Köckeis, 1963). Assistance to elderly parents is therefore provided as needed, often on the basis of emergency. The assistance must be planned, arranged, and scheduled in a much more formal, calculated manner than is usual when persons are living under the same roof 24 hours a day.

About two thirds of the elderly in Britain and the United States report receiving help from their families, including occasional or regular money allowances or gifts (Shanas et al., 1968:428–429). This is less common in Denmark, but still almost one third report such family assistance. Help includes housework, preparation of meals, shopping, bathing, and dressing. In all three countries those who are ill or bedfast rely heavily on members of their families.

The Semang of Malaysia honor and respect their aged (Tomashevich, 1981:29). If elders are incapable of providing for themselves, their children take care of them, even carrying them on their backs when moving camp. Likewise, old age is relatively secure among the Baganda, thanks again to the family (Queen and Habenstein, 1974:89). An elderly male may improve both his status and security by adding more wives to his harem. He is never without a home. If he has no home of his own, he may dispose of his property and join the family of a son. Another option open to either a man or a woman is to secure a grandchild to join one's household and assume many of the responsibilities of making a living.

As a Toda of central India grows older, his personal fortune is likely to increase (Tomashevich, 1981:29). Some are able to add a private wife to an otherwise polyandrous household. There is some security in numbers, as the family, whatever its composition, will absorb the risks of any of its members, including the cost of an elaborate funeral that may include the sacrifice of a buffalo for the use of the deceased in the next life. In the Gwembe tribe of south central Africa, the men used to marry women considerably younger than they, and they could rely upon several of these to support them in their old age (Colson and Scudder, 1981:135). The women in turn, as they were widowed, might be inherited by one of their husband's kinsmen or could rely upon their sons for support.

The Modoc Indians of northern California provide separate housing for the aged (Tomashevich, 1981:29–30). The dwelling is furnished with extra insulation. Families of the occupants provide wood for a fire that is kept burning continuously in the winter and also carry food to them. The family is also the chief resource of the elderly among the Old Order Amish of Pennsylvania (Tomashevich, 1981:27). Elderly parents traditionally retire to a separate dwelling or a separate section of the family residence known as the "Grossdawdy House." They are free to do as much or as little as they wish and to participate in the affairs of the extended family as their health and interest may dictate.

So families function in different ways in different societies to serve as support systems for elderly members. Although they are the primary units for such support in all societies, there are many supplemental systems in both primitive and modernized societies.

Communal Sharing

Glascock and Feinman (1981:25) found that 56 percent of the societies included in their sample from the Human Relations Area Files (HRAF) were supportive in their treatment of their elderly members, and Simmons (1945:32–34) found communal sharing of food in about one third of the primitive tribes included in his study. For the most part these tribes were characterized by collective or fishing economies; some were hunters. Such sharing, including sharing with aged members, was most characteristic of peoples living in areas where climate was severe and hazards of food shortages were common. Severe cold, as in the polar regions, and excessive aridity, which posed risk of drought, were conditions most commonly associated with this cultural trait. It was noted among many Eskimo communities, the Lapps, and various Siberian tribes, such as the Yukaghir, Chukchi, and Yakuts. But it was also found among such desert-dwelling peoples as the Navahos of the southwestern United States, the Seri of Baja California, and the Xosa of southern Africa. It is inferred that people living under such rigorous climatic conditions experience erratic changes in availability of food, alternating between abundance—when weather is favorable or fish are plentiful—and famine in hard times. One cultural adaptation to such uncertainty is sharing, an elemental kind of insurance. Simmons could find no significant difference in the treatment accorded to aged men and aged women in such societies. Men and women shared equally in the fruits of abundance and the privations of lean periods.

It is no mere coincidence that in some of these same societies we encounter reports of abandonment, exposure, killing, and suicide of the aged (Glascock and Feinman, 1981:25). In such marginal societies, when conditions become generally intolerable, the least productive people will be considered expendable. When harsh choices must be made, or when the individual has become a severe burden or handicap to an already hard-pressed community, it is understandable that the elderly may at times have been selected or have selected themselves for sacrifice. Simmons (1945:240) assures us that such practices result from dire necessity, "the hardness of primitive life, not the hardness of savage hearts." The action is often taken on the initiative of the elderly person and may be marked by rites of passage indicating honor and compassion. Such actions take place in accordance with cultural norms. This is in contrast with the horrible neglect and starvation of the elderly members of the Ik tribe, who, according to Turnbull (1972), were among the first victims of a totally individualistic, anomic struggle for survival during a recent famine in northern Uganda. Community standards and cultural norms completely disintegrated as individuals sought only their own survival, leaving the elderly and children to starve in isolation.

In some societies some of the elderly are provided for through gifts because of their roles as priests, shamans, sacrificers to the dead, or members of privileged secret societies (Goody, 1976:121). These may take the form of meals cooked for special holidays, or they may be individual gifts of food, money, or other wealth signifying the achievement of religious merit. In Buddhist societies some widowers and elderly men enter the priesthood, and apart from the merit-making and religious aspects of such a late-life career, they also gain some modicum of economic security. The women of the community are obligated to provide food that traditionally was collected by the priests themselves, circulating with their bowls through the community. More recently, especially in urban areas, the food may be taken to the temple, the responsibility for its provision being organized and agreed upon on a regular schedule.

In addition to sharing food on a communal basis, the elderly are often provided with other services, either formally or informally. In a public housing development in Wisconsin, Jonas and Wellin (1980:222) found neighbors voluntarily providing services to ill or impaired elderly in the following percentages: domestic chores—cooking, cleaning, laundry, and so on—44 percent; socioemotional support—visiting, reading to, checking up on—24 percent; personal care—nursing, administering medication, exercising, grooming—20 percent; and running errands—mainly to the market or pharmacy—12 percent. Within a two-week period, one third of the residents were recipients of some form of help from friends or neighbors within the project.

Communal support of the elderly is a customary aspect of life among the Hutterites of the northwestern United States and Canada (Eaton, 1964:95–96). Such support includes health care, coverage of medical bills, and funeral expenses. Likewise, the *Kibbutzim* of Israel are reported to provide complete economic security and exemplary communal services for their elderly (Tomashevich, 1981:24). However, being physically located in such a setting, be it segregated by age as in the Wisconsin case or age integrated as in the *Kibbutzim*, does not assure the development of communal services. Angrosino (1976) reports on a middle-class retirement housing development in Florida that has not jelled into such a community; there is little semblance of mutual concern or community consciousness. Angrosino attributes the lack of communal feeling to the fact that the residents had no part in planning or managing the development.

Private Insurance

Private insurance, providing annuities as well as other benefits, has become an extensive source of economic support in old age in modernized societies, but except in the form of burial societies, it is still rare in premodern or developing societies.

Burial societies have sprung up in the early stages of urbanization in many societies. The extensive migration by detached individuals typical of that stage of development, with the consequent living among masses of strangers, gave rise to the specter of death with no one caring and no one to contact relatives or take appropriate action. Thus in the mining cities on the copperbelt in Africa, tribal membership often became the basis for fraternal organizations, the chief function of which was to notify kin in case of death and to guarantee transport of the corpse back to the native tribal community. Lodges, fraternal orders, and national language societies served the same purpose among immigrant populations in American cities during the nineteenth century. Over time some took on more extensive insurance functions, such as the building of hospitals, nursing homes, and retirement homes available to their members.

A form of burial insurance existed even in imperial Rome, where *collegia* (associations of artisans), in return for the payment of an initiation fee and monthly premiums, paid funeral expenses to the surviving dependents (Manes, 1932:97). But few such institutions survived into the Middle Ages.

Private insurance to provide annuity income is a recent and modern development, and for the most part its growth has followed that of public old age insurance (social security). It is used to supplement the Social Security System and other pension systems operated by corporations or unions.

Corporate Pensions

Pensions provided to employees under plans by corporations or unions have recently become significant in many modernized countries. In 1972 the Social Security Administration estimated that 44 percent of wage and salary workers in private industry in the United States were included in private pension plans (Kolodrubetz, 1974). Only 21 percent of the retired population was actually receiving income from this source in 1980 (Beattie, 1983:406). Little is known of the extent of coverage or the size and security of benefits in private pension systems in other parts of the world. In a few countries, such as Finland and Switzerland, private pensions have been mandated by governmental legislation, and in France and Sweden 80 to 90 percent of wage and salary workers are covered by industry-wide collective agreements with employers. The trend is toward earlier vesting and easier portability of such pensions. In some areas such systems preceded public social security and are now tending to be displaced by the public systems (Cheit, 1968:201), but in the United States the private pension plans have grown along with the Social Security System. They appear to be regarded as "a comfortable second story to the 'floor' of protection offered by social security."

Thus most modernized noncommunist countries have evolved extensive but quite varied mixes of public and private pensions (Schulz, 1976:584–585). There have been protracted debates over the relative merits of private voluntary versus public compulsory systems, with the issue ultimately tending to be resolved in favor of the public compulsory system with varying degrees of supplementation as determined by individuals, unions, or corporations.

Social Security

Some years ago the United Nations (1956:81) drew a contrast between the ways in which agricultural and other types of societies supported their elderly. In agricultural societies, it was stated, both young and old are maintained by the family. In what was called the "capitalist stage," the young continue to be supported by the family, but the aged live on savings. Finally, in the "social stage" the support of the aged is by way of social security with the assumption of community responsibility, while children are still cared for by the family. This appears to be somewhat idealized and oversimplified. It is doubtful that there are capitalist or social stages in any uniform pattern of development, and it is also doubtful that most of the elderly have ever lived on their individual savings. It does appear true that in preindustrial societies the elderly, as well as other dependent persons, relied upon the family and that in modern industrialized societies the trend is toward reliance upon a wider sharing of risk in the general form of social security.

By 1977 there were 114 countries that had some form of old age, disability, and survivors' insurance (U.S. Social Security Administration, 1977). All the European and North American countries, about two thirds of the Middle Eastern and Latin American countries, about half of the Asian countries, but less than half of the African countries were included. Fifteen other countries reported no general social security system but did have some kind of pension system for public employees. This was the situation in Afghanistan, Botswana, Burma, Chad, Ethiopia, Gambia, Indonesia, Jordan, Kampuchea, South Korea, Laos, Malawi, Sierra Leone, Somalia, and Thailand. Obviously, these are all countries with limited economic development and slight modernization.

In most countries the old age benefits become payable between ages 60 and 65, although the statutory retirement age is as low as 45 and as high as 70. Most impose a retirement test, but in Canada, Denmark, Finland, Iceland, New Zealand, Norway, and Sweden, payments are available to every resident past a specified age without regard to employment or past contributions (Cheit, 1968:199). In Australia, South Africa, Trinidad, and Tobago, pensions are potentially available to any aged resident, but a means test is required. Of course this tends to blur the conventional distinction between old age insurance, under which the insured have a vested right to the benefits, and old age assistance (or relief), under which the payments are based upon financial need.

Old Age Assistance

Most countries have some kind of governmentally administered program under which people in dire need, including old people, may be given assistance. Under the English Poor Law of 1601, such assistance to older people was supposed to be provided in the institution originally called the almshouse. Its counterpart in the United States was often called the poorhouse or—because many of them were located in rural areas with land attached, the produce of which was to provide partial support of the institution—the "poor farm." In addition to these institutional programs, over the years in both England and the United States, programs of outdoor relief also developed. During the nineteenth century, poverty and pauperism among the aged became widespread in England. Charles Booth's classic study in the 1890s (1894:53–54) reported that nearly one third were receiving parish relief. This led to the appointment of the

Royal Commission on the Poor Laws and subsequently to the establishment of old age pensions in 1908. In the United States prior to 1935, outdoor relief was the responsibility of states and counties, but in addition to setting up the Federal Old Age Insurance system, the Social Security Act of 1935 established a joint federal-state program of Old Age Assistance. Initially the minimum age of eligibility was 70, but this was later reduced to 65. In addition to age, the primary basis of eligibility under this program was need, and a means test was required. In 1974 this Old Age Assistance program was taken over by the federal government and was incorporated into what became known as Supplemental Security Income, still retaining the means test.

Though most countries have some kind of relief programs, as long as the main consideration is economic need, few find it necessary or advantageous to treat the elderly as a separate category for this purpose. In other words, when the primary issue is alleviation of hunger, most societies do not bother to classify the recipients by age.

Property and Security in Old Age

Simmons (1945:46) concluded that the effort to accumulate property had been nearly universal as a hedge against old age dependency. However, he also found significant variations in the extent and success of this effort according to the type of economy. It was much less extensive in collective economies than among farmers and herders.

Perhaps one of the few exceptions to Simmons' statement is to be found among the Bushmen of the Kalahari Desert in southern Africa (Thomas, 1959). These people subsist by hunting giraffes, elands, and other sparse game, supplementing their diet with tubers and melons. It is a precarious existence that forces them to move about over a wide hunting area. There is practically no possibility of accumulation of property by individuals. Certainly there is no concept of private ownership of land, and game and other items of food are divided on the spot, following strict, culturally prescribed rules. Individuals carry all their personal property—consisting of minimal clothing, hunting weapons, digging sticks, and a few ornaments—with them on the frequent moves about the desert. And most of these personal possessions are likely to be broken and scattered on one's grave at his or her burial (Thomas, 1959:127). In such an environment there is little security at any age, but despite this tenuous existence, Thomas asserts that they do not abandon the aged or handicapped (1959:239).

Among herders and agriculturalists, who have more extensively developed concepts of property, we find older people making greater use of ownership or control of property to assure their own futures. As Silverman and Maxwell (1983:51) demonstrate, the control of such resources correlates strongly with deference toward the aged. Furthermore, retirement contracts securing the rights of the elderly to specific services or resources after transfer of ownership or control have been used for several centuries in Europe and the United States to provide for security in old age (Queen and Habenstein, 1974:415; Quadagno, 1982).

The Sidamo of southwest Ethiopia mix herding of cattle, sheep, and goats with the cultivation of bananas and maize, and in this society the elder generation wields so much power that it is referred to as a 'gerontocratic society" (Hamer, 1972:15). The control of land and cattle and their allocation among the younger generations are the primary means by which the older men exercise their power over the younger men and the rest of the society. Similarly, among the Bantu peoples of southern Africa, whether they are pastoral or agricultural, the elders are responsible for allocating rights to the use of the land that is the property of the sib or tribe (Fuller, 1972:52–53). This is characteristic of the Zulu, the Tswa, the Shona, and the Sotho tribes. The right to make use of tribal lands is the most cherished perquisite of tribal membership, but a senior member is invariably responsible for the specific allocation, which of course places a lot of power in that person's hands. This is equally true of both patrilineal and matrilineal tribes of central and west Africa. Among the patrilineal Ibo of Nigeria, the elder male apportions the land to younger males and receives payment from them in return (Shelton, 1972:38). This means that the older person may retire from farm work and spend his time and energy in the role of administrator. The goods and services he receives in this capacity usually exceed those of any other person in the lineage, providing not only economic security for him in his old age but also high honor and status.

Similar principles apparently apply in other parts of the world. Among the Kapauku Papuans of western New Guinea, elders who have managed to accumulate considerable estates, and thereby to provide work for many others, are accorded prestige and high status (Boyd, 1973:36). However, it appears that both the wealth and status are achieved; they are not automatic ascriptions based on age.

There is also no guarantee of success and security in rural Yugoslavia. Some who work hard and contribute faithfully to the common enterprise of the patrilocal joint family household known as the *zadruga* may be among the "winners," who are rewarded with a secure niche and an honored position, but others who have perhaps been less diligent and less mindful of their responsibilities to the common enterprise may be among the "losers," who become "charity cases" living in a home for the aged (Simic, 1978:77–103).

Rural Ireland presents another illustration of the use of property by older males not merely to ensure their own security but also to hold adult sons in a subordinate role (Streib, 1972:171–174). Here it is customary for an older man to retain ownership and control of the family farm until very late in his life. Meanwhile his sons continue to work as unpaid family laborers, totally dependent upon the father for economic support and unable to marry because of the lack of an independent means of supporting a family. In the absence of a definite and unambiguous system of inheritance, the father may play one child against another, using the prospect of inheritance as "a form of blackmail" to keep the children (in their thirties or forties) submissive to his will. Ultimately he may turn the farm over to a son, being careful to reserve the "west room"—the most spacious and best furnished—for himself and his wife and to provide for financial support for the rest of their lives (Arensberg and Kimball, 1968; Kennedy, 1973).

Though not usually holding the children in such complete thralldom and not blocking marriage for such extended periods, some seventeenth-century New England farmers reportedly used property and potential inheritance in a similar manner to retain control and safeguard their old age (Fischer, 1977:52–53).

No doubt other forms of property are also used to provide security in old age, but agriculturalists provide some of the most pertinent examples of this approach to old age security. Once land becomes acknowledged as a form of property, whether individually or communally owned, the person who controls its use or transfer acquires power. If this power can be retained into old age, it provides, as Simmons (1945:46) said, "a hedge against old age dependency." Many other forms of property are less tangible and less durable, and in urban industrial societies the average worker, being a wage or salary employee, apparently has a lower probability of accumulating sufficient property to provide such a hedge. This is particularly true because he or she is much more likely to have a lengthy old age and to be deprived of continued employment during much of that extended lifetime.

Economic Roles of the Aged

Age is one common basis of division of labor, even though it may be less important in this regard than sex and other conventional criteria (Herskovits, 1952:33). But obviously cultures differ in the significance they attach to age and therefore in the ways in which age impinges on the economic life of the community. Indeed there may be systematic ways in which age is related to different economic systems as they have been sketched. For example, the debilities common to old age may limit the participation of elderly males in the economic life of a hunting society quite as effectively as chronological age and supposed vocational obsolescence do in an industrial society. Some have suggested that the relationship between continued occupational activity and the level of technological development may be curvilinear, with relatively low levels of participation by the aged in fishing and hunting societies (which require vigorous physical activity), rising levels of continued input in agricultural societies, followed by falling levels during industrialization (Williamson, Evans, and Powell, 1982:5–7; Sheehan, 1976).

Certainly the factory system of production broke up the apprenticeship system that had earlier fostered age grading of the workers. Under that system progressively increasing levels of skill were associated with rising status and pay, providing a lifelong ascending ladder of economic achievement and reward (Warner and Low, 1946; Whyte, 1946:32–34). The factory system also separated the workplace from the place of residence, converted most workers into employees, and propelled them into a money economy. Working for someone else for wages in a large, impersonal system favored the development of impersonal standards of efficiency that militated against the elderly worker and fostered the development of the retirement system. Some elements of age grading remained in the industrial work plant in the guise of seniority, abetted by labor unions, but seniority's impact was limited to providing a new concept of the normal work life and providing job preference, promotions, and honorific rites of passage only within that favored period (Miller and Form, 1951:358). At the end of that period, retirement abruptly terminated such preferences and prerogatives.

Thus for the first time age itself became the reason for the elderly's nonparticipation in the workforce. In a society in which one's status depended mainly upon his or her work role (Warner, Meeker, and Eells, 1960), to be abruptly separated from that role, sometimes with little preparation, and plummeted into a workless existence (Rosow, 1974), left the elderly not only in a "roleless role" (Burgess, 1960) but also "statusless" (Cowgill, 1974). Thus, for reasons of age alone, the aged industrial worker became a nonparticipant, returned to approximately the same level as the senescent hunter no longer able to hunt.

But before pursuing this theory further, we must look more closely at the various ways in which the elderly, both men and women, are in fact related to economically productive tasks in various societies. For the moment I shall attempt to classify these relationships into those that: (1) provide a lifelong ladder of promotion and advancement in status, (2) provide for continuity in participation, (3) afford the opportunity of easing up and phasing out, (4) prescribe a definite system of retirement based on age, and (5) provide new roles and opportunities for participation. Naturally these are not always mutually exclusive categories, and they may not fit into any neat historical sequence, but I shall return to that theoretical issue at the end of the chapter.

Ascendancy

In many societies, both past and contemporary, an individual's life is a continuous progression. Each transition represents a movement toward greater responsibility and higher status. This means that old age is the pinnacle of life, the ultimate achievement (Linton, 1942:597).

In some societies the progression toward this summit is quite gradual, and there are few if any rites of passage to mark the transitions from one status to the next. In others the transitions are quite abrupt and formally recognized, often by public events such as initiation ceremonies or installation services. Foner and Kertzer (1978:1092) found only 2 (Latuka and Nyakyusa) out of 21 age-set societies in which the transition to old age involved dramatic role discontinuity. There are many variations on the theme of ascendancy, only a few of which can be illustrated here.

The Sidamo of Ethiopia represent one such pattern (Hamer, 1972:16–21). The life cycle for the male is a progression from birth and early childhood to young manhood (marked by initiation rites), marriage, promotion to elderhood, exalted old age, and death. During childhood he is schooled to perform services for and to show respect for his elders. The son runs errands, works, and cares for his parents. He learns to herd the cattle that are the principal form of wealth in his society. He learns to plant and cultivate maize and ensete. Initiation marked by circumcision and a period of seclusion celebrates his ascendancy to manhood, and marriage usually takes place shortly thereafter. At marriage he can expect an allocation of land from his father, and he will begin to accumulate wealth, both by working his land and by raiding the cattle herds of neighboring tribes. Daring and bravery during these raids and the resulting warfare are honored but so also is excellence in oratory and debate. Promotion to elderhood is a major transition that usually takes place in middle age. Thereafter he ceases to do manual labor and gives up raiding and warfare. He becomes part of the paternal generation, which directs the work of the younger people and exercises judicial functions, settling disputes and restraining the rivalry and competition among the youths. As an elder he is deferred to in both speech and services, and he is revered for his wisdom. Furthermore, as he moves on toward old age, his status and influence increase. Eventually an old man (approximately 70) may become a *woma*, one who personifies the highest ideals of the culture. Such a person embodies courage, truth, justice, and wisdom and is even believed to possess the power to foretell the future.

In most respects the female life cycle parallels that of the male, although the female is always clearly subordinate to the male, and her role is always related to reproduction or food preparation. The young girl is also taught to honor her elders. She is served last at meals, following the elders, the young men, and the adult women. Very early she begins to assist her mother in food preparation. There are no puberty rites, aside from private instruction in personal hygiene, but pubescent girls are carefully supervised and chaperoned to guard against bride stealing and premature loss of virginity, a disgrace and financial loss to the family. At marriage—which is arranged by her father after he bargains with the suitor's family and consults with all agnatic kinsmen, the girl's mother, and the girl herself—she undergoes significant physical preparations. She changes her hair style, pierces her right ear for an earring, has her clitoris removed by surgery, and undergoes a two-month period of seclusion, after which the marriage may be consummated. She then goes to live in the village of her new husband and becomes subject to the tutelage and control of her mother-in-law. As she gives birth to children, her status and degree of freedom increase, but only when her sons marry and bring daughters-in-law under her control does she approach the culmination of her career. She may even demand that a grandchild be given to her to raise so that the child can serve her in her old age. With the assistance of such a personal servant, in addition to her various daughters-in-law, her workload may lighten. When she becomes the oldest woman in the village, it will devolve upon her to initiate housewarmings and harvest rituals. Furthermore, after menopause the sexual taboos are relaxed, and she is much freer to move about and to associate with whomever she wishes, even in cross-sexual groups (Hamer, 1972:21–24).

This principle of lifelong ascendancy appears to apply generally to the Bantu-speaking people of southeastern Africa (Fuller, 1972). Among the Thonga tribes of Mozambique, the headman is called "father of the people," and it is the eldest male in a lineage who speaks to the ancestral spirits in times of famine, supplicating them to make the fields produce to feed his people (Fuller, 1972:56).

Far to the northwest, in Nigeria, the Ibo people follow a similar life course. Until his marriage at age 20 or so, the young boy works on his father's land, and all his efforts contribute to the communal supply. Even after marriage he continues to work some of his father's lands and to live patrilocally. However, he will also clear some additional land and farm it for himself, thereby beginning to accumulate some personal wealth, a lifelong goal. In time he will begin to benefit by his children's labors and with his wealth purchase honorific titles, additional wives, and various other symbols of status (Shelton, 1972:37–38). Eventually he can expect to live off of the largess of his descendants' labors and be relatively free to spend his time in visiting with friends, settling land disputes, and caring for the ancestral shrines. But the climb to wealth, power, and status is not always smooth and untrammeled. The transition from dependent servant in his father's household to independent household head is fraught with ambiguities that result in considerable generational tension and conflict (Arth, 1969).

In traditional Corsican society the elder male was absolute economic chief of the household (Cool, 1980:153). He was the owner of the animals and land that provided the economic support, and he retained the respect of the community through both this economic power and his knowledge and experience. But the elder woman, too, was a power within her own realm—the home. Even after the death of her husband, she continued as mother, grandmother, and matriarch of the home. Her knowledge of the community and her experience in problem solving gave her a secure position, and her status tended to rise with age (Cool and McCabe, 1983).

In the highlands of Ecuador, Peru, and Bolivia, the life pattern is one of ascendance, and the village elders of Vilcabamba gained a world-wide reputation for longevity based on their tendency to exaggerate their actual ages (Mazess and Forman, 1979). However, this proclivity toward overstatement of age is itself evidence of the honored status of old age in that society. In the highlands in general, however, high status does not automatically accrue with age. Instead it depends upon wealth accumulated through hard work and thrift, service to the community in the form of offices in the politico-religious heirarchy, and discharge of one's kinship obligations (Finley, 1981). Because it takes time to acquire all these merits, such a person is likely to be well along in years when he achieves them.

Rural Ireland has often been cited as the archetype of male ascendancy. In his classic study more than forty years ago, Arensberg (1937:107) stated:

Ireland is in many ways an old person's country. Where emigration carries the youth away, old age is disproportionately numerous. But that fact is not all the story, for the rural Irish are long-lived. . . . They live long because they have much to live for. In their own sphere of life, *they are honored: they have power.*

And elsewhere, Arensberg and Kimball (1968:163) indicated that the elderly female shared to some degree in the benefits accruing from the ascendancy principle:

Place of honor and privilege within the household belongs to the old couple. In their families they are objects of respect and a mild sort of veneration on the part of all younger members. This respect is as much folk custom as the norms of family life.

The traditional family in rural Ireland has been a stem family, with one of the sons destined to succeed to ownership and management of the family lands. However, the elder male has been very reluctant and slow to transfer this control, so the son has often had to wait until his thirties or even forties to assume the role of farm manager. Because marriage was also delayed until this point, the Irish are noted to be among the latest marrying people in the world. The elders have used this power of control of inheritance to provide for their own security, often causing the younger generation long delays in launching their careers.

However, Scheper-Hughes (1983) asserts that this system has now broken down in some parts of western Ireland, where the land has become very unproductive and a high proportion of the farmers have no visible heirs. In this circumstance the elders have become objects of pity and contempt rather than honor. Scheper-Hughes portrays them as unenvied scarecrows watching over wasted, worthless fields.

Something akin to the traditional Irish situation may have obtained in New England during the seventeenth century. Fischer (1977:53) tells of the Holt family of Andover, Massachusetts:

The family patriarch was Nicholas Holt (1603–86), a prosperous yeoman with a handsome property and five sturdy sons to work it. And work they did, for almost as many years as their hardy father clung to life—and land. They married at the usual age in New England—twenty-six on the average—and each soon moved into a home of his own. But their homes were built upon their father's property, and they did not even begin to receive land of their own until 1681, when

Nicholas Holt was seventy-seven. The eldest son finally gained his independence at the age of forty, after having been married for twelve years! By 1685 all the sons had received their land, at an average age of thirty-two, which was very near the New England average. But even then it came with strings attached. Full financial independence did not really begin until Nicholas Holt died in 1686. There was, by the way, no sign of open hostility between fathers and sons in the Holt family, or in their town. The historian of Andover doubts that any such enmity existed. In seventeenth-century Massachusetts that pattern of generational relations seems to have been accepted by young and old as the way of the world.

Among the Hutterites, where land is communally owned, there is less ambiguity about the transitions, and they apparently take place gradually and with little stress. There is gradual lightening of workloads. Women do not work in the fields after about age 45, and they may no longer take their turns at cooking and baking for the whole community. They may continue with some chores, but they tend to spend more time supervising children of daughters or neighbors. Men too may ease their loads and be promoted to supervisory roles. There is little tension about this withdrawal; it is a mutually arranged matter (Eaton, 1964:96–97). The consequence of this process is that the oldest men tend to serve in executive posts or as members of the managerial council. The pattern is for one to progress to positions of higher status as he or she grows older (Boyd, 1973:39).

Continuity

The norm favoring continuity of activities and life experiences well into old age appears quite widespread, although allowance is always made for declining competence. There are varying degrees of the norm's strength and differing personal and social criteria for enforcing it or making exceptions to it. Havighurst (1978:31–33) has noted that continued interest and involvement in the worker role is a favored lifestyle of aging in seven Western societies. This is true even though retirement has become a widespread practice in all these countries. Apart from full-time remunerated employment, involvement in the worker role may include part-time or occasional employment, volunteer service with the former employer or with a different employer, continued work activity on one's own initiative, a hobby that is work related, continued activity in professional or union organizations, continued reading of professional journals, and so on. Significantly, Havighurst noted that there was a greater tendency toward continuity among teachers than among steel workers. This is in accord with the finding that there are higher proportions of older workers in the professions, crafts, service occupations, and in self-employed work (Riley and Foner, 1968:51). The same is true for farmers, proprietors, managers, and officials (Miller and Form, 1951: 358–359). It is also easier to maintain continuity if the work can be performed at or near one's home, as with the Thai lacquer workers and silversmiths (Cowgill, 1968:161).

In many societies it is difficult to differentiate between work and leisure activity, between employment and retirement. In modern societies the distinction is made chiefly on the basis of remuneration. In other words, a person who is being paid for the activity in which he or she is engaged is defined as employed, but a person who is not being paid may be viewed as a volunteer or merely as a participant in leisure time pursuits. This reveals how arbitrary and shallow the distinction actually is. Identical behavior engaged in by two people side by side may be called employment in one case and volunteer work in the other.

In preindustrial societies this kind of distinction is seldom made, and it would never be made in a subsistence economy. It can occur only when some workers are employed by other persons and are paid for their activity in some accepted medium of exchange, that is, money. If most of the production is for home consumption and little of it gets into a market where it is exchanged for money, there is little reason or occasion to raise the issue of work versus leisure or employment versus retirement. In most preindustrial societies older people continue their daily activities without consciously distinguishing between work and retirement. In fact the idea of retirement does not exist, and the practice is unknown.

Among the Inuit Eskimo, everyone is encouraged to continue working as long as possible, and cessation of work occurs only because of physical incapacity (Guemple, 1983). The same appears to be true of the Bushmen of the Kalihari Desert in southern Africa (Thomas, 1959). Indeed older women are usually the key figures in the small bands that constitute the effective communities among these people. Such older women are the most knowledgeable about where and how to find berries and tubers in the barren veld (Thomas, 1959:103). They not only find the food, they distribute it among the band (Thomas, 1959:215). Older men participate in hunting game to the extent of their physical abilities and assume responsibility for distributing the meat after the kill (Thomas, 1959:116). They also decide when to move on to a new hunting area and what the destination will be (Thomas, 1959:55).

The aged of Samoa are permitted to engage in any form of labor they are capable of performing (Holmes and Rhoads, 1983). There is a smoothly flowing continuity to the life cycle, and the aged are fully integrated into their society. They perceive themselves to be valuable, participating members in all family and village activities.

A similar continuity is to be observed in Mexico. Adams (1972) reports that the elderly continue as much economic activity as they can manage and that their work is indistinguishable in kind from that of their children. The children treat them with respect, which does not necessarily connote admiration. Lewis (1963) notes the same continuity in the village of Tepoztlan but points out that there are slightly divergent patterns for males and females. The elderly male is more likely to reach a plateau in activity and esteem, and perhaps even manifest some decline, while the elderly female shows a greater tendency toward an ascendancy pattern, often achieving a dominant position in the household (Lewis, 1963:419–420).

In the Colombian Andes to the south there is also much continuity in life, and older people maintain a high level of activity in family and community affairs. Their advice is sought in regard to matters in which their knowledge and experience are relevant, and reduced activity in one aspect of life is usually compensated for by increased participation in another (Kagan, 1980).

In India older women normally continue to manage their own households as long as they are physically able (Vatuk, 1980:144–145), but as daughters-in-law are brought into the household, the younger women may take over the heavier, more onerous aspects of housekeeping, while the older women shift to more managerial roles: handling the family finances, shopping, dealing with tradesmen, planning and supervising family ceremonies, and arranging for gift exchanges. Older women are also very much involved in the care of grandchildren, and they are usually responsible for the care of the cows, attesting to the value placed on such animals in that society. In present-day China most older persons continue to work as long as they are able; no one is forced to retire, but lighter tasks are often assigned to the elderly (Missine, 1982:6).

On the island of Truk most older men continue to be actively involved in the cultivation of taro, but they are heavily dependent upon their spouses or daughters for its preparation (Borthwick, 1977:212). Older women rarely work in the taro fields, but they usually continue to assist in its preparation.

Japan is an anomaly, a mixture of traditional and modern, of continuity somewhat eroded but partially masked by continued verbal iteration of traditional norms. Though retirement has become widespread and customary in the larger enterprises in Japan, continued employment of older males is still the rule. This apparent contradiction is explained by the fact that upon formal retirement, the male worker gets another job, often in a family enterprise. One reason for this high rate of employment of older males is the exceedingly low level of the pensions, which are often not available until several years after formal retirement. For the older woman in Japan, as in many other parts of the world, there is more continuity than for her husband. She often continues full responsibility for management of the household, although in recent decades daughters-in-law have assumed much more of this responsibility in three-generation households (Masuda, 1975). Certainly grandmothers as well as grandfathers are much concerned in the care of grandchildren, but both may also assist in the work performed by their children. This is especially likely when the family is engaged in a self-employed enterprise such as farming, retail trade, small restaurants, and so on (Maeda, 1978:66).

Tapering Off

Perhaps the most common pattern of aging around the world is a gradual and permissive reduction of participation in economic production. It was the most widely favored lifestyle of the aged in the seven Western countries surveyed by Havighurst (1978:33), and Simmons (1945:88) noted a tendency even in primitive societies for older people to shift to tasks that were less physically demanding, requiring less mobility, agility, and strength.

Of the Baganda in Uganda, Nahemow (1983:108) says that the most apt characterization of older people is "continuity from the past at a reduced level." Both young students and the elderly themselves attested that older people did not hold any particular position or status in the society; as a rule they do only light work, usually concerned with housekeeping and cultivating, but they spend much of their time sitting around visiting, smoking, and drinking. Nahemow likens this roleless role to the situation in modernized Western nations and attributes it to an individualistic value system that was quite compatible with the Western values that began to penetrate Bagandan society. Because of this individualism, older people in Baganda have never occupied a secure or exalted position, and the current situation cannot be attributed to modernization (Nahemow and Adams, 1974:161).

The fishermen of Newfoundland are forced to give up the strenuous life of fishing at a fairly early age to become land-based workers employed at the local fish plant or to subsist on unemployment insurance (Davis, 1979). This is a severe blow to the egos of many, and there is considerable depression as a result.

Though the Inuit Eskimo fisherman is encouraged to continue

fishing as long as he is able, he is permitted a gradual withdrawal (Guemple, 1983:25). Members of a household share equitably in the proceeds of their joint activities, and as long as there are younger, able-bodied workers in the household, the interests of the elders are secure. An aging hunter can expect his unmarried sons and his sons-in-law to do much hunting for him. Furthermore, there is much communal sharing of the proceeds of a hunt, and successful hunters are honored for their prowess and are proud to be able to contribute to the community well-being. Making and repairing the tools and weapons used by the hunters and fishermen require much labor, and older men and women keep the active foragers equipped with the tools of their trade. And of course the older women are usually also occupied with other domestic labors—sewing, cooking, cleaning, baby tending, and so on. Advancing age does not limit the effectiveness of women nearly as much as it does that of men; older women can continue their normal activities into very advanced stages of debility.

Until wage labor and a new religion destroyed their power base, older men among the Salish of the northwestern United States and western Canada were honored and deferred to. Like the Inuit, older men were eventually forced to give up active fishing and hunting, but they still had important and honored roles, which included leading the ceremonies and rituals that accompanied the annual cycle. One such ceremony of major importance to the Salish was the First Salmon Ceremony. But the Shaker movement, which swept through that Indian tribe in the 1880s, undermined allegiance to such traditional dieties and in the process destroyed the role of the elderly as keepers, interpreters, and teachers of tribal lore and ritual. Recently there has been a revival of interest in the past and in the traditions of the tribe, and with this revival has come a renaissance of this role for older people because only they remember the proper ways of observing the First Salmon Ceremony and the intricacies of the Winter Dance. Older people have thus regained their role as a cultural resource, even though this is now more of a cultural than an economic role (Amoss, 1981a:230–231).

The shift from active to more passive roles is also illustrated by the Druze of Lebanon and Syria, among whom older men have powerful and highly valued functions as keepers of tradition and leaders of ritual (Gutmann, 1969).

In the rural-industrial community of Kahl, West Germany (Weatherford, 1981), where farming is systematically articulated with factory labor, life cycle transitions seem to occasion minimal stress. Stem families are common, and retirement has become a gradual process. Part-time work and piecework employment are regularly coordinated with farm labor needs and are easily adjusted to health needs. Extended vacations and liberal sick leave (often spent at a spa) are also utilized to make the transition to full-time retirement or part-time farming very gradual and adjusted to individual needs. In the case of housewives, older women also find it possible to taper off at will. Caring for grandchildren and prolongation of household management responsibilities can serve to continue usefulness, but these are also roles that can be diminished as needed.

As noted earlier, Japanese male workers continue employment at a much higher rate than in Western industrialized societies, but there are also numerous ways in which they can taper off. First, after formal retirement at a fairly early age (55–59), they are commonly reemployed at a less strenuous, lower-status position for a time (Maeda, 1978:54; Kii, 1976:75). Then, after the second retirement, they continue to live with a son in a stem family arrangement, which provides opportunity for both the elderly male and female to carry out many active roles in relation to the junior members of the household. At the same time the demands of these roles can be informally adjusted to the capabilities of the elderly performers (Maeda, 1978:68–69).

While the Niolan woman of Corsica is following an ascendancy pattern within her domain, her husband is likely to be tapering off. He is no longer the chief provider, and though he may for a time be an advisor, arbitrator, or adjudicator, these roles are somewhat ephemeral and his authority is often more apparent than real (Cool and McCabe, 1983:65).

Another case that can be described as tapering off is that of the Fulani. The older generation gradually divests itself of livestock as the children marry, keeping only such animals as they can comfortably care for. At the same time the older woman has been giving calabashes to her daughters, symbolizing the assigning of milking rights. Ultimately all of her calabashes are gone, and she is retired from milking (Goody, 1976:121).

In Taiwan, Confucian teachings are still strong, and the elderly are shown deference and respect. In the rural areas there is no definite age of retirement, and many are still active in farming and trade, as well as in political and community affairs, well beyond 65 years of age. Yet men do begin to taper off, even more than required by ill health or permitted by wealth, and women begin to turn household management over to daughters-in-law. Furthermore, there is now a strong tendency for the joint family to break up as sons are able to assert their independence. Rarely is the elderly couple left unattended, and there is usually no mark of disrespect, but there is a diminution of responsibility as well as control (Harrell, 1981:194–195).

To the south and east on the island of Etal in the Caroline group, life is not as easy as in the Western stereotype of the tropical South Seas. Indeed adult life is strenuous and physically demanding, and people are consequently adjudged to be old when they can no longer keep up the pace in gardening and fishing. Older men and women therefore find it necessary to begin to transfer responsibilities to children and grandchildren. This does not mean that they become inactive, only that they change the nature of their contributions. After relinquishing their former roles as farmers and fishers, they begin to devote most of their energies to management of their property, arranging inheritances, settling disputes, and instructing both children and young adults in the fine points of making a living in that habitat. They also play an active role in educating and supervising their grandchildren (Nason, 1981:163).

The pattern of growing old among the !Kung Bushmen of the Kalahari Desert is mixed. In terms of the major occupation of the men, hunting, there comes a time when older men can no longer keep up the pace, and an increasing amount of their time and energy will be spent in camp, repairing and perfecting weapons. They may go on solo hunts for small game or trap birds rather than participate in the exhausting tracking of such big game as giraffes. But they certainly do not become useless or unimportant. They are always repositories of important knowledge; they have spent a lifetime building a network of trading and mutual aid relationships, which serve in their old age as their only accumulated assets. Living the precarious, nomadic life that they do, there is not only little opportunity to accumulate tangible property, there appears to be a systematic effort to avoid it (Biesele and Howell, 1981:94). Instead, through a lifetime of gifts and services to others, one has amassed credits that may be cashed in the form of reciprocal obligations in case of need. Older women persist in gathering berries and tubers as long as they can walk. But the oldest male in the band is likely to have a very important politico-economic responsibility, that of "hosting" the water hole. In this arid region it is vital that someone know the available water sources and who makes use of them. This is usually the responsibility of the eldest male in the band (Biesele and Howell, 1981:85).

Another set of hunters in far off northern Canada does not taper off so gracefully. The Chipewyan people occupy an area much too far north to engage in agriculture. Instead their economy has traditionally been geared to hunting the barren-ground caribou. This too is a strenuous occupation, requiring physical stamina as well as experience and cunning. But success in hunting is believed to derive not from experience but from magical power; declining achievement is attributed to the loss of this power. To cease to be a competent hunter means that you have been deserted by the essential force that makes you a man in this society, and growing old makes you useless. The main substitute activity is gambling, which provides a poor substitute indeed in terms of status and self-esteem. The older women, however, continue their household activities with little moderation, so eventually the once bold, dominant hunter and head of his household is reduced to relative futility and subservience to his now dominant wife (Sharp, 1981:100–103).

The long-living Abkhasians of the Caucasus continue working to quite advanced ages, but eventually they too slow down. About half begin to taper off in their eighties and the other half during their nineties. Those over 100 put in about a four-hour workday (Benet, 1974:15–16).

Retirement

Retirement from a lifelong economic role solely because of age is a modern phenomenon developed in industrial societies (Donahue, Orbach, and Pollack, 1960; Atchley, 1976:10; Streib and Schneider, 1971:4) and only recently being imitated in some developing societies. In preindustrial societies the complete cessation of productive economic activities is rare (Goody, 1976:119). There is no mention of such a phenomenon among the Sidamo of Ethiopia (Hamer, 1972), the Ibo of Zaire (Shelton, 1972), or among the southern African Bantu (Fuller, 1972). In Samoa an older man may retire from the position of household head and cede his position on the village council to a younger man, but this by no means entails idleness or withdrawal from other aspects of community life (Holmes, 1972:89). In Thailand there is a similar sloughing off of community political responsibilities such as village headman and council membership, and just recently all of the civil service has been put under a mandatory retirement rule, but the ordinary worker, especially in rural areas, is unaffected (Cowgill, 1972a:100–101).

Some kind of formalized system of retirement, with associated pension or insurance programs providing some degree of economic maintenance, has been adopted in all modernized societies. Cumming and Henry (1961:146) refer to it as "society's permission . . . to disengage." It is, says Orbach (1962:53), "the creation in modern society of an economically nonproductive role for large numbers of persons whose labor is not considered essential or necessary for the functioning of the economic order." This appears to be a constant and predictable accompaniment to industrialization. The United Nations (1962:12) reports that withdrawal of older workers from the labor force is directly proportional to the extent of industrialization. At the time of its study, only 38 percent of the males age 65 and over in 21 industrialized countries were still in the labor force, as contrasted with 70 percent in 21 predominantly agricultural countries.

Historian David Hackett Fischer (1977:4) has pointed out that 200 years ago in America, scarcely anyone retired in the full modern sense of the word: "Most men worked until they wore out. So also did many women, whose maternal tasks normally continued to the end of life." He continues with some history of its development (1977:135): "Forced retirement at a fixed age was rare in early America, and first appeared for public offices in the late eighteenth century. But not until the late nineteenth century did mandatory retirement become common in most occupations."

By the time of the economic recession of 1908, compulsory retirement was so common but pensions so rare that widespread hardship provoked a strongly worded message from President Theodore Roosevelt to the Congress (Fischer, 1977:160); however, it took another more prolonged depression and another President Roosevelt to drive the Congress to the passage of the Social Security Act of 1935.

Streib and Schneider (1971:v), in the preface to their study *Retirement in American Society*, declare that there are three basic prerequisites to the widespread adoption of the practice of retirement: (1) longevity, which permits a large proportion of the population to live to advanced ages; (2) productivity, which makes it possible for the society to dispense with the labor of a significant fraction of the labor force; and (3) social insurance, which provides a systematic mechanism for economic support of nonproductive members. Thus an increasing number of nonproducing elderly may be provided for from the margin of surplus of a highly productive labor force. Such a mechanism inevitably involves some transfer of resources from the working segment of the population to the nonworking segment and thereby sets the stage for a conflict of interest between the two segments. The resolution of this conflict is usually a compromise in the amount of support to the nonproductive elderly, ranging from token payments at minimum subsistence (if that) to continuance of normal wages and prior standard of living. Seldom is the latter achieved. In Japan the pensions are exceedingly low, forcing many workers to seek further employment in order to subsist (Kii, 1976:70–72). In the United States in 1973–74, social security benefits replaced 32–49 percent of the average income received during the final years of employment (Schulz, 1980:98), while in China urban retirees are supposed to receive 70 percent of the wages they received prior to retirement. American economist John Kenneth Galbraith (1958:338) has argued that a society affluent enough to dispense with the potentially productive labor of its elderly is also affluent enough to maintain them at their customary standard of living, but obviously this is seldom done.

Despite the near universality of retirement in industrialized countries, there is little uniformity in the timing of the event of retirement. Public policies vary from 50 to 70 in the statement of ages at which retirement is permitted or expected, and sometimes the stated age is different for males and females. A recent compilation by the United Nations for 29 countries is shown in Table 5.1. Clearly the modal age of normal retirement for males among these countries is 65. Seventeen of the 29 countries listed in the table specify that age, and almost half of these hold to the same age for females. It is interesting that when a higher age for males is specified, the same age is designated for females, but when the normal retirement age for males is lower than 65, a still lower age is listed for females. I know of no particular reason for this; indeed it is difficult to ascertain the rationale for such a differentiation at any age level.

Thailand is not listed in the table, but the normal age of retirement from the civil service there is 60 (Cowgill, 1972a:94). In China the nominal ages are still lower; for manual laborers the ages are 50 and 55 for females and males, respectively, and for other workers they are 55 and 60 (Haber, 1979:8). However, during a study tour there in 1978, I discovered that these nominal ages at which persons may retire with pension are seldom observed in practice; all the retired people whom I interviewed had retired at later ages.

This points up that the normal ages of retirement as stated in Table 5.1 are not necessarily the actual ages of retirement. For example, whereas 65 is listed for the United States as the normal age of retirement because it is the age at which full social security benefits become available, more than half of the workers retire earlier, many at age 62, when reduced benefits become available (Pendrell, 1979:305).

Among the countries that have adopted a stated normal retirement age—and these are mostly modernized societies—it appears that the more modernized they are, the later the normal retirement age. Those developing countries that have specified normal retirement ages for any part of their labor force appear prone to designate somewhat earlier ages, in the range of 55 to 60 rather than 60 to 70, as in the most developed countries. If this observation is true, it is still difficult to account for it, though it is probably a product of interaction among physical, demographic, and economic factors. In less developed societies people are perceived to be old at younger ages. They will have relatively few elderly, most of whom will be cared for in a family context, so very few will be dependent upon public transfer of payment mechanisms. Provision for these few from the public treasury may be justified by their scarcity and

Table 5.1. Normal Retirement Age as Defined by Public Policy, Selected Countries

Country	Age (Years)	
	Women	Men
Norway	70	70
Ireland	70	70
Denmark	67	67
Iceland	67	67
Sweden	67	67
Canada	65	65
Luxembourg	65	65
United States	65	65
Spain	65	65
Portugal	65	65
Netherlands	65	65
Switzerland	65	65
France	65	65
Finland	65	65
Israel	60	65
United Kingdom	60	65
East German Democratic Republic	60	65
West German Federal Republic	60	65
Australia	60	65
Belgium	60	65
Greece	57	62
U.S.S.R.	55	60
Czechoslovakia	55	60
Japan	55	60
Italy	55	60
Hungary	55	60
Yugoslavia	55	60

Source: United Nations, *The Aging: Trends and Policies* (New York: United Nations Department of Economic and Social Affairs, 1975), p. 33.

high status, even though that treasury is limited and strains to meet the needs of a younger, growing population. On the other hand, in more developed and more affluent countries, where there is a much higher proportion of elderly people, many of whom can be expected to live to quite advanced ages, it still strains the resources and will of the society to provide adequate transfer payments for the support of a large proportion of the population. It may therefore be a protective economic reaction to define old age more conservatively in order to limit somewhat the growing public liability.

However, it is necessary again to caution that normal ages of retirement as expressed in public policy may not correlate very closely with actual practice. Hence we may be straining to explain something that does not really exist.

There is no clear relation between labor supply and either the age or the sheer practice of retirement. Though the adoption of a policy of retirement and the inducement (or reward) of a pension have often been motivated by the desire to provide an opportunity for younger workers to move into and through the system (Schulz, 1980:4), this need actually fluctuates. What was a tangible need during the depression of the 1930s in the United States disappeared during the following decade, when World War II produced a shortage of labor that definitely retarded retirement (Riley and Foner, 1968:53). Even in less pressing times, some countries encourage workers to stay on the job beyond pensionable age. In fact Schulz (1980:63) found that half of the noncommunist, industrial countries imposed no retirement test for the payment of social security. Workers in Sweden and West Germany became eligible for benefits at age 65, regardless of whether they continued to work and to receive income from such employment. It is interesting that communist nations are more insistent upon the retirement test than are noncommunist nations.

Among 25 industrialized countries, the proportions of older persons of both sexes who were economically active during the early 1970s ranged from 2 percent in East Germany to 35 percent in Japan (Schulz, 1980:56). Whether these represented lower levels of physical activity than we would find among people 65 and over in nonindustrial societies is unknown. Such societies do not keep statistics on such matters, and as noted earlier, they probably do not distinguish between work and play, certainly not between employment and retirement.

Despite the trend toward official retirement of older workers in industrial societies and a trend toward earlier retirement in many, there has been a general lengthening of the work life. In the United States the work life of the average male worker increased from 32 years in 1900 to 42 years by mid-century (Wolfbein, 1963:11). The reason for this increase was, of course, the lengthening of life expectancy, which permitted more and more workers to continue working until retirement instead of dying on the job. However, earlier retirement has produced a slight reversal in this trend since the 1950s (Riley and Foner, 1968:424).

Needless to say, there is selectivity in the determination of the types of workers who continue to work to older ages, as contrasted with those who retire early. Professional workers continue to work to later ages than manual workers (Friedmann and Havighurst, 1954), while self-employed workers continue longer than employees. Males in rural areas, especially farmers, stay active in the labor force longer than most urban workers (Riley and Foner, 1968:51). Highly educated male workers continue longer than those with less education. Marital status also makes a difference: married men are more likely than single men to continue working to late ages; but the opposite is true for females, single women continuing in greater proportion than married women. While these evidences of selectivity in continued employment give some clues as to the reasons for declining employment among older persons in industrial societies, Riley and Foner (1968:53–56) offer the following more general reasons for that decline: (1) the concentration of older workers in slow-growth sectors of the economy; (2) the relative decline of the agricultural sector, in which older people are concentrated and in which they may continue to work without regard to any arbitrary rules of retirement; (3) the decrease of self-employment in all sectors of the economy; (4) the increasing size of establishments, which not only curtails self-employment but fosters the development of bureaucratic rules, including rules concerning retirement; (5) the upgrading of jobs, which increases the educational specifications and gives advantage to younger, more highly trained workers; and (6) automation, which produces obsolescence of many jobs of older workers.

However, a further factor has been the development of corporate pensions and state social insurance programs that provide an alternative means of economic survival. Such programs are not only humanitarian necessities for workers who are coerced into retirement, they may also induce others to retire voluntarily and even to retire earlier than the usual retirement age. It is not coincidental that labor force participation rates by older workers are lower in those countries with higher retirement benefits (Gordon, 1963:442–449).

Increased leisure is widely regarded to be a consequence of retirement. Whether this is a positive attribute or not depends on the values of the person and the society. Societies in which the "work ethic" is especially strong appear to be less positively disposed toward retirement than societies that are less compulsive about the virtues and benefits of labor. Some older Americans are reluctant to retire and have difficulty adjusting to an abundance of unstructured time. Clark and Anderson (1967) report frequent mental conflicts among older Americans because of the fear of dependency, which is seen as one hazard of old age in the absence of adequate physical or economic resources. However, in India older people say that old age is a time for rest and leisure, a time when one has the right to take it easy and be cared for by others (Vatuk, 1980:142).

On the surface the literature on the effects of retirement upon individuals is contradictory and confusing. This ambiguity appears to result from the commingling of reports of reactions at different stages of the process, both personal and historical. Persons who have been fearful of retirement have usually found that the reality is not as bad as the anticipation (Streib and Schneider, 1971:125–126). Before retirement became commonplace, there was much concern about losing one's utility, becoming isolated, being unable to maintain one's independence, having to lower one's standard of living, and keeping busy (Havighurst and Albrecht, 1953). Such attitudes were reported not only in the United States but also in Norway (Pihlblad, Beverfeld, and Helland, 1972:234) and Australia (Bower, 1974:135). It may also be true that retirement was most difficult for the first cohorts to encounter it (Foner and Kertzer, 1978:1100) and that conditions have improved for more recent retirees in the United States. The continuing trend toward early retirement seems to testify to more favorable attitudes toward it in recent years (Bixby, 1976:3).

Actual research into the consequences of retirement, all of which has been published since 1960, has failed to confirm the earlier fears and dire expectations. Though retirement is sometimes precipitated by ill health, there is no empirical evidence that the act of retirement is injurious to either physical or mental health (Streib and Schneider, 1971:69). Retirement has a more positive than negative impact on marriage (Atchley and Miller, 1982:28–29, 36). There is no decrease in life satisfaction (Streib and Schneider, 1971:116) and no effect on the proportion of people who identify themselves as "old." Nor is there much evidence of feelings of uselessness, isolation, or loneliness (Harris and Associates, 1975:129–173). Of course retirement does result in a sharp reduction of income, an average of 56 percent, but this does not produce a significant increase in "worry" about money (Streib and Schneider, 1971:163).

Retirement Activities

Older people in modern societies are faced with a dilemma. On the one hand, they are expected to cease paid employment. On the other hand, they are expected, if not urged, to keep busy. What are retirees to do?

We have already noted that in Japan many retirees, out of economic necessity, get other jobs, which means that they are not really retired. Similar patterns may be observed elsewhere. Second and third careers have become commonplace in the United States. After retirement from an initial career, the person, often after a period of preparation or retraining, enters another career and pursues it for economic gain. Some initial careers, such as professional sports, are notably short lived, and one rarely enters them with the expectation of continuing throughout his or her lifetime. Professional athletes nearly always expect and prepare to enter a second career after they retire from their sport. Many professional military people follow a similar pattern.

Another option, which has become so popular in the last 20 years that it resembles a social movement, is volunteering. Harris (1975:94–98) found that 22 percent of a national sample of older people were already volunteering, and an additional 10 percent wanted to. In 1981 these figures were essentially unchanged—23 percent volunteering and another 10 percent wanting to (Harris and Associates, 1981:29). As to the types of activities these people were involved in, Harris has the following to say (1975:95–96):

> The types of volunteer work that older people are most involved in include health and mental health (e.g., working in hospitals and clinics, programs for the emotionally ill, disease prevention), transportation (e.g., driving the ill, the aged, handicapped or others in need), civic affairs (e.g., vote registration, lobbying and advocacy activities), psychological and social support services (e.g., friendly visiting to the homebound, programs in nursing homes, outreach programs to find people in need, hot-line counseling, telephone reassurance for shut-ins), give-away programs (e.g., providing emergency food, clothes, household equipment, thrift shops), and family, youth and children-oriented services (e.g., programs for foster children, teaching home management skills, working in residential facilities for dependent children, day care services).

Activities that were mentioned less frequently included the following: organizing and administering volunteer programs, such as information and referral programs; educational activities, such as serving as teacher aides, tutoring, or working in literacy programs or library services; recreational services, such as coaching and teaching arts and crafts; working on community problems such as race relations; cultural activities, such as teaching art or drama or serving as museum tour guides; working on community housing problems, such as organizing home improvement or home maintenance programs; assisting in law enforcement and crime prevention programs; offering career counseling; and assisting in meals-on-wheels programs. The list is varied and extensive, and many of these activities are obviously socially valuable. Many are functional equivalents of those performed by older people in nonindustrial societies; they involve assuring and assisting other persons, maintaining social institutions, transmitting the culture, and solving social problems. This raises anew the issue of conflicting values in the dilemma posed above. If these are socially valuable activities, why do we expect people to perform them without remuneration?

Partly because of this conflict, there are variations among societies in the extent of volunteering. The people of Sweden apparently assume that if a thing is worth doing, the person should get paid for doing it. Therefore, volunteering is much less prevalent there than in most other Western countries. From this perspective, volunteers, particularly elderly retired volunteers, are being exploited. They are required to retire from remunerated employment, and then they are urged to volunteer their time, energy, and talents without full economic return. A parallel consideration is the extent to which they become involved in competition with younger, paid employees. Theoretically, volunteers are supposed to perform activities that are so marginal that no one would be employed to do them if payment were required. But in fact one may often observe volunteers and paid employees performing the same duties. Furthermore, volunteers, who are mostly middle class in status and usually have considerable education, often complain that they are assigned only menial, boring, and inconsequential tasks. The dilemma has not been resolved, but volunteerism is still flourishing.

In the United States the establishment of the Peace Corps during the Kennedy administration lent a new glamour and exotic mystique to volunteer activities. At the same time it modified the definition because Peace Corps workers are not totally unpaid; they receive a subsistence allowance and travel expenses (Blatchford, 1974:16–30). In 1965 the Johnson administration added a parallel domestic program called Volunteers in Service to America (VISTA). Though neither of these was designed for retirees, both were open to them. Above all they signaled the entry of the federal government into the business of promoting volunteerism. Shortly, several programs that were intended to enlist primarily retired workers were also launched—the Foster Grandparent Program, which recruits and trains older people to provide companionship and guidance to handicapped, institutionalized children; the Service Corps of Retired Executives (SCORE) and the Active Corps of Executives (ACE), which use experienced, retired executives and professionals as consultants to small businesses that are having operational problems; and the Retired Senior Volunteer Program (RSVP), which is less specialized and offers men and women aged 60 and over a variety of opportunities for volunteer service in their own communities. Early in the Nixon administration, a cabinet member, George Romney, was named chairman of the National Program of Voluntary Action, with the assignment of working out a policy and a coordinated program for the federal government's use of volunteers. This effort eventuated in the Cabinet Committee on Voluntary Action, with Romney as chairman, responsible for coordinating the volunteer efforts of all the various government departments. At the same time the National Center for Voluntary Action was privately established to inform, educate, and assist interested parties in learning about opportunities for volunteer service in both government and the private sector. Early in 1971 the six federal programs named earlier were consolidated under one agency, ACTION.

In addition to these federal programs, most of the states have some kind of formal office for the coordination and assistance in the use of volunteers, including retirees, in state and local government as well as in the private sector.

All this illustrates the scope and significance of volunteering as a social movement in one Western society. Some years ago Havighurst (1960) surveyed the roles of elderly persons apart from work and family in six other Western societies. Though these were explicitly noneconomic roles, the survey indicated that exclusion from the workforce did not reduce people to inactivity. Their various activities included club and church membership, informal activities with friends, continued citizen duties, recreational and leisure pursuits, reading, and study. In a comparative study of three Western industrial societies—Denmark, Great Britain, and the United States—Shanas and her associates (1968:285) found that only a very small minority (4 percent or less) of old people were living in extreme isolation and also that only a few were often lonely, 4 percent in Denmark and 9 percent in the United States (1968:271). Yet Barker and Barker (1963:246–272) found that older people in a Yorkshire village were less active and less involved in community life than those in a midwestern American town. They observed that retirement appeared to be a more formal process in England, resulting in more extensive disengagement.

Pihlblad, Beverfeld, and Helland (1972:237) noted the relative isolation and inactivity of retirees in rural Norway. Deprived of former roles, these older people had difficulty developing new ones.

The situation is much less bleak in Australia, where everyone is eligible for pension at retirement, but Wild (1978:171) reports that most people lose some economic power when they retire, and the options of the lower class in particular are limited. The aged poor are becoming increasingly concentrated in a few suburbs of large cities (Wild, 1978:162), and Earle (1980) reports that those who have been forced to move there to obtain public housing have thereby often isolated themselves from former friends and opportunity for continued participation. Lacking means of transportation, the relocated poor not only sever contacts with former friends and neighbors but also have limited access to opportunities in the city at large. However, Wild (1978:163–164) notes that no such limitations apply to the upper- and middle-class aged. To be sure, the wealthy usually live in suburbs, but they do not lack transportation or contacts, and many of them have second homes in vacation spas to which they migrate seasonally. In recent years many middle-class aged have retired to the Blue Mountains and the southern highlands.

Specialized Roles of the Elderly

The urge toward continued activity on the part of elderly people appears nearly universal, and social norms generally sanction such behavior. This gives rise to many specialized activities performed exclusively or primarily by the elderly. These too vary widely in different parts of the world. By no means can I catalogue all of them, but perhaps I can illustrate something of their range and variety. Here I shall be concerned with roles and activities that are primarily economic in nature, leaving the examination of familial, political, religious, and educational activities for discussion elsewhere in this book.

The types of activities in which older people specialize (1) tend to involve extensive knowledge, skill, and experience; (2) are usually somewhat sedentary—they require less mobility and can often be done close to one's abode; (3) tend to require less strenuous physical activity; (4) are often supervisory in nature, requiring organizational and social skills; and (5) may include dealing with magical or supernatural forces, including spirits of ancestors.

Older women, while not usually required to participate in the heavy physical labor of farming, are frequently engaged in later phases of food preparation and processing. Among the Crow Indians, older women usually cut up the meat brought home from the hunt and hung it up to dry. One responsibility of elderly Hopi women was to shell the corn. Among the Xosa, aged women tended the gardens and frightened the birds away, and older people also served as scarecrows for the Incas.

Elderly Bakongo women shelled peanuts and cracked pumpkin seeds, while the aged of both sexes among the Sema Naga stayed in the village and dried the paddy, protecting it from pigs and fowl (Simmons, 1945:84–87).

Among the Chippewa Indians, while the rest of the family slept with their feet to the fire, an old man kept the fire burning and kept watch. Older men are often utilized for making tools and weapons. In Malaya older Semangs were noted for the blowguns they made. In fishing societies older people often made and repaired the nets that the active fishermen used. Among the Seri, elderly women made the poison for their arrows. Older people are often skilled woodcarvers and basket makers. Aged Lengua men made string puzzles and miniature bows and arrows as toys for the children (Simmons, 1945:84–85).

Older people are favorite storytellers, genealogists, and historians. Since this is more a cultural and recreational activity than an economic one, I shall reserve detailed discussion and illustration for Chapter 7.

A conspicuous role of older women in many societies is one that might be called "beauty expert" or beautician, but it includes a wider range of activities than is conventionally associated with the latter term. In addition to barbering, the role may include such related activities as tattooing, scarification, tooth filing or extraction, perforation and orna-mentation of nose and ears, and painting actors for participation in ceremonies and dances. Older women in Samoa are the only ones who burn candlenut and collect the soot used in tattooing (Holmes and Rhoads, 1983:123). Other societies in which tattooing is practiced as an art chiefly by older women include those of the Albanians, the Kalahari Bushmen, the Sema Naga, and the Todas of southern India (Simmons, 1945:89). However, it is older men who knock out the front teeth of young Arunta men in order to make them acceptable to women. Elderly men of the Dieri tribe perform the nose perforation on young children five to ten years old so that they can later put ornaments in the holes. Scarification of the thighs, shoulders, and breasts of young Tasmanians was the prerogative of older women, and older women were exclusively in charge of painting the bodies of young Crow women in preparation for various ceremonies (Simmons, 1945:89–90).

Another specialty over which older women have a monopoly in many societies in midwifery. Simmons (1945:91–92) noted such activi-ties in more than 20 tribes in various parts of the world. Various tech-niques were employed, and sometimes the services extended to abortion, but older women were always in charge.

I have noted in the discussion of the ascendancy pattern of aging how older men often graduate to supervisory and managerial roles. Since this overlaps political functions, I shall have more to say about this kind of specialization in the next chapter. In many societies women also progress to become household managers in their old age. To the extent that older people specialize in educational and religious roles, they will be reviewed in Chapter 7.

Summary

We have seen that in most preindustrial societies, older people continue as a part of the productive labor force as long as they are physically competent. Though there is some reduction in the arduousness of physical demands and even some tendency to move older workers toward advisory, judicial, tutorial, and managerial roles, there is scant evidence of the elderly's withdrawal or disengagement from active involvement in the vital business of community life. Only in industrial economies do we encounter the institution of retirement.

Late in the twentieth century, retirement of the elderly from paid employment is apparently approaching universality in industrialized societies. Current trends are strongly in the direction of more general and earlier retirement, but there is still considerable variability in the age at which retirement occurs. Newly developing societies apparently tend to establish somewhat earlier chronological ages for retirement than the older, more highly industrialized countries, but this may change as their populations age and the health of their older people improves.

Economic support of the elderly and the destitute in preindustrial societies has usually been the responsibility of the family or local community. The family has been the first line of defense in all societies, but in those in which communal sharing of consumption goods is customary, the elderly usually participate fully. Increasingly large populations and greater mobility have brought new problems and new adjustments. Begging and individual charity tend to be replaced by organized programs that range from ecclesiastical charity to public assistance.

In nearly all societies individuals have sought to assure their own survival in old age through the acquisition or control of property. This appears not to have been successful except in stable agricultural societies where ownership or control of land provided a means of exercising power over younger workers.

Private insurance is a recent development found only in modernized societies, but it has proven inadequate as a general provision for old age. Most people have been unable to secure enough coverage to provide adequate annuities to provide a comfortable level of living. Consequently, private insurance is usually merely supplemental to corporate pensions and social security.

Social security, in the form of either old age insurance or governmentally administered pensions, has become the major provision for financial support of the elderly in all modernized societies. Nations frequently initiate such programs with pensions for government employees but progressively extend the coverage to employees in the private sector and eventually to self-employed persons. A few countries now have universal pensions for all older residents. Corporate pensions, like private insurance, are in the main supplementary or complementary to such governmental social security. Public assistance based on need is often viewed as a transitional program pending complete coverage and adequate benefits.

We have found a variety of career patterns and many different ways in which older people relate to the world of work. In some cultures one is expected to follow an ascending pattern throughout one's life, and in these societies the "hoary head" is indeed "the crown of glory" (Proverbs 16:18). This ascending pattern appears to be most typical of pastoral and agrarian societies. In such societies the high status of the elderly is partly based on their accumulation of property and use of property as a means of social control. Another factor undoubtedly is older people's accumulation of valuable information.

A second pattern of economic activity in old age is one of continuity. There is a very widespread tendency for older people to continue their lifetime patterns of activity into old age; this is so extensive that it is impossible to identify it uniquely with any particular type of society. We have found it among hunters, fishers, and farmers, and there is even an effort to maintain the pattern in industrial societies.

Still, all societies make allowance for declining capabilities. In most preindustrial societies people are permitted to taper off in a very natural and informal way, with little strain or discontinuity.

Only in modern industrial societies or societies feeling their influence do we encounter the highly discontinuous pattern known as retirement. Here, instead of continuity or a natural tapering off, we find careers abruptly terminated because of age alone.

In all societies there are economic or quasi-economic activities that are largely if not exclusively the province of older people. In modern industrial societies, however, no one is automatically channeled into these activities simply by reason of age. The types of activities in which the elderly specialize tend to require exceptional knowledge or skill, be somewhat sedentary, demand less strenuous physical activity, be supervisory and managerial in nature, and often include behavior relating to supernatural forces.

In all societies the elderly constitute a diverse category. Roles and activities differ significantly by gender. Although there may be some general tendency toward convergence of male and female roles in old age, there is probably no society in which there is not some residual differentiation by sex. The appearance of convergence often simply reflects changes taking place in opposite directions—males becoming less active, less aggressive, and more submissive, while females are becoming more assertive, less inhibited, and more dominant. Indeed, in terms of the nomenclature of this chapter, in some societies the lifetime pattern of women's economic activities might be described as ascendant while their husbands' pattern could better be described as tapering off or retirement.

There are also significant variations by social class. These have not yet been well researched in any society, but Wild's (1978) general descriptions of class differences in the behavior of elderly people in Australia provide some intriguing glimpses of possibilities in this direction.

Chapter Six

Political Roles
of the Aged

Older people not only participate in family life and to varying degrees become involved in economic activities, they also often occupy such significant political roles as administrators, elder statesmen, judges, and legislators. In this chapter I want to illustrate the variations and patterns of political roles of older people around the world. I shall point out some of the structural features of political institutions that influence the degree and form of participation by the aged. I shall describe extreme forms of political control in the hands of elders, known as gerontocracies. I shall illustrate the various types of political roles and discuss their relation to life cycle stages. Differences in the political roles of males and females will be given attention, and the mechanisms utilized to exert power or influence will be analyzed. Finally, I shall consider whether any historical trends or general principles emerge.

Structural Features

Every society has some degree and some form of age grading. By this I merely mean that some general age categories are recognized as significantly different stages of the life cycle through which all persons must pass.

Such age grades are invariably identified in the language of the society, and in general terms different roles are ascribed to each grade.

They therefore form the basis for age stratification (cf. Riley, Johnson, and Foner, 1972). Because the different grades or strata are assigned different roles and functions in the society, they are also differentially rated and valued. Whether these are arranged in a hierarchy of power that impinges upon political institutions is another variable dimension of comparative gerontology, but obviously if increasing age carries with it increasing influence and power, this is a very important facet of the society.

Older people, even if only middle aged by modern standards, probably wield little power in nomadic hunting and gathering societies (Simmons, 1960; Sheehan, 1976; Williamson, Evans, and Powell, 1982:5). In such societies there are few material goods to be controlled and used as leverage on younger generations. Such people often live in areas where climatic extremes and the migratory way of life place a premium upon youth and vigor. Furthermore, they are too preoccupied with the practicalities of survival to give much time and attention to ritual, ceremony, and tradition—areas in which older people often have an advantage. However, on the basis of a study of 49 traditional societies, Sheehan (1976:436) finds that in more complex, tribal societies, seniors hold much stronger positions:

> Tribes are more attached to the land, inhabit friendlier ecologies, number more persons, up to several thousand per village, possess much more real and movable property, have complex family and kin networks to govern every aspect of personal interaction, believe in complicated religions and mythologies, and practice a formally ritualistic life. The stability and tradition of tribal living gives seniors far more play for social role and status than that to be had by their nomadic opposites.

The process of detribalization and the concomitant forging of larger nation-states, as in Africa since World War II, have often taken on overtones of conflict between generations. For example, in a leadership training operation in Zambia during the summer of 1962, just prior to independence, young adult enrollees faced with the challenge of writing a constitution and setting up a new national government frequently asked: What shall we do with the chiefs? These young leaders in the national arena clearly viewed the tribal chiefs, most of whom were older, as potential stumbling blocks to nation building. The younger persons were casting about for ways to include the older tribal leaders in the national process without also providing them with an opportunity for obstruction.

Seniority is a common criterion in the selection of tribal, clan, and lineage leaders, and hence the incumbents tend to be elderly. They often are viewed as the owners or stewards of the lands and other corporate assets of the tribe or clan, and the stewardship usually passes by inheritance from the elderly incumbent to a suitable descendant in the oncoming generation, middle aged at the time of succession.

Older people appear to hold the strongest positions in agricultural societies. According to Sheehan (1976:436):

> In pastoral and especially in agricultural economies, daily preoccupation lies not with foraging for food for existence, as in nomadic bands, or with the constant threat of warfare in tribal societies . . . but with the relatively complicated means of subsistence and the comparatively complex, but in some ways flexible, social organization entailed.
>
> Heightened socioeconomic development may combine with the security of a relatively productive and peaceful environment to allow for nurturing the rich cultural and religious traditions associated with peasant life. The premium placed upon preservation of the heritage and the wide field for senior governance of ritual likely explain much of the high prestige and power enjoyed by older persons in peasant communities.

Leaders in a system that relies upon inheritance as the primary criterion of choice will probably be older than leaders in systems utilizing other principles of succession, such as popular election or seizure of power by force. But this principle needs testing. It is certainly subject to the qualification that once in office, incumbents usually try to consolidate and perpetuate their hold on power, and to the degree that they are successful in this endeavor, they then age in office. Thus, under any system leaders may become old, and any differences in predominance of elders will be relative.

Societies that retain a vertically extended form of the family as a residential unit are probably more favorable than others to the retention of power by their older members. Sheehan's study (1976:438–439) of 49 traditional societies supports this proposition. Illustrations may be found in the societies of prerevolutionary China, the ancient Hebrews, and classical Greece and Rome.

Another structural feature of societies that has implications for the political power and influence of older people is the mode of tracing descent. As noted in Chapter 4, patriliny is favorable to the perpetuation of influence and power by older men, and matriliny tends somewhat to enhance the position of older women. However, in the latter case, actual power still usually resides in the hands of males, frequently a maternal uncle (Fuller, 1972:66), hence called the avunculate.

Gerontocracies

In a few societies the power of the oldest generation is so great that the term *gerontocracy* has been employed to describe them. Literally, the term means government by old men, but in the societies so identified, an outstanding feature is polygyny, in which the old men hold a virtual monopoly over the women, especially the younger women, and young men must delay marriage inordinately or be content with those women who are unattractive to their elders (Spencer, 1965:300). Gerontocracies of this kind are found in Africa, Australia, and Melanesia (MacLeod, 1931:637).

One such society is that of the Sidamo of southwest Ethiopia (Hamer, 1972). Here males are initiated into age sets in their youth, any time between birth and middle age. Each age set covers a span of 7 years, and in one 35-year cycle there are five distinctively named age sets; but there are two cycles in process at any given time, that of an older generation and that of a younger one. A young initiate enters the age set just ahead of that of his father in the older cycle; thus he is separated from his father's age set by four intermediate sets, representing an age span of 28 years.

A young man is initiated into his age set only after his father's set has been promoted to elderhood. The modal age of initiation is about 18 to 20; hence the age at which the father's set is promoted must be about 46 to 48. Theoretically, two full cycles would require 70 years for completion, but actually one becomes a member of the oldest set after 63 years.

During his childhood a boy runs errands, works at assigned tasks, cares for his parents, and plays at adult roles. After initiation into his age set, he is considered an adult; he may marry if an appropriate female is available. He will be allocated a share of land along with some cattle and money by his father. During his junior cycle he is expected to amass further wealth, to participate in warfare and cattle raids, and to develop his skills in oratory in preparation for elderhood. Promotion to elderhood in middle age is likely to be the most important event in his life. He ceases to do manual labor and rarely participates in further military actions. Thenceforth he assumes the more circumspect role of judge and arbitrator of disputes. A high proportion of the disputes concern land boundaries because of the intense competition among the younger men and actual or suspected favoritism by fathers in making assignments to their sons. Thus the senior years are largely concerned with curbing the excesses of the junior generation. One who completes two full cycles, approximately 70 years, is eligible to become a *woma,* one who is designated as the highest personification of the ideals of the culture. Old men exercise much power and are accorded high respect.

The female life cycle is not so elaborately structured. During their early years girls learn adult roles by helping mothers, grandmothers, and other female relatives. Females have no puberty ceremony per se, but marriage is the all-important transition of their lives. It is marked by a two-month period of seclusion, during which the girl undergoes a clitorectomy, changes her hair style, and has the right ear pierced. Marriage may be to a well-established elder or to a younger man who has already experienced some success. From then on the woman's life will be concerned with reproduction and feeding her family. If and when she is widowed, she may enter a leviratic marriage with her former husband's brother or live under the protection and support of a son. In her old age she will continue sustenance activities but with lightened workloads, because she will have daughters-in-law whose activities she supervises and even grandchildren who may be assigned to assist her.

A similar gerontocracy is found among the Samburu (Spencer, 1965). This is a complicated, rigid system based not only on age grading, within which an individual moves from boyhood to young manhood to elder, but also on a system of age sets, each spanning 12 years. A new set is constituted every 12 years, and these age sets form the basis for junior and senior ranks within each age grade. Older men control marriage, and young men are prevented from marrying until they are about 30 years of age. Meanwhile the older men monopolize the younger women in polygynous marriages. This of course engenders resentment on the part of the younger men, but they apparently submit to it in the expectation that one day it will be their turn. They will become elders in due course and will hold power over the society, including the power to monopolize the women (Spencer, 1965:315).

The monopoly of women is such an important indicator of the extensive power of older men in this society that Spencer actually used it to construct a *gerontocratic index.* This was the "polygamy rate of older men [over 40] divided by the polygamy rate of younger men" (Spencer, 1965:301). For one Samburu clan the index was 5.4, and all the Samburu clans had higher indexes than three neighboring tribes. Spencer used this index to justify labeling this society a gerontocracy.

There are also some gerontocracies in Australia. Roth (1897:169) reports on some aborigines of north-west-central Queensland:

When the individual reaches full development of puberty, he or she undergoes a ceremony which entitles him or her . . . to a certain social rank or status in the community. As life progresses, other ranks are progressively attainable for each sex, until the highest and most enjoyed by an old man, or an old woman, is reached.

Lowie (1947:315) speaks of "the absolute dominance of the elders" in this society, and Birket-Smith (1960:51) adds, "Nowhere else in the world have old men so much say in affairs. Though there is no strictly organized form of government, they do in fact form a gerontocracy." And, reminiscent of the gerontocracies of Africa, Roheim (1926:51) points out that one of the consequences is that "the old men get the young women and the young men have to content themselves with old hags."

These are some of the contemporary societies that have been called gerontocracies, but there are others, both historical and contemporary, in which older people are very influential or powerful, although these have not usually been thought of as gerontocracies. The ancient Israelites accorded to their tribal elders power of life and death, as illustrated in the story of Abraham preparing to sacrifice his son Isaac, who was saved from such a fate only by divine intervention. Not only did the father and tribal patriarch hold such fateful power, he controlled the marriages of children and the disposition of tribal property. Furthermore, the rights of elders were buttressed by an ethic of obedience on the part of the children, who were taught to "Honor thy father and thy mother." Indeed Philo Judaeus attributed an element of divinity to parents: "Parents are something between divine and human nature, partaking of both. . . . What God is to the world . . . parents are to their children; they are 'the visible gods' " (Tomashevich, 1981:23).

Within the family domain, early classical Greek society also bordered on gerontocracy. In the seventh century B.C., the Greek husband and father was definitely master of his household. The wife had to have the husband's permission to leave the premises, and children were completely subservient to their parents. The ethic of filial piety was almost as strong in Greece as it was in the Orient. Later, when democracy was instituted in Athens, the power of elder men was restricted and sometimes mocked. Plato emphasized children's duty to their parents, but his pupil, Aristotle, associated old age with declining powers (Williamson, Evans, and Powell, 1982:40).

In classical Rome the *paterfamilias* was, in theory at least, absolute ruler of his household, even more so than in Greece, where his power was seen as a trust to be administered for the welfare of the family rather than as something to be used for his own whims (Smith, 1942:65). The Romans reputedly revered their parents almost as profoundly as they did their gods and goddesses (Westermarck, 1922:350). The concentration of land in the hands of elderly males, along with a profound reverence for ancestors, gave much power to older men. However, the expansion of the empire brought more emphasis on military prowess and began to undermine the authority of elderly males; at the same time it wrought some improvement in the position of older women (Williamson, Evans, and Powell, 1982:42).

The classical expression of the doctrine of filial piety is to be found in the writings and teachings of Confucius. They gave expression to an ethic that in time pervaded China, Korea, and Japan. The ways in which this doctrine affected the patriarchal, patrilineal family structure of classical China were traced out in Chapter 4, and we need only review it briefly here and note its significance for the power of the elderly in that society. Filial piety meant absolute obedience to and obligation for support of parents on the part of sons and daughters-in-law. The obligations included care and support in old age. Disobedience or failure to support meant disgrace not only for the negligent child but for the whole family. Under such a system, older people obviously had great power. Though this was mostly true of older men, particularly the eldest male in the patriliny, it was true to a lesser degree of older females. The matriarch of a household, though technically subject to the authority of a male— father-in-law, husband, brother-in-law, or son—nevertheless exercised de facto power in domestic matters over all the junior females. The extent of the elderly's power in traditional China may be reflected in some observers' view that the Revolution of 1949 in large part was a rebellion of the young against the "tyranny of the aged" (Tien, 1977:1– 7). One of the first and most sweeping bits of legislation under the new regime was the Marriage Law of 1950, which nullified the one-sidedness of the structures of filial piety by prohibiting the exploitation of one generation by another and affirmed mutual responsibility of caring for each other (Chapter IV, Article 13):

> Parents have the duty to rear and to educate their children; the children have the duty to support and assist their parents. Neither the parents nor the children shall maltreat or desert one another.

It is a bit early to assess the impact of the revolution, the legal change, the collectivization of the land, and modernization upon the power of older people in China, but for the most part they appear to be respected, secure, and well cared for (Treas, 1979; Haber, 1979; Cherry and Magnuson-Martinson, 1981). Yin and Lai (1983) even predict a temporary resurgence of the authority of a better-educated older generation before modernization begins to have its usual effect.

The ethic of filial piety is still quite strong in South Korea. The eldest son is still expected to remain in the home of his parents and assume primary responsibility for their welfare in old age (Koo, 1977). Only in the large cities are there clear signs of a weakening of the power of the elderly deriving from this principle.

The Confucian teaching of filial piety was also very strong in Japan under the rule of the Samurais. The Japanese family, however, was more nearly a stem family in form rather than the laterally extended family of China. In other words, in Japan there was more emphasis upon primogeniture and the responsibility of the eldest son. Still, the ruling authority within the patrilineal family, called the *ie* by the Japanese, was the *koshu,* the eldest male. He retained his power as long as he wished (Kii, 1976:22), and he and his wife had first claim under the Meiji Code to the support of their children, ranking ahead of the younger couple's own children in priority of support. Again, the legal basis for both this priority and the excessive power of the elders was changed under the Constitution of 1948, which moved far in the direction of democratization of status within the family and asserted mutuality of responsibility between generations. But change of legal status does not automatically effect the intended changes in actual relationships. The power of the elders has doubtless diminished under the new regime, but they still typically live with their children and perform their ceremonial roles for the *ie.* There probably have been greater changes in the roles of elder females than in those of their husbands. Older women traditionally dominated their households in domestic matters and tyrannized their daughters-in-law. This situation appears to have changed drastically, and now, even if the mother-in-law is still living in the same household as her daughter-in-law, the latter is in control (Masuda, 1975:57).

According to Tomashevich (1981:24–25), paternal power was very great in prerevolutionary Russia. A father was the tsar of his household, holding such authority by a similar divine right. Children in aristocratic families reportedly stood in mortal fear of their fathers' curses. But again that situation has changed both legally and actually; the family law of 1930 emphasizes mutual responsibility.

Types of Political Roles

Simmons (1945:130) noted that older people frequently played political and judicial roles in primitive societies. One very common designation was as chief of a tribe or lineage. Among the Ibo of southeast Nigeria, this is found in terms of the administration of "political, legal and moral obligations" (Uchendu, 1965:85). The rival Yoruba cultivators also observe the principle of seniority, and "the headman [of a village] is usually the senior man in the largest and wealthiest of the families" (Tomashevich, 1981:29). His powers include allocation of the use of land and supervision of the rituals and games of the youths. Among the pastoral Kirghiz of Afghanistan, the elderly have great political power, gained primarily through their control of economic resources, but they are also thought to be very wise, possessed as they are of extensive knowledge of the history, local ecology, and curing rituals of their society (Shahrani, 1981:188). "The household head alone owns the family's *yurt* and its contents, the herd, and any other tangible goods the family may have claim to, and he may dispose of them without the consent of other members" (Shahrani, 1981:179). In addition, he arranges the marriages of his children, often with an eye to the future security of himself and his spouse. For this reason both father and mother may wish to keep sons and daughters near at hand; consequently, lineage endogamy and cousin marriage are frequent.

The joint family of Taiwan is derived from the prototype of the Chinese family of the mainland. Like its classical forerunner, it is "a solidary economic corporation for property management and the control of production and consumption" (Harrell, 1981:200). The head of the family, usually the senior male, manages the corporation, exercising firm control over the entire family economy. In addition, he is the family representative in all village political affairs.

Older people were the political leaders and administrators in the traditional culture of the Coast Salish of Washington and British Columbia, managing all political affairs except warfare. They dominated village politics and were responsible for maintaining intervillage alliances through networks of marriage and potlatch alliances (Amoss, 1981:233). Here we note, in addition to managerial and administrative roles, that of diplomat. Political leaders were supposed to be wise, gentle, courteous, and forbearing. They achieved their ends through persuasion and influence rather than raw power.

Not only do older people perform executive and administrative roles as chiefs, headmen, and the like, they are also often legislators and policymakers. This is a chief connotation of the term *elder*. In fact Hamer (1972:25) notes that the most visible feature of the gerontocracy of the Sidamo is the assembly of elders. Whether such an assembly is formally organized or not, some body of elders is a common characteristic of preindustrial societies. Koo (1977:13–14) observes that in rural villages of Korea in which a single patronymic clan predominates, social control is maintained by the elders of the clan. However, she also points out that this situation is changing in two respects. First, there are fewer such villages; second, the tightness of control is slackening, and in some villages the elders may only be the nominal leaders.

Among the Mapuche Indians of Chile, there is a chief and a council of elders, but their responsibilities are sometimes delegated to other elderly persons who are heads of lineage branches (Boyd, 1973:38). The headmen of the Dusun tribe in Borneo are chosen for life. They cannot be removed or recalled; they remain in authority until they die or voluntarily retire (Boyd, 1973:38). The senior males and lineage heads make up the body of elders of the Gururumba tribe of New Guinea; they are the most prestigious members of their society (Boyd, 1973:37). Boyd notes that among the Ngoni of southeast Africa, older people, both male and female, are honored and looked to for leadership. It has also been remarked that in societies characterized by age sets, it is usually the elders who schedule the initiation rites and thus determine the lifelong associates of their junior cohorts (Foner and Kertzer, 1978:1088).

In such societies legislation and policymaking decisions are seldom separated from judicial decisions about particular cases. Settling quarrels, disputes, and feuds is another role that is often ascribed to older people. In the Kamba tribe in Africa, a trial presided over by elder judges becomes a spectacle and serves to entertain as well as effect adjudication (Simmons, 1945:120). Such a trial takes place in the open and draws large crowds. After the disputants have aired their grievances, the oldest and the most experienced judges withdraw and decide on a verdict. If either or both of the contending parties fail to submit to the decision, the elders will reassemble, beat their staves of authority upon the ground, and pronounce a curse upon the recalcitrant parties. Only by public apology and payment of an additional fine can the curse be lifted. So is the power of magic added to the authority of age in the administration of justice.

In Konduru, India, the village elders and the oldest men of the senior lineages of the castes concerned in any dispute act as an ad hoc council of judges in settling local problems (Hiebert, 1981:212). These informal councils are a highly effective, traditional alternative to the modern legal system; few local disputes ever get to the formal courts.

Older men among the Bontoc Igorot of the Philippines used a type of lie detector to help them determine who was the guilty party. All suspects were required to chew a mouthful of rice, which, when thoroughly masticated, was spit into a dish and examined. The person with the driest rice was adjudged guilty, since it was believed that nervousness during the trial would check the flow of saliva (Simmons, 1945:121–122). Milne

(1924:240–241) reported on an analogous procedure that was used at a Palaung trial in northern Burma:

> Twelve elders were present and it was a solemn affair, the elders sitting on the ground in a row, and in front and facing them were the accused men. At a little distance was a crowd of onlookers, who were ordered to keep silence. The proceedings began by each man swearing that he was not guilty. Then each took off his jacket baring his body to the waist, and raised his jacket on a line with his forehead, when he again swore by the Buddha and the spirits that he was innocent. The elders addressed each man in turn with these words, "If thou art guilty may thy back show that it is so." The jackets were next laid on the ground in a row, between the elders and the accused, each in front of its owner. Then one of the elders, a worthy and learned man . . . took in his hand the "oath stick," a small rattan cane which was kept in the house of the headman and was used for no other purpose. All the elders prayed to the spirits to come down and to point out the guilty man. The stick was blown upon four times, and the jackets were struck with it five times. The accused then put on their jackets. Their backs were examined, and those of the guilty displayed red blotches. I have been assured by many old men that they have seen those red marks appear. They said that they were quite visible but that they faded very quickly.

Turnbull (1983:226), seeking to generalize from his long and varied experience as an anthropologist, says, "In some societies the political role of the old is formalized, their long years of experience being called on to help in the resolution of otherwise intractable disputes; having so little to gain or lose, the old make admirable arbitrators."

The role of judge and arbiter shades into that of elder statesman. That seems to be the essential capacity of the *tu'ua* in Samoan villages (Holmes and Rhoads, 1983:123). The *tu'ua* is an elder renowned as an orator and possessed of extensive knowledge of village and district affairs. The village looks to him for definitive pronouncements on disputed issues. He is entitled to the central position at any public gathering, and should he arrive after the post is already occupied, it will be immediately vacated in his favor (Grattan, 1948:19).

Amoss and Harrell (1981:17) report that in many traditional societies, wise elders are relied upon for their expertise in technical, social, and legal matters. Among the Asmat of Micronesia, elders were appealed to on the basis of their organizational and political knowledge, and older people were valued for their legal knowledge, which was useful in settling disputes. Werner (1981), upon investigating the basis for the extraordinary prestige and influence of elders among the Mekranoti Indians in central Brazil, concluded that the main foundation of their role as elder statesmen was their knowledge, particularly their knowledge of rituals and ceremonies. And Fuller (1972:67) found that almost all elders in Bantu tribes were highly respected as wise counselors.

There is a council of elders and a "Soviet of the Long-Living" among the Abkhasians of the Caucasus. The chairman of the collective uses them as an advisory group, presenting them with complex problems that they usually solve (Benet, 1974:20).

Of course we also find instances of the elder statesman role in Western modernized societies, as illustrated by Winston Churchill, Bernard Baruch, and Dwight Eisenhower, and, on a lesser scale, by the overrepresentation of elders in the power structures of local communities (Presthus, 1964:287). But it appears clear that in developed societies, such persons are exceptions among the elderly populations, and the elder statesman role is based upon their prior achievements, not primarily upon their age (Cowgill, 1972b:251).

Older women have rarely played dominant political roles (Simmons, 1945:130). There are of course prominent exceptions, such as Golda Meir, Indira Gandhi, and Margaret Thatcher. But these are definitely exceptions, and their prominence is or was based either on their own unique abilities and accomplishments or on the particular events that brought them to power; indeed it appears that they have held their positions despite rather than because of the fact that they were elderly women.

Overall, women have held stronger political positions in societies that are matrilocal in residence and matrilineal in inheritance, succession, and authority. But even in matrilineal societies, actual administrative and executive functions are commonly vested in males of the lineage, as attested to by the frequently accompanying custom of the avunculate, under which a woman's brother exercises authority over her children—presiding at family functions, instructing the children in family customs and secrets, arranging their marriages, and so on.

Nevertheless, older women often exercise considerable authority and influence within the limited domain of the family household. We have already noted, for example, the traditional dominance of the mother-in-law over daughters-in-law in the management of their joint households and extended families in prerevolutionary China, Korea, and Japan. Although this authoritative role has been severely eroded in recent decades, one can still see vestiges of it in the frequency with which older women manage the purse strings, pay the bills, and make up the budget. For example, after prolonged questioning about the income and expenditures of a 14-member extended family household living in a commune southwest of Shanghai in 1978, I asked, "Who decides how the money is spent?" Two granddaughters-in-law who were participating in the interview immediately pointed to their 73-year-old grandmother-in-law.

Although somewhat less ascribed by the traditional culture, a similar phenomenon may be observed in many Latin American societies (and perhaps in Spain itself), where many older women become dominant matriarchal figures to the families of their adult children, who tend to live close by and in some respects operate as extended families. A similar pattern has been observed in American black culture, although in this case it is probably generated by the high rate of instability of marriage, which results in many black women becoming accustomed to playing the role of head of the household throughout their adult lives. Many continue in this role as grandmothers.

In modernized societies the loss of powerful individual roles and the growing awareness of common problems have led older people to organize special-interest groups for mutual support and exertion of influence upon political institutions. In the United Kingdom the National Organization of Old Age Pensioners presses for higher pensions (Selby and Schechter, 1982:163). In Israel the National Organization of Retirees, a confederation supported by the Labor party, seeks to influence the regulation of retirement funds. The Federal Congress of the Elder Generation in West Germany exerts pressure upon the major political parties on behalf of the aged. In Poland the Union of Fighters for Freedom and Democracy, an organization of elders, is considered influential. Political consciousness is apparently on the rise among the elders of France, but they prefer to exert their pressure as members of mainstream organizations rather than establish separate, age-segregated organizations. Pension groups are powerful in Sweden but relatively weak in Japan. In the United States the largest organized group of the elderly, with some 15 million members, is the American Association of Retired Persons, allied with the National Retired Teachers Association.

Late Life Patterns of Political Involvement

As with economic roles, there are changing patterns of involvement in political roles at different stages of the life cycle. Though there are similarities and correlations with the patterns of economic roles, there are also differences. In gerontocracies, the lifetime pattern of political power and activity must be described as one of ascendancy. The acme of political leadership is achieved only in old age. Sometimes this is a matter of gradual progression, but more commonly it is an abrupt, culturally prescribed ascent to the status of elder or chief.

As noted earlier, the promotion to elderhood is the most important event in the life of a Sidamo man (Hamer, 1972:18). The same is true among the neighboring Samburu (Spencer, 1965:315), and in both tribes accession to elderhood means withdrawal from warfare and strenuous economic activities in favor of full-time political and judicial roles. There is a more gradual ascent in political influence among the Bantu of Kavirondo, where the authority of the aged is related to their proximity to ancestors. They are presumed to be free of selfish motives and capable of exercising influence over living relatives and associates (Tomashevich, 1981:28).

Among the 71 "primitive" societies included in Simmons' (1945) study, he found 56 in which chiefs were always or usually old men. Though neither the polar nor the Point Barrow Eskimos had formally designated chiefs, the de facto headmen of their villages were the oldest men. Among the Haida Indians, even when a chief became incapacitated and had to turn effective leadership over to a younger man, he retained the formal title for life. Chieftainships were also for life among the Kwakuitl, the Chippewa, the Crow, and the Omaha. And when a young man, by accident of hereditary succession, was elevated prematurely to the chieftainship of the Pomo tribe, he was awed by the heavy responsibility placed upon him and distressed that thenceforth he was expected to act old, including not participating in any strenuous physical activities. In a similar instance in Samoa, when a young man of only 27 was made a *matai*, he complained that his hair was already turning gray and that he had to act like an old man, including looking after the affairs of a household of 31 persons.

The Bakongo people at one time had leaders who were too infirm to travel, but they were still revered and obeyed (Simmons, 1945:108). A Xosa chief was estimated to be about 70 and had more than 20 wives. Old chiefs were traditional among the Dahomeans; one who was about 90 was described as "old and venerable." Some other societies in which an ascending pattern of authority with age is characteristic are: the Hottentots, the Mongols, the Semangs, the Chukchis, the Palaungs, the Aruntas, the Ainus, and the Trobrianders. Increasing prestige and authority with age appears still to be characteristic of Korea (Koo, 1977:13), and even among the contemporary Hutterites, older men are usually elected to the *zeugbruder* (board of directors) of the community enterprises (Eaton, 1964:97).

However, there are many societies in which the opposite tendency is noted—a pattern of "easing out," retirement, or disengagement from political roles. Often this is informal, gradual, and perhaps only partial, but in other instances it may be abrupt, total, and final. Keith (1980:351) notes that in India there is strong pressure on older people of both sexes to withdraw from positions of authority and seek more meditative and spiritual roles. But the elders thereby gain a claim on younger members to look after their physical comfort. At the same time they may actually expand their social activity. Vatuk (1980:146–147) noted these same tendencies in Rayapur. Usually it appeared to be a truly mutual disengagement process as far as the political roles were concerned, but again the elders tended to compensate by increased social participation.

Several observers have commented that local political leaders in Thailand are usually in late middle age, but few are actually old. Concerning the northern village of Ku Daeng, Kingshill (1960:70) states:

> The leadership in the village is in general in the hands of the middle-aged. Shortly after our arrival the *Kamnan* called a meeting of the village leaders. Of the fourteen men present the average age was fifty-one, but only four men were less than fifty. . . . We made out a list of thirty-six villagers to whom we gave a set of prestige rating cards. . . . The average age of this group was forty-seven.

Cowgill (1972a:98) found the same pattern for active political leaders in the craft village of Ban Khern, but he found a much older average age for a more select group (eight) of prestigious persons. Kaufman (1960:75) noted that while some *kamnan* remained in office for life, they usually resigned at about age 60. It is for a different reason that older immigrants of Oriental origin in Israel are ceding power to the younger generation. Lacking experience with both the programs for older people and the bureaucratic modes of administering them, they look to their juniors, who have become more sophisticated in such matters, to run interference for them (Weihl, 1972:209).

Retirement has not only become characteristic of Japan in the economic sphere, it now appears to characterize dominance and headship in the household. Elderly parents now relinquish authority within the household, the father as head and the mother as supervisor of the daughter-in-law (Kii, 1976:99), and according to Kiefer (1974b:171), they gain the right to be indulged and "spoiled" by the younger members. A similar process of displacement appears to be underway in Taiwan (Harrell, 1981:193).

Disengagement from both economic and political roles now appears to be the norm in Australia. Bower (1974:121) reports that the elderly "show no hunger for power . . . and disengage themselves in a curiously passive way from life around them." In that setting the disengagement is reported to be so extensive that it breeds a sense of "uselessness, obsolescence and resignation" (1974:128).

In Chapter 5 we noted some instances of convergence, if not actual inversion, of economic roles of males and females with increasing age. The same phenomenon may be noted with respect to power relations and political roles. For example, Cool and McCabe (1983:65–67) report that older men in Lebanese villages have lost whatever power they once may have held in the marketplace. They perceive themselves as unsuccessful and are so perceived by their women, and they are aware of it. Consequently, when older women tell their husbands to do something, instead of remonstrating with them as they once would have, they now meekly submit and carry out their wives' orders. Thus the men have become increasingly impotent, while their wives have become increasingly confident and dominant.

A similar inversion is reported in Chipewyan society by Sharp (1981:101–108), where a man's decline in physical prowess is interpreted as a failure of his magical power. This brings on a decline in his influence in domestic and community affairs, but at the same time his wife's influence is likely to be rising. The husband's power and influence are based upon his competence in a single area—hunting; when he can no longer perform in this area, he is useless to himself and to the community. By contrast, his wife, with at least three traditional roles (mothering, handicraft work, and food processing) that are not as drastically curtailed by failing physical health, carries on and becomes increasingly influential. Her mothering role does not necessarily end with the maturity of her own children, given the prevalent custom of adoption and the expectation that she can "borrow" a child from each of her own children's marriages. This not only prolongs her mothering role, but under her tutelage the grandchildren can perform many valuable services in running the household and thereby lighten her burdens. The same tendency is noted in Mexico (Adams, 1972:110–111), where with increasing age some women become more outgoing and domineering and, even though this is not the approved norm, come to dominate their husbands.

Another illustration of role reversal, limited to the realm of magic, comes from the Comanche Indians of the American plains. Kardiner (1945:65) states:

> Women, with few exceptions, had no power before the menopause. After the menopause a woman could acquire power as readily as a man. It was common for a medicine man to have his wife assist him, teaching her

everything that was required for curing, except rituals for the actual transfer of power. Immediately after the menopause the husband gave power to her. . . . The distinction between the sexes, as far as medicine power went, was largely disregarded.

Mechanisms of Power

In surveying the literature on aging in various societies and specifically the political roles that older people play, I have encountered at least six different means that older people employed to place themselves in an advantageous position for exercising power or influence over others. These include (1) using magical powers, (2) playing intermediary with ancestral spirits, (3) controlling property, (4) building exchange obligations, (5) employing the ethic of filial piety, and (6) retaining and using a monopoly over valuable information. There is some overlap between these categories, and there are doubtless still other mechanisms that have not been included in this list. But a few illustrations of each of these will clarify their meaning and give an impression of the variety of means by which older people get, maintain, and exercise power.

Illustrations of the use of magic to influence or control the behavior of others abound. Here I shall discuss it only as an instrument in the hands of elderly persons. The above account of medicine men and women in Comanche society is one such illustration. Among the Embe of east Africa, it was said, "It is only by means of the rankest superstition that the old men are able to maintain their supremacy over the hot-blooded youths" (Chanler, 1896:247). Writing about the use of magic as an instrument of social control, Honigman (1963:278) says, "An oldster sometimes manages to maintain dominion over grown sons even though they seethe with frustrated rebellion."

One way in which magic is employed for these purposes is through the invocation of curses or the threat thereof. Westermarck (1922:350) reports that children of the aristocracy in prerevolutionary Russia used to stand in mortal fear of their fathers' curses. However, such children may have been in as much fear of disinheritance as of the actual efficacy of the curses. Some southern Slavs are also said to believe that if a son does not fulfill the last will of his father, the soul of the father will curse him from the grave. Thus the magical control may continue even after one's death. Among the Mpongwe of western Africa, "There is nothing which a young person so much deprecates as the curse of an aged person, and especially of a revered father" (Westermarck, 1922:350). Among the Nandi,

If a son refuses to obey his father in any serious matter, the father solemnly strikes the son with his fur mantle. This is equivalent to a most serious curse, and is supposed to be fatal to the son unless he obtains forgiveness, which he can only do by sacrificing a goat before his father.

If curses are the negative means of prohibiting certain actions, blessings are the positive means of encouraging and rewarding behavior that is approved, and the blessings of parents and of elders are believed to be efficacious and necessary in many societies. Among the Bogos, no one takes an important step, such as getting married, opening a business, or accepting a job, without the blessing of his father or master (Westermarck, 1922:351). Wherever curses are employed to constrain actions, the same supernatural forces may be called upon for blessings, that is, rewarding proper behavior. Numerous instances of such actions by elders and parents are reported among the ancient Israelites and the Greeks of the classical era (Westermarck, 1922:348–350).

Sometimes the supernatural forces being invoked are the spirits of ancestors, and at this point the use of magic as a control merges with ancestor worship and the employment of ancestral spirits for similar purposes. But the elders of a society are often thought to be in an especially favorable position to intercede with ancestors; after all, the elders are expected shortly to join the company of ancestors and other spirits of the dead. For this reason deathbed wishes, deathbed blessings, and deathbed curses are especially powerful. Among the ancient Teutons, a deathbed curse was the most powerful of all (Westermarck, 1922:351). And in those parts of the Orient where Confucian teachings have been most influential, reverence for and obedience to parents is linked with reverence for ancestors, and one duty of the elderly in these societies is to care for the ancestral shrines and conduct the appropriate rituals in relation to them. This custom is still quite strong in Japan.

A primary mechanism that older people have used to keep younger generations in line and to get them to do their bidding is the control of valued property (Simmons, 1945:36–49). When laws or mores recognize property rights and such rights can be husbanded and retained by individuals into old age, this undoubtedly is one of the most effective means of maintaining control, ensuring personal security, and retaining high status and prestige. According to Simmons, its importance can scarcely be overrated. Of course there are many different concepts and types of property. Property can include songs, charms, names, money, ornaments and trinkets, clothing, houses, blankets, family heirlooms, land, trees, livestock, slaves, and women. From the standpoint of exercise of power by older people, perhaps the most important forms of property are land

and livestock. Simmons and many others (Dowd, 1980; Maxwell and Silverman, 1970; Sheehan, 1976) have noted that the ascendancy of the power and status of older men is correlated historically with agriculture and herding. Those who control land, either as individuals or as lineage conservators, in an agricultural society have a powerful leverage over other people, especially potential heirs. However, Simmons (1945:49) notes that older women fare somewhat better from the standpoint of property control in collective and hunting and fishing societies.

Among the Nyakyusa, men strive to accumulate many cattle and many wives (Tomashevich, 1981:28). These are not only symbols of status, they are instruments of power and security in their old age. In this particular society, older people also garner authority as mediators between the younger members of the society and their dead ancestors. Older men of the Tiwi tribe reinforce their power and ensure their comfort by marrying additional wives, particularly young ones (Keith, 1980:351). As was noted earlier, in societies that have been called gerontocracies, it is alleged that the old and powerful men tend to monopolize the young women.

In Ibo society the elder male of the lineage is the steward of the lineage property, the patrilineage, including its lands. He apportions the land to the younger members for their cultivation, and in return he receives tribute from them in kind. Although he probably no longer engages in active farming himself, he doubtless receives more in goods and services than anyone else in the lineage. He also shares in the bride wealth received by the lineage for daughters who marry and move to other villages, but of course he must furnish the bridal price for sons and grandsons of his own lineage (Shelton, 1972:38).

Although Truk is in the process of modernization, the elderly have been fairly successful in maintaining control over land and using it as an instrument of authority (Borthwick, 1977:247–250). The prospect of a generous inheritance is a subtle incentive to one's children to provide the best of care, lest a sibling rival gain a larger share of the patrimony (Borthwick, 1977:196). A Maori youth is carefully instructed by his elders concerning land boundaries, and an aged man's deathbed wishes concerning the distribution of his property are considered as binding as a written will (Simmons, 1945:46).

Exchange obligations are also a way to exercise influence over others in one's old age. In prerevolutionary Chinese villages, debts and favors were long remembered, and in times of adversity the obligations could be collected (Ikels, 1980:87). This provided additional security in old age beyond that inherent in the extended family and the ethic of filial piety. Among the Kiwi, one pathway to power and influence was through reproduction, for a man could exchange daughters for additional wives (Werner, 1981:15).

As we have noted, the ethic of filial piety has been especially strong and well defined in those parts of Asia where Confucian influence has dominated, particularly in China, Korea, and Japan. This is certainly a powerful cultural device for retaining authority in old age. Though it has been eroded by democratizing and modernizing forces in recent decades, at its height it was a very effective mechanism for ensuring authority in old age. When children, especially sons, were taught from earliest childhood that their most sacred obligation was to their parents and that the most shameful disgrace for them and their families was disobedience or failure to support their parents, they were bound to feel constrained to fulfill the duties of that ethic. Similar feelings of obligation and duty have been observed in other parts of the world, although they are not so clearly delineated. The power of the *pater potestas* in classical Rome was supported by similar obligations, as was the authority of parents in both the Greek and Hebrew civilizations.

Though actual behavior may depart somewhat from the norm, Adams (1972:108) finds that "absolute obedience" is expected of Mexican children. Older people consider themselves the heads of their households, and they give orders to household members (1972:118). The Ainu of northern Japan also expect strict obedience to parents and deference to all older persons (Tomashevich, 1981:29). Whether this is a peripheral extension of the Confucian influence is difficult to say.

Another mechanism that elders employ to undergird their authority is their reputation for wisdom if not an actual monopoly over certain valuable knowledge. Hamer (1972:17) noted that the elders in Sidamo society were supposed to be wise and circumspect. They were supposed to examine all sides to a dispute before arriving at a decision. Maxwell and Silverman (1970) found that control of valuable information by the elderly is a major factor explaining their relative status and esteem. This finding is further documented and confirmed in a recent comparative study of 95 societies with data drawn from the Human Relations Area Files (Silverman and Maxwell, 1983).

Changes in Political Roles of the Aged

From our review of the political roles of older people in various societies, it seems possible to distill some general principles as to the types of societies in which they play the most prominent roles and even to make some tentative suggestions of historical trends.

In societies where leadership roles are ascribed by inheritance, elderly people are likely to predominate. To be sure, early death of an incumbent may on occasion catapult a younger person into power prematurely, but in general such societies seem to favor those who are senior in age.

As Simmons pointed out, the power of the elderly appears to be at its highest in herding and agricultural societies. This is primarily because of their greater opportunity to gain and retain control over the main economic resources in such societies—livestock and/or land. All gerontocracies have occurred under these circumstances.

In Western society this converts into a curvilinear historical trend: little political power is attributable to the elderly in prehistoric collective or hunting and fishing economies; it rises with the development and advancement of agriculture; then it declines again with industrialization. Industrialization, with its corporate enterprises, individualized labor, money economy, high mobility, and rapid social change, militates against the maintenance of power on the part of older people. In fact, as we have seen in Chapter 5, retirement from positions of economic importance appears to be an inevitable adaptation to industrialization, and for the general populace this also means a loss of political power and influence. Only a few well-placed or particularly charismatic people are able to retain positions of political leadership in old age.

Older men have been much more successful than older women in achieving and maintaining positions of political authority. Although some early evolutionists wrote fanciful works about a primordial stage of female dominance (Briffault, 1931; Bachofen, 1861; McLennan, 1886), anthropologists have looked in vain for any real matriarchal societies. There are matrilocal and matrilineal cultures, and in these older women tend to have higher status and influence than in patrilocal and patrilineal ones, but even in these the real authority is vested in the men, usually older men.

In less developed societies there is less differentiation of institutions and therefore of leadership positions. Hence, when older people do hold power in such societies, that leadership tends to include authority in family, religious, and economic affairs, as well as political. In modern societies leadership roles are more specialized, and to be a leader in family or religious matters does not entail any broader political authority.

Furthermore, the scope of the primary political units defines the range of authority of the leaders of those units. In societies in which the most significant political units are clans or lineages, headship of those clans or lineages coincides with the dominant political positions. However, the process of nation building, which accompanies modernization, subordinates tribes, clans, and lineages to a higher political authority and in the process downgrades the leadership positions in those subordinate units. Older people are much more likely to hold leadership positions in family- or lineage-based social organizations than they are in secular nation-states. The downgrading of familial institutions relative to the larger nation-states has therefore reduced the potential for older people to play significant political roles (Cottrell, 1960).

At the same time, modernization has reduced the size of the nuclear family and dispersed the extended family. Even though the lineal descendants in the second and third generations from a common ancestor may act as a "modified extended family" in a few limited service functions, such as visits, household chores, and response to crises, they are neither a residential unit nor a corporate body in modernized societies. Hence, to be the head of such an attenuated body is no longer a real political leadership role. There may be some residual prestige attendant upon such a role, and such persons may be loved and venerated, but they have no real authority. Even control over inheritance means only control over individual property transfer from a member of one generation to a person who may be a member of another generation; it is not the control or channeling of the corporate property of a lineage or clan. Furthermore, the threat of cutting one out of a will loses force when the prospective heir has other resources to fall back on, such as income from his or her own job.

Summary

There are numerous structural features of societies that affect the political roles older people play in them. The general forms of government—whether highly centralized or decentralized, whether democratic or autocratic—make a difference. Also the type and degree of age stratification and the extent to which this is hierarchical in terms of the relative prestige and power of the various age strata are obviously important. Other structural features that are influential in determining the extent of power or political leadership include the use of inheritance as a principle of succession to positions of leadership, the form and degree of extension of the family, and the customary way of tracing of descent. Some societies have been identified as gerontocracies; a few illustrations of these were reviewed.

The types of political roles that older people perform in various societies range from executive or administrative, as tribal chiefs or village headmen, to legislative, as members of councils of elders, to judicial, as arbitrators and peacemakers, to diplomatic, as elder statesmen looked to for their wisdom and circumspection in all matters. Older males have been much more prominent in these roles in all societies than have older women.

In some societies the pattern is one of continuing ascendancy in political power and authority with increasing age, but we also observe a tendency for older people to retire or withdraw from positions of authority and responsibility. The ascending pattern is apparently most characteristic of societies in which the predominant economic activity is either herding or agriculture. Certainly retirement has become the dominant mode in modernized societies, although this is less predictable for political roles than it is for economic roles.

Among the mechanisms older people use to get and retain power are magic, reverence for ancestors, control of valued property, accumulation of exchange obligations, a culturally imposed and reinforced ethic of filial piety, and monopoly of valuable information.

Older people have greater opportunity to play significant political roles in societies in which such roles are inherited through bloodlines. Historically, the relative power and authority of older people appears to have reached its zenith in herding and agricultural societies and to have declined with industrialization. Older men play much more powerful roles than older women in all known societies. In earlier societies in which older people had more prominent political roles, those roles were less specialized than those of the relatively few elderly who are able to achieve or maintain leadership roles in modern societies. Headship of tribes, clans, or lineages in many preindustrial societies constituted significant political leadership roles, but head of a modern nuclear family is an insignificant political role.

Chapter Seven

Religious and Educational Roles of the Aged

In addition to familial, economic, and political roles, the elderly often perform religious and educational functions. In his survey of primitive societies, Simmons (1945:175) states:

> It can be stated explicitly that in primitive societies aged men and women have been generally regarded as repositories of knowledge and imparters of valuable information, as specialists in dealing with the uncertain aleatory element, and as mediators between their fellows and the fearful supernatural powers.

In assessing the valued roles of elderly people in preindustrial societies, anthropologist Turnbull (1983:229) identifies "wise men, witches, and saints."

Like the other roles discussed earlier, religious and educational roles vary in the extent to which they are specialized and the degree to which they are differentiated from other roles of life. In general it appears that they are less specialized and less clearly differentiated from other roles in preindustrial societies and that, conversely, they have become much more specialized and sharply segmented in industrial and postindustrial societies.

In this chapter I want to describe and illustrate some of the religious and educational roles fulfilled by older people in various societies, and in those societies where seniority is an advantage in the selection and performance of such roles, I shall try to uncover explanatory clues. In that quest I shall often raise the question: What kinds of societies favor specialization by the elderly in certain kinds of religious and educational functions, and why? We may again discover not only correlations but suggestions of historical trends in these matters.

Some Religious Roles

Many different roles may be roughly identified as religious leadership roles, and the lines of demarcation between them are often blurred. These include magicians, sorcerers, conjurers, necromancers, wizards, witches, witch doctors, medicine men, healers, curers, shamans, prophets, diviners, seers, priests, preachers, ministers, nuns, clergymen, clergywomen, theologians, divines, and pastors. I would like to group these into four major categories without worrying too much about the fine shades of difference within those categories. The four major divisions under which these roles will be discussed are: (1) magicians, which will include all varieties of sorcerers, necromancers, and witches; (2) medicine men, which will include all kinds of healers employing supernatural forces; (3) prophets of all kinds, including fortunetellers; and (4) priests, including all types of clergymen and clergywomen. In addition to these leadership roles of religious professionals, older people may be involved in religious behavior as followers, celebrants, supplicants, or laymen. I shall give some attention to these lay roles as well.

The term *magician* is commonly used as a synonym for the term *sorcerer*, which is defined in Davies' *A Dictionary of Anthropology* (1972:121) as, "A man who practices and invokes magic in a community." Davies speculates that "sorcerers may have started when someone, unable to hunt, perhaps through injury or old age, turned to other ways of keeping his place in the tribe."

Magic is sometimes believed to be a special endowment that not only permits one to manipulate the environment but also protects the magician. It may even provide protection from the infirmities of old age (Sharp, 1981:105). To live a long time without becoming senile is a sign of supernatural power. No doubt most magicians are convinced of their own powers and try to use them responsibly for social service objectives, but of course there are also charlatans who simply exploit their clientele, such as the old Eskimo who confessed to Peter Freuchen that he was "a big liar" and "a foolish old man" (Hoebel, 1972:586). A layman among the Eskimos expressed strong belief in and support of their *angakut*; he had confidence in the magician's ability to make their lives and particularly their food supply more secure (Simmons, 1945:144).

Elderly magicians are sometimes suspected of taking unfair advantage and prolonging their own lives at the expense of others. The Tonga, for example, believe that very old people steal portions of the lives of others by the exercise of powerful medicine and human sacrifice (Amoss and Harrell, 1981:22). Extreme old age arouses suspicions of malevolent power. The deaths of children are attributed to old men's ambitions (Colson and Scudder, 1981:142).

Noting the widespread association of witchcraft with old age, Turnbull (1983:233) says:

> Where old age is associated with witchcraft . . . it . . . provides a considerable measure of . . . social security for the elderly, . . . because their proximity to power makes them all potential witches. Since nobody wishes to offend a witch, in case he turns into a malevolent sorcerer, the elderly are treated with extra respect and consideration.

Older women also are often thought to possess supernatural powers (Bever, 1982:157). Westermarck (1922:346) noted that among the Moors, while old men acquired saintly qualities, old women became *jinnia,* or evil spirits—there was an element of the supernatural in both. Likewise, among the Kapauku Papuans, an aged woman gains power because people fear her spirit, and after her death she may become a "female ghoul" (Pospisil, 1963). The Ainu too fear aged women both before and after death. They used to burn the house in which an elderly woman had died in an effort to prevent her return, lest she bring calamity upon the survivors (Simmons, 1945:161–162).

Shamans are always old in Salish society. They monopolize ritual roles that have the power to bring on or cure fatal illness (Amoss, 1981a:240–241). They can see ghosts, and through their knowledge of the appropriate magical rites, they can placate spirits intent on evil. Dieri patriarchs communicate with spirits and through them can produce rain or even direct thunderbolts (Simmons, 1945:157).

A frequent part of the shaman's role is that of predicting the future. Gray-haired leaders among the Iban of Borneo examine the content of dreams, the flights of birds, and the hearts of pigs in order to predict the course of future events. In this society no important undertaking is launched without consulting the omens, that is, without consulting the elderly shaman, who in turn consults the omens (Simmons, 1945:152).

Because all human societies are afflicted to some degree with sickness and disease, the possessors of magical powers are inevitably called upon to cure those ailments, and thus the role of magician shades into that of medicine man or woman. Among the Gururumba, who greatly

venerate age, older men are the only curers; their skill is highly specialized and important (Boyd, 1973:39). Older women as well as men are
involved in the trance medicine practiced by the !Kung Bushmen (Biesele and Howell, 1981:91). Singing and dancing are intensified in old
age to the extent that they are deemed necessary preludes to the trance,
during which the nature of the problem and the method of treatment are
revealed. We must not assume that this is mere play or philanthropic
activity; it is an occupation and it is serious business. An elderly Xosa
medicine man is quoted as saying, "No pay, no cure" (Simmons,
1945:159). Older women often made "soul flights" to the realm of the
dead to obtain the magical formulas—the proper words to repeat—in
order to effect a cure (Simmons, 1945:142). Elderly Asmat women were
both curers and sorcerers, usually concentrating their attention, for good
or ill, upon the abdomen of the patient or victim because that was where
the primary soul was supposed to reside (Van Arsdale, 1981b:115).

Among the Witoto, the position of shaman was usually inherited by
the eldest son, who was taught the art by his aged father but was not
permitted to practice until after the death of the old man (Simmons,
1945:152). However, their medicine was supposed to be so powerful that
even tribal enemies would not knowingly kill a shaman for fear of supernatural revenge. Only older men can be shamans among the Kirghiz
because young men are unable to see the *jin* with which they must deal.
The shamans, or *bakhshi*, spend years in cultivating a relationship with
benevolent *jin*, who then become their collaborators in coping against
malevolent ones (Shahrani, 1981:188).

The elderly are frequently the ones called upon to prepare the dead
for burial or cremation and to tend the burial shrines of ancestors. Older
women are the caretakers of the family graves in Samoa, keeping the area
free of weeds and well supplied with cut flowers (Holmes and Rhoads,
1983:124). Priestlike offices are held by elders among the Bantus of
southern Africa. These are the representatives of the living to the dead
ancestors. Indeed it is reported that a man too old to work and too feeble
to hunt or fight is the most suitable representative of his people when
religious rites are to be performed (Fuller, 1972:65). In a Chukchi family
the oldest wife is assigned responsibility for the sacred things of the
household, and the older women perform most of the funeral rites (Simmons, 1945:161). In Japan one of the filial duties that a man must still
carry out in his old age is the preservation and care of the ancestral shrine
(Tomashevich, 1981:25).

Elderly persons in the various societies not only perform such religious roles as shaman, diviner, and priest, but even as laypersons older
people are the repositories of knowledge of the mythology and ritualistic

practices of their culture. Part of the lore related to Thomas (1959:76) by an elderly !Kung Bushman of the Kalahari Desert was their story of creation. In a society in which rapid change is going on, older people may be the only ones who know the traditional practices. And if there is an interest in preserving or reviving the traditional culture, the elders are brought to center stage in the process. Thus a religious revival among the Coast Salish has increased the prestige of the elders because only they know the words to the old songs and the steps to the dances that were central to the former religious rituals (Amoss, 1981b).

Magic has been employed to solve all kinds of problems. For most people the weather is important; for some it is critical. The Inuit used magic to calm the storms so that their fishing operations would not be jeopardized. The Haida also employed magic on their fishing expeditions. Many people have sought to ensure the success of their efforts in hunting and fishing through magical means of control over their quarry. The !Kung Bushmen of the Kalahari not only use great skill and endurance in stalking their game, such as giraffe, they call on occult powers as well.

As we have seen, many people use magic for healing and curing sickness. The Shilluk and the Xosa are only two examples. Magic can be used to keep evil spirits away or propitiated. On occasion it has even been purported to stop an eclipse, although cynical modern observers suspect that in these cases the magicians were also astronomers. Manifold are the examples of people making use of magicians and diviners to select the propitious time to undertake a project. Rainmakers abound everywhere, even in societies dominated by modern concepts of science. A common objective of such efforts is to save or increase harvests.

But magic is not only efficacious against the natural elements, it is also employed against or on behalf of other humans. A common objective is to defeat one's enemies, as among the Dieri, the Berbers, and the Shilluk. One may also seek to force someone else to obey one's will, in war or in love. Predicting the future is a never-ending quest, and if magic or communication with the dead or with all-seeing spirits is useful, it will be used. Magic is also applied to prolong life and to provide security in old age.

Simmons (1945:174) found that older people were especially likely to be cast in formal priestly roles in more complex and highly developed social systems:

> The aged have also found many opportunities to exercise their powers in more formalized religious and ceremonial roles. They have served as guardians of temples, shrines, and sacred paraphernalia, as officers of the

priesthood, and as leaders in the performance of rites associated with prayers, sacrifices, feast days, annual cycles, historic celebrations, and the initiation of important and hazardous enterprises. They also have been prominent in ceremonies associated with critical periods in the life cycle such as births, puberty, marriage, and death.

Among the Kirghiz, a *mullah*, or religious teacher, is likely to be an older man with great experience and knowledge, and he is expected to teach the young the basics of religion (Shahrani, 1981:189). Schweitzer (1983:173) also finds that older people are usually the ritual specialists among the American Indians, providing expert consultation concerning the tribal dances and the various ceremonies at their yearly encampments. Older men lead the chants and sacrifices around the sacred fires of the Creeks, and a Hopi priest carries the heavy burden at the winter solstice ceremony of persuading the sun to return from his winter wandering (Simmons, 1945:166–167). Older men held the highest offices in the religious organization of the Aztecs and were referred to as "the ancients of the temple." Only men over age 60 were admitted to certain orders of the priesthood. They attended to all matters relating to religion and the religious instruction of youths. Their province included sacrifices, divination, care of the temple and sacred vessels, composition of hymns, and arrangement of rituals and festivals (Simmons, 1945:167).

In the regions permeated by the teachings of Confucius, filial duties toward parents shade into religious responsibilities toward ancestors, and the eldest male of the lineage performs some priestly functions. One such function among the Chinese was the committing to memory and reciting for the benefit and edification of younger descendants one's genealogy covering 20 or more generations (Ikels, 1980:86–87). As noted earlier, filial duties also entailed the care of family shrines and burial sites and performance of the appropriate rituals. In the eastern Solomon Islands a man keeps the relics of his dead father in a special case, and when difficulties arise he prays to his ancestors for help (Tomashevich, 1981:30). Ancestors are feared and revered by the Igbo of Nigeria, and their eldest living descendants have priestly roles to perform. The older men perform daily ceremonies for their placation (Arth, 1976:355; Shelton, 1965:20–23).

There is little doubt that older people are prominent in the performance of magical, shamanistic, and priestly functions in various societies, but there is disagreement on whether older laypeople turn increasingly to religious preoccupations as they age. In cross-sectional research in the United States, older people appear to be more likely to identify with a particular religious faith, express more positive theological beliefs, and say that religion is very important to them, but their attendance at religious services is slightly lower than that of younger cohorts (Riley and Foner, 1968:484–494). However, there are two basic questions about this kind of evidence. Do the differences result from change in people as they get older or from different experiences of different cohorts who have grown up and been socialized at different periods of time? This question has not yet been answered definitively, although the evidence seems to point more heavily toward the latter interpretation. And is the lower attendance by the very old due to poorer health and less mobility?

At the same time there is considerable anthropological testimony that at least in some parts of the world, there is an increasing preoccupation with religious matters in old age. Several observers have noted an apparent increase in religious merit-making activities in old age in Buddhist Thailand (Blanchard, 1957:427; Cowgill, 1972a:99, de Young, 1958:67–68). These activities are not limited to more frequent and regular attendance at the religious services at the *wat*, or temple. Older women in particular spend more time in preparing food for the priests and cleaning and caring for the temple, and some actually sleep at the *wat* during periods of intense religious activity. Some older men, usually widowers, reenter the priesthood in their old age and thus become full-time religious functionaries.

Similarly, in India it is reported that religion becomes increasingly important in the lives of older women as they disengage from family responsibilities (Hiebert, 1981:226). They spend time propitiating the gods in their homes; they take offerings to the temple and sometimes even leave their homes to become disciples of a Hindu saint or guru.

Older people acting in their religious capacities tend to be called upon to minister to the needs of the people in all of life's major crises and transitions. Older women are often midwives in attendance at childbirth, and if a magical or supernatural element is added to their knowledge of the practical medical art, their value is enhanced within the framework of the traditional culture. Christenings, infant purification ceremonies, top-knot cutting, circumcision, and other early childhood rites that help establish the individual's identity and ensure its welfare are always attended by elders and are frequently administered by them. Initiation rites marking the end of childhood and the beginning of adulthood are nearly always decided upon and presided over by elder members of the family or tribe. Weddings call for the wisdom, example, and magical aura of those who have lived long and successful lives. In Thailand an elderly couple thought to have had an exemplary marriage are designated to prepare the marriage bed. And of course, as noted earlier, older people, especially because of their proximity in time to ancestral spirits and their presumed influence with them, most often officiate at funerals, burials, and cremations.

These are the predictable events in the life cycle of most individuals, but chancy and erratic crises also demand the wisdom of age and the powers of the occult. Sickness, accident, drought, famine, defeat or victory in war, flood, hurricane, and so on require explanations and survival techniques. In traditional societies these are most likely to be possessed by the elderly, and this possession provides them with valued roles and therefore status.

But social change can quickly render such arts and roles obsolete and leave the elderly with baggage that is deemed useless. Elderly Asmat are now said to be living in a "ritual void" (Van Arsdale, 1981b:112) because the rituals the older men knew and conducted during that tribe's warring and headhunting days have lost their validity in a pacified subculture of modernizing Indonesia. The same thing happened to the Coast Salish of the American Northwest when they shifted from hunting and fishing to wage labor (Amoss, 1981a:235). Their intimate knowledge of the salmon runs and of the rituals associated with that annual event became of little value as they were set to work digging clams or cutting timber. It is doubtful that the current revival of ethnic traditions will furnish anything more than a temporary respite from their technological unemployment. A major activity of this revival almost guarantees that the resurrection of the skills of the elderly will supply but a transitory interlude; as rapidly as possible their knowledge is being committed to tape, film, and print. As this task is completed and their knowledge is deposited in libraries, they can again be dispensed with.

This is doubtless an illustration of what Franklin Henry Giddings called the "costs of progress" (1900:67–96). Around the world the sweep of modernization is destroying the utility and validity of the traditional religious roles of the elderly in many societies. As a wise old diviner told Charles Edward Fuller (1972:60) upon giving Fuller the divining bones with which he once earned a living, "People do not consult me any more."

The Aged as Teachers

Almost forty years ago, Simmons (1945:40) asserted: "Few generalizations concerning the aged in primitive societies can be made with greater confidence than that they have almost universally been regarded as the custodians of knowledge *par excellence* and the chief instructors of the people." Maxwell and Silverman (1970) hypothesized that control of useful knowledge is a primary basis of the high esteem in which older people are held in such societies. Later, Watson and Maxwell (1977) confirmed this hypothesis after correlating an information control scale with a scale for esteem of elderly in 26 societies. This implies that control of useful information partially explains the high esteem of the elderly in primitive societies, but, conversely, the loss of such control in modern societies helps explain the decline in the status of the elderly in these societies.

Among the Aleuts in the late nineteenth century, every village reportedly had one or two men whose special function was to educate the children (Elliot, 1886). In many societies this becomes the particular prerogative of grandparents. Thus it is the grandparents, not the parents, who represent the chief transgenerational conveyors of a society's culture (Tomashevich, 1981:21). So it is among the !Kung Bushman, where the grandparents care for small children while their mothers are away on their gathering forays (Biesele and Howell, 1981:89). The elder generation spends much of its time in teaching the grandchildren the skills, traditions, and values of the society. In fact the Baganda define a good grandparent as "one who teaches, loves and cares for his or her grandchildren" (Nahemow, 1983:112). Though grandparents of both sexes are included in this definition, it seems to apply with special force to the grandmother. This is true also in Dahomean society, where older people spend much of their time educating their grandchildren, using storytelling as the chief medium (Tomashevich, 1981:28). But this is neither a matter of convenience nor of blood relationship; it is very much a matter of age and experience. Age and wisdom are so closely identified that it is not unusual for an African, regardless of blood relationship, to refer to a person noted for his or her wisdom as "grandfather" or "grandmother" (Fuller, 1972:58).

It is natural that such wise persons should be advisors as well as teachers. Among the Igbo of Nigeria, the elders not only transmit information, they are also recognized as the moral agents of youth (Boyd, 1973:37). Elders are revered as advisors among the Kogi of Colombia (Reichal-Dolmatoff, 1951) and the Haida of British Columbia (Tomashevich, 1981:29). Older women admonish the young, and the male elders serve as advisors and interpreters of tradition to all ages among the Hutterites (Boyd, 1973:39). Older men are often sought out for advice by younger Thai villagers (Blanchard, 1957:405).

The content of the elders' teaching is as wide as the term *culture*. Certainly it includes the history, mythology, and folklore of the society itself. Among the Incas, certain elders were assigned the task of remembering the important events of their history and recording by means of knots and threads all of the laws, the succession of kings, and the time in which each ruled (Simmons, 1945:136). As an aid to memory, songs were composed in which historical events were recounted. These then could be memorized and handed down from generation to generation. Otherwise, among a nonliterate people, the history is bounded, as Bleck said of the Bushmen, by the memory of the oldest person (Simmons, 1945:139). When their hair turns gray, Kapauku Papuans stop working in the fields and spend much of their time educating their grandchildren in the history and folklore of their society (Pospisil, 1963). The elders are considered repositories of tradition in Swaziland and among the Semai of Malaya (Boyd, 1973:39). Pritchard gave an account of elderly Samoans assembling in an evening to rehearse the deeds of their ancestors or relate the legends of their gods (Simmons, 1945:137).

Creation stories are usually among the legends. Such a story was related by the elderly teachers, along with historical events and tales about the old style of life, in a Mexican village (Adams, 1972:111). Another feature of lore that is preserved and transmitted by the elderly is the genealogy of the lineage. This has been noted among the Gwambe (Fuller, 1972:59), the Tiwi (Boyd, 1973:39), the Toda (Simmons, 1945:137), the Samoans (Holmes, 1972:81), and certainly it is a prevalent preoccupation of the elderly among the Chinese.

Another area in which the knowledge of older people is extensive and relevant is the physical environment within which the people live. Fuller notes (1972:59) that among the Zulu, information supplied by him about the natural environment was distrusted because he "was not old enough to know." The only credible information came from their own elderly. The elderly of the Maori are a veritable storehouse of nature lore. The names of all living things are known (some 280 plant names, 100 birds, and 60 insects), and this represents only a fragment of the information stored in the memories of elderly Maori people (Simmons, 1945:138). The older men among the Aranda of Australia teach the young the tracks of various animals and the location of the best sources of food (Tomashevich, 1981:30). Most elderly Kirghiz men are steeped in local history and ecology, and some are noted for their veterinary skills (Shahrani, 1981:189).

Perhaps even more notable among the teaching skills of the elderly are those in the realm of arts and crafts. These range broadly through music, art, pottery, weaving, tanning, dance, flower arranging, and calligraphy. Among the Omaha Indians, only the older men knew the old songs perfectly and could teach them to the oncoming generations (Simmons, 1945:133). The Hopis are noted for their crafts, and the aged among them are the best technicians, the older women in pottery and basketry and the older men in weaving and tanning. In Japan the folk arts in which older people excel and which they in turn teach to the young include calligraphy, flower arranging, the tea ceremony, *bonsai* horticulture, and several stylized forms of poetry (Maeda, 1978:66–67). Among the Bantus of southern Africa, an elderly male or female usually initiated a dance, performing the first steps, and an elder began the first drumming (Fuller, 1972:63). The treasured knowledge of the elders of the Coast Salish included methods of construction and canoe making (Amoss, 1981a:227). On the island of Truk, the art of traditional massage is a monopoly of the elderly, who only reluctantly pass it on to the younger generations (Borthwick, 1977:201). In instances where social change involves change of language, it is the elderly who retain the old language and, to the extent that it is taught at all, teach it to the young. In the old lacquer village of Ban Khern in northern Thailand in 1965, most of the older people still spoke Khern (from the Shan states of Burma), but less than 20 percent of the children understood the language. In modern China older people are the most frequent participants in the daily early morning meditation/exercise known as Tai Chi (Haber, 1979:7), and some of them proudly display their certificates as teachers of the art.

A favorite medium through which the elderly carry out their educator role is storytelling. Some develop this to a high art, and the education is at the same time amusement and entertainment. Such was the case with the old men of the Asmat tribe. Beginning at about the age of eight, boys would gather at the fireplace of their grandfather to listen to the adventures of fictional characters, the Asmat equivalent of the American "Dick and Jane," or of animals such as a dog, or a bird such as a cockatoo. In the course of such stories, the children would learn much about their jungle environment and the natural resources of the area (Van Arsdale 1981b:116–117). The young defer to the elderly among the !Kung Bushmen, and the elderly take great delight in telling and retelling stories of their own exploits or those of mythical beings (Biesele and Howell, 1981:88–89). Oratory is a prized art form in Samoa, and the young orator chiefs often gather in the evening to listen to their elders as they discuss myths, legends, customs, family history, and genealogy. The aged are considered storehouses of information, and this is the customary method of imparting it (Holmes and Rhoads, 1983:123). Incidentally, the Samoans employ another interesting art form, the chanting of legends (Simmons, 1945:97). This is akin to the songs and song contests that will be discussed later. Turnbull (1965:120) tells of the involvement of the aged Mbuti pygmies in storytelling, recitation of myths and legends, and even imitation of the behavior of various animals, all for the edification and entertainment of the children.

I observed an interesting variation in the use of older people for oral history in China in 1978. Here the elderly were encouraged to tell about their lives before the Revolution of 1949. The intent was the opposite of most oral history; instead of glorifying the past, the purpose was to portray the horrible conditions that obtained in China before the revolution and in the process to justify it and attest to the progress since then. Haber (1979:7) observed the same phenomenon and was told that the elderly often visit schools to tell their "bitterness stories." In performing this role, the elderly are presented as heroes in Chinese society (Missine, 1982:7).

Borthwick (1977:194) observed singing contests between villages on the island of Truk. These were not especially for older people, but some older people participated. Months of rehearsal preceded the actual contests. Rivalry was also involved in the posing of riddles by elders among the Bantu (Fuller, 1972:63). In addition, they vied with each other in telling myths and legends.

What do older people get in return for these activities? Often the returns are very tangible and very practical. In fact the simplest answer to the question is: they get a living. In some societies this is supplied in a quid pro quo exchange; that is, in return for a given bit of valued information, the elder may receive definite remuneration. Aged men among the Navaho charged high prices for information about cures, sacred names, legends, secrets, and songs (Simmons, 1945:135). They were paid in sheep, cattle, or horses. Elders in the secret societies of the Akamba actually held a monopoly over certain information and charged dearly for sharing it. When a person needed knowledge about a certain custom, he or she had to go to an elder for it and pay with a goat or, if he or she was rich, a bull (Simmons, 1945:139). Such a monopoly was planned and husbanded. The elders would resist sharing all of their treasured knowledge until very late in life. Aged Dieri systematically kept certain knowledge from the young in order to increase their power over them (Simmons, 1945:138).

In other instances the exchange was less explicit and less crassly economic. Marshall (1976) reports that among the !Kung Bushmen, a hunter is expected to share any kill with his parents and with his wife's parents. Such sharing is not conceived of as payment to those elders for their roles as educators, but in a general sense that is the nature of the bargain.

But apart from the economic rewards, which may be specific and explicit or quite general and implicit, there are other rewards. When the information imparted is valued, its possessors and teachers will also be valued, and this implies some other intangible dividends in the form of prestige, honor, respect, and a sense of importance to the community. The feeling of being a significant member of the society and having a secure and accepted role in it is certainly a part of the role of the aged in the preindustrial societies that have constituted the bulk of our examples in this chapter. It is a role that tends to be eroded in the process of modernization.

We can see the beginnings of this erosion in many places around the world and its veritable completion in many modernized countries. The current fad of preservation and revival of traditional ethnic cultures is symptomatic of the process. There is a temporary nostalgic satisfaction in recalling the old days and the way things were, and the recording of these recollections supplies the occasion for a curtain call for some elderly people. They may enjoy a brief round of applause before the old theater finally closes. The former life of the Coast Salish can never return. Some of the current cohort of elderly may remember and tell us about it; we may even revive parts of it in pageantry, but it is all playacting. The reality is gone, and shortly those living memories will be replaced by books, films, and tapes stored away in our modern libraries. Even the oldest of the Oklahoma Indians can no longer recall earlier forms of ceremonial behavior, past lifestyles, or the movements and exploits of a hunting and gathering existence (Williams, 1980:109). Indeed the current demand for revival produces some stress among their elderly because they are being pressed to recall and reproduce events they never actually experienced.

The fact of the matter is that rapid social change, such as the contemporary process of modernization, renders older people obsolete. Their classic role as conservators and transmitters of vital information is destroyed. Much that they know is no longer pertinent, and much that they don't know is essential. Watson and Maxwell (1977:55) note that in Samoa the elderly are becoming less and less useful as sources of information, and Adams (1972:119) notes the "increasing irrelevancy" of the knowledge of elderly Mexicans. In fully modernized societies the aged are reduced to "a roleless role." They have not only lost their economic function and some political influence, their roles as religious and educational leaders have also been eroded.

However, modernization not only renders useless much of the knowledge possessed by older people, the new forms of education and the values that accompany them also expose the deception that the elderly have sometimes used to bolster their privileged positions. Finley (1981) notes that in Guatemala modern education has undercut the traditional "cargo" system through which men worked themselves up to positions of power and status, resulting in extremely powerful roles in old age. Modernized people no longer share the mystical beliefs that supported such a system.

Summary

We have seen that the aged have generally been revered for their knowledge, experience, and wisdom in preindustrial societies. This reverence often allocated to them positions of leadership in religious and educational matters. They were commonly magicians, seers, medicine men and women, shamans, and priests. They were looked to for explanations of life and life's events. They foretold, arranged, and presided over life's crises and transitions.

Their memories were the storehouses of preliterate culture, and they inculcated that culture in the oncoming generations. They preserved and transmitted the history, myths, legends, and lore of the people. A favorite art form was storytelling, but the elderly taught by deed as well as word, and they were the master craftspeople in an era when excellence owed more to long experience and practice than to the precision of the program in the computer.

The acceleration of social change—along with the developing technology of recording, storing, and retrieving information—has largely destroyed the traditional role of the elderly as teachers. The pace of social change is now so swift that one's knowledge and skills are obsolete by the time one is old, unless of course he or she participates in lifelong learning, as a few are belatedly coming to do. But even here the emphasis is upon the renewal of technical skills or the development of idiosyncratic forms of personal expression. There does not appear to be anything on the educational horizon that would renew the grandparent-to-grandchild teaching-learning relationship.

Chapter Eight

Theories of Aging and Types of Societies

I have sought in this volume to collect and compare information about elderly people from all over the world. I have paid attention to the conditions surrounding them and the ways in which differing institutional structures have influenced older people, and I have noted some of the roles that older people play in various societies. In this concluding chapter, I want to summarize and integrate these materials, not only to review where we have been but to draw broader theoretical meaning from them.

At the outset I noted the high proportions of older people in modern industrial and postindustrial societies. This is one consequence of the demographic transition that promises to become a worldwide process. Death rates have already fallen in all parts of the world; birth rates have done so in the most modernized areas and are beginning to show significant and rapid decreases in some of the less developed countries (China, Taiwan, Korea, Thailand). Populations in these areas are already aging, and as other developing areas lower their birth rates, they too will experience demographic aging. During the twenty-first century, this will probably become a worldwide phenomenon.

If institutional modernization accompanies this demographic process—and I think it will in many ways and at various speeds—we may now begin to anticipate some of the problems that will be encountered and some of the opportunities that will open. Be it noted that I consider this aging trend the most pertinent and valid evidence of human progress. What greater achievement can we point to than that most of the babies now being born will live to become old? The further challenge of the future will be to see that those long lives are also full and happy ones.

In Chapter 3, I noted that certain value systems are favorable to high status and active roles on the part of elderly people; these include filial piety, so extensive in the Orient, and familism. Where these value systems prevail, they promote continued ascendancy of elders and appear to inhibit the erosive tendency of modernization. Another set of values, however, often accompanies modernization and accelerates its down-grading momentum; this includes the work ethic, egalitarianism, individualism, and the cult of youth.

In reviewing family and kinship systems in relation to their elderly members, I found that extended forms of the family accorded older people high prestige and psychological security. It was also noted that within these systems, the older members sometimes abused their power and monopolized resources. The trend toward neolocal marriages and nuclear family households in modernized societies not only leaves some elderly people in rather precarious circumstances, it also must be seen as freeing the younger generations from domination by their elders. In these modern societies the state has assumed some of the responsibility for financial security of older members, while family interaction continues at a relatively high level. Furthermore, this interaction and mutual aid, being no longer fraught with so much obligation and duty, is now more based upon affection and love.

The family is doubtless the most important social group for older people in all parts of the world. Though elder parents do not usually live with their children in modern Western societies, they do live nearby, and there is much interaction and mutual assistance. In many nonindustrial societies grandparents not only live in the same household with one or more of their children, they often are more significant figures in the socialization of their grandchildren than are the parents of those children. In modernized societies, partly because of the separation of residence, grandparents have less continuous contact with grandchildren, and the relationship is less intimate and more formal. However, for demographic reasons, children in those societies are more likely to have grandparents who are living and many even have the opportunity to see their great-grandparents occasionally.

A small proportion of older people in all societies have no children or grandchildren. In societies where some form of the extended family is traditional, these individuals are usually included in the membership of some such family unit and are cared for within it. Lacking that, they may be attached to another family unit in a kind of foster family arrangement, an arrangement observed in a Chinese commune a few years ago. Because of low birth rates, high mobility, lower marriage rates, and neolocal marriage, a higher proportion of the elderly in modernized societies are left in a familyless situation in their late years, and when physical infirmity besets them, there is no alternative but a long-term-care institution. Though such institutions are not unknown in nonindustrial societies, such as China (Haber, 1979; Olson, 1981; Treas, 1979) and Kenya (Moore, 1978), they are much more extensive and the proportion of the aged population residing in them is much greater—about 5 percent—in modernized societies.

In premodern nonindustrialized countries older people usually continue their normal work activities as long as they are physically able. Only in modern industrialized areas has retirement become a prevalent practice, and only in these societies do we find a general tendency toward disengagement on the part of the elderly. It is also in these societies that we find the most highly evolved pension and social security systems. When older people can no longer support themselves through employment in societies where income is linked with individual work and where families have become nuclear in residential patterns and also subsist from individual paychecks, it has become necessary to make extrafamilial arrangements for their financial security. Thus in both capitalist and socialist countries, governmental pension systems have been devised to meet this need.

It is probably true, as Simmons says (1945:46), that people in all societies have sought to save to provide for their security in old age, but only in pastoral and agrarian societies in which private property exists in reasonably durable form, such as cattle or land, has this been a very viable possibility. In collective economies and among hunters and fishers, in the absence of the technology for long-term preservation of produce, older people, along with the rest of the populace, depend upon the current catch, find, or kill. If they cannot provide for themselves, they must either depend upon the productivity of others, usually members of their families, or do without. Herders and agriculturalists, however, have the opportunity to accumulate resources with future productive potential. If they can establish individual or group property rights and maintain those rights into old age, they have a margin of safety. Because this has been feasible only for herders and farmers, it is in these types of societies that we find the highest status, the greatest power, and the most prestige of the elderly.

It is also in these societies that we find the greatest tendency toward a pattern of age stratification in which each higher age bracket represents a higher status and increased power. This constantly ascending pattern stands in contrast with the modern pattern of disengagement and discontinuity in roles.

Nevertheless, in all societies we find much diversity among the elderly. Their status and financial security always vary by gender; older men have usually had a considerable advantage over older women, and the scales are not balanced by some evident tendency toward convergence of roles in old age. Certainly there are also differences in economic security, comfort, and lifestyle by social class in nearly all societies. These differences have always been wide, but they may be widest in modern capitalist societies.

Gerontocracies such as those of the Sidamo and the Samburu provide us with illustrations of extreme political power on the part of the elderly. In such societies, at least for males, there is an ascending line of power and influence throughout life, culminating in old age. But in many societies not so rigidly stratified by age, older people are nonetheless amply represented among the headmen, chiefs of tribes or clans, and councils of elders. They perform executive, administrative, legislative, and judicial functions. Older people's political roles appear to be most powerful and most extensive in pastoral and agricultural societies. In fact political leadership by the elderly is sometimes maintained in societies where extensive retirement from economic roles is practiced. Techniques for gaining and retaining power include the use of magic, monopoly of valued resources, collection of exchange obligations, and exploitation of culturally reinforced reverence for age. Democracy tends to open the system for more extensive participation by the young, but it by no means eliminates the potential for a few elderly to hold on to positions of power by invoking principles of seniority, by collecting on accumulated exchange obligations, by controlling valued resources, or by sheer individual ability or charisma.

In traditional societies older people have generally been revered for their knowledge, experience, and wisdom. This has often led to leadership roles in religious and educational realms. Their memories are the libraries of preliterate societies, and their storytelling is a favorite form of education and entertainment of such peoples. This role has clearly and irrevocably been lost in advanced societies, where social change makes older people obsolete within a lifetime and where technological development has produced superior ways of preserving and retrieving accumulated knowledge and experience.

Theoretical Issues

A number of theoretical issues were raised in Chapter 1 with the implied promise that a review of aging around the world might throw some light upon them. Therefore, it seems appropriate that I should return to these issues and forthrightly address the question. Have we indeed learned anything about those issues?

Is disengagement an inherent and necessary aspect of human aging? The comparison of aging in many different societies and cultures provides a rather firm negative answer to this question. There is a very strong tendency toward continuity of familial roles even when social pressures and/or cultural traditions sanction separation of residence of adjacent generations. Furthermore, in many societies continuity or even ascendancy characterizes the life patterns in economic, political, and religious roles. Disengagement from those roles, particularly from economic roles, is typical only of modern industrialized societies, where retirement has become almost universal. It is also in these societies that the educational role of the aged has been almost completely lost. In general, disengagement occurs in preindustrial societies only because of disability, rarely on the basis of age alone.

Among agriculturalists and herders we see a much more general tendency toward continuity of earlier roles and continued activity and involvement in family and community affairs. Even in the face of the widespread practice of formal retirement in modern societies, there is continuity of other roles and extensive substitution of volunteer activity. Among active retired people, one frequently hears such remarks as, "I was never so busy in my life" and "How did I ever find time to work?"

There is much evidence of feelings of mutual obligation between adjacent generations in all types of societies. Parents feel a duty to support, shape, and discipline their children, and when children become adults, they generally feel an obligation to assist and support elderly parents in need. In many societies such obligations are explicit and formally stated; sometimes they are embodied in law. Undoubtedly there is much implicit and informal balancing of accounts in the exchange obligations felt by one generation for another, but this is rarely a cold-blooded calculation, and genuine love and altruism are intertwined with duty and obligation as motives in the relationship. Exchange theory has its applications in all societies but has limited utility in explaining social change or the differences between societies in their treatment of the elderly. Exchange takes place in all societies, but what is exchanged and what value is placed upon the goods and services involved are functions of the particular culture. Furthermore, the conditions that determine the ability of the different parties to fulfill their part of the bargain are different in different societies and change over time. Exchange theory does not explain these differences. It merely predicts that when one party can no longer fulfill its obligations or offer valued goods or services, that party's value and status will diminish, and there will be a tendency to reduce the amount of interaction. Exchange is an ongoing process; we need to know which factors alter the terms of that exchange and the abilities of the parties involved to meet societal expectations.

Modernization theory has much more explanatory and predictive power. It speaks to issues of change over time, and because different societies are in different stages of modernization at any given time, it may help us to understand some of the differences among those societies. However, because modernization is such a key factor and concept, I will merely call attention to it here and discuss it more extensively in the following section.

We have not found a general or universal negative stereotype of old age. The strongly negative themes in Western literature (Fowler, Fowler, and Lamdin, 1982; de Beauvoir, 1973) may or may not truly represent the attitudes of the people of the times; in any event they reflect only Western views, those of literate people and those in the vanguard of modernization. Nonliterate people generally have more sanguine views of the elderly, perhaps because the elderly have an obvious value for cultural preservation and transmission. Some of the literary references patently confuse aging with decrepitude, although it has been asserted that senility and invalidism are seldom used as criteria for defining old age (Glascock and Feinman, 1981:21). Those societies characterized by ascendancy patterns in economic, political, educational, and/or religious roles certainly do not reflect negative stereotypes of aging; and regardless of the validity of their claims of longevity, the long-living people of the Caucasus, Pakistan, Ecuador, and Greece (Holmes, 1983:68–83) have positive stereotypes of old age. In fact in some instances (Mazess and Forman, 1979) the positive view of aging leads to overstatement and exaggeration of the actual age.

The existence of "Shangri Las"—where biological aging supposedly takes place at an abnormally slow pace and where, in consequence, there are alleged to be unusually high proportions of very old people—still has not been proven. In the case of Vilcabamba, Ecuador, the appearance of such longevity must now be accredited to exaggerated statements of age (Mazess and Forman, 1979). In the absence of substantiating documents, we cannot be certain that the Abkhasians or the Hunzas really represent particularly long-lived people. In the case of Paros, Greece, 5 centenarians in a population of only 2,703 is certainly a high rate, but five cases scarcely demonstrate a general tendency, and in any event the computed life expectancy of the island is only 77 years (Beaubier, 1980), which is comparable with that of Sweden and Japan.

Certainly definitions of old age vary widely. Even the criteria by which such a late stage of life is identified differ from society to society and from time to time. Though a functional definition is more commonly used (Glascock and Feinman, 1981:20), when a chronological definition is employed, there appears to be no reason to revise Cowgill and Holmes' (1972:322) statement that "the concept of old age is relative to the degree of modernization; a person is classified as old at an earlier chronological age in a primitive society than in a modern society."

It has been asserted that there is more heterogeneity and variability within the older generation than within any of the younger generations of any specific society. A survey of older people in various societies cannot confirm or disprove such an assertion, because in very few societies has such a proposition been put to the test; however, I see no reason to doubt it, and certainly a worldwide perspective increases the range for such variation.

Modernization Theory

Throughout this volume, modernization has emerged as the massive form of social change that has most frequently and most irresistably operated to undermine the formerly privileged position and power of the elderly.

The idea of modernization, in one form or another, has inhered in all modern social science. Auguste Comte, the French social scientist who coined the word *sociology* about a century and a half ago, posited this new field of knowledge upon the basis of his belief in a regular progression in humans' ways of thinking about the world. According to Comte, humans' earliest explanations were in terms of supernatural forces, beginning with animistic spirits and progressing to anthropomorphic gods. This was the theological stage, during which the source of human knowledge of these spirits was revelation. It was succeeded by a metaphysical stage, in which humans sought explanations in terms of universal natural law, using reason to arrive at their conclusions. Ultimately they reached the positive, or scientific, stage, in which the test of truth was observation. Scientific laws then depended neither upon the whims of supernatural spirits nor the mysterious forces of nature; they were merely humans' generalizations about regularities as they observed them in the universe. Comte also believed that there was a regular and predictable order in the kinds of phenomena to which humans applied this positive method. This was in the order of decreasing generality and increasing complexity, which resulted in the following sequence:

mathematics, astronomy, physics, chemistry, biology, sociology. Thus the world's first sociologist made the positive or scientific way of thinking the essential element of modernity.

With this as the beginning rationale of sociology, and given the added stimulus supplied by Darwin's evolutionism, it is not surprising that theories of social change have constituted an important part of sociological theory ever since. Herbert Spencer was a contemporary of Darwin and a rival in that he also propounded a theory of evolution, but Spencer's theory was intended to be universal in its application, whereas Darwin's theory applied only to biological organisms. I need not go into the exceedingly complex and abstruse aspects of Spencer's theory here. What is relevant to modernization theory is his statement that the modern tendency in social evolution is from a military form of society to an industrial one. He viewed primitive humans as basically predatory and warlike and therefore amenable only to an autocratic, military form of social organization. But a more highly differentiated and interdependent form was evolving, based upon peaceful cooperation of enlightened individuals who, in seeking their own interests, also served the interests of a higher form of society. Spencer obviously adopted this dichotomy from Comte, although he denied the extent of Comte's influence. In any event here was a statement of the direction of contemporary social change—from simplicity to complexity, from undifferentiated homogeneity to highly differentiated and specialized heterogeneity.

Durkheim, the great French successor to Comte, expounded very similar ideas. In his terms the trend of modern social change was away from a mechanical form of social solidarity to an organic form, that is, from a form of society in which the individuals were characterized by their similarity and conformity to the same uniform customs and an unquestioning identification with the whole, in which individuality was submerged in the collective consciousness, toward an organic form in which individuality became the very basis of solidarity. Division of labor demanded specialization, which emphasized unique skills and differences that made an individual valuable to the society because of the unique role he or she could play. But because such division of labor made everyone dependent on each other, all were bound together in an organic solidarity of mutual interdependence. Clearly Durkheim was describing what he saw to be the essential difference between primitive society and modern society. In other words, he was describing the fundamental changes in the form of European society at the beginning of the twentieth century.

At about the same time, German sociologist Ferdinand Toennies was elaborating very similar ideas under the rubrics *Gemeinschaft* (community) and *Gesellschaft* (society). Gemeinschaft consisted of the kind of group life into which one fitted naturally. Relationships were maintained and actions engaged in for their own intrinsic value to the individual, not for any ulterior purpose. Kinship groups, neighborhoods, and small towns were prototypes of Gemeinschaft. On the other hand, Gesellschaft consisted of relationships that were entered into by deliberate rational choice; a person decided to join the group or engage in the action with some specific end in mind. Contractual relationships and special-purpose associations were typical of Gesellschaft. Originally Toennies developed the concepts as a framework for the historical analysis of the evolution of modern society. He believed that primitive society was basically Gemeinschaft-like and that the modern social trend was toward a Gesellschaft-like society. Relationships were becoming more calculated and rational.

Later, Robert Redfield put these concepts in an ecological context and applied them to specific communities and societies in the process of change. Redfield's term for the earlier form of society was *folk society* (1947:293):

> Such a society is small, isolated, nonliterate, and homogeneous, with a strong sense of group solidarity. The ways of living are conventionalized into that coherent system which we call "a culture." Behavior is traditional, spontaneous, uncritical, and personal; there is no legislation or habit of experiment and reflection for intellectual ends. Kinship, its relationships and institutions, are the type of categories of experience and the familial group is the unit of action. The sacred prevails over the secular; the economy is one of status rather than of the market. These and related characterizations may be restated in terms of "folk mentality."

He contrasted such societies with urban societies, but he did not delineate as explicitly the characteristics of such societies. This task had been done by his colleague at the University of Chicago, Louis Wirth, a few years earlier (1938:1):

> A city is a relatively large, dense, and permanent settlement of heterogeneous individuals. Large numbers account for individual variability, the relative absence of intimate personal acquaintanceship, the segmentalization of human relations which are largely anonymous, superficial, and transitory, and associated characteristics. Density involves diversification and specialization, the coincidence of close physical contact and distant social relations, glaring contrasts, a complex pattern of segregation, the predominance of formal social control, and accentuated friction, among other phenomena. Heterogeneity tends to break down rigid social structures

and to produce increased mobility, instability, and insecurity, and the affiliation of the individuals with a variety of intersecting and tangential social groups with a high rate of membership turnover. The pecuniary nexus tends to displace personal relations, and institutions tend to cater to mass rather than individual requirements. The individual thus becomes effective only as he acts through organized groups.

Both writers viewed modern social change primarily as the disintegration of folk societies and the development of urbanism.

Following World War II, when former colonial empires were being dismembered and many new nations were being established from the remnants, and when much attention was being directed to help these new nations establish themselves as viable political and economic entities, the earlier dichotomous theories of modern social change coalesced into more macroscopic theories of modernization. Still, one searches in vain in the literature of this era for a concise, meaningful definition of the term *modernization*. Dore (1969) defined it as "the transformation of one's own society or segments of it in imitation of models drawn from another country or society." This did not say what kind of society the model was. Bendix (1968) was only slightly more explicit when he said that it was the process whereby "backward" countries imitated advanced countries. This is tautological and says little more than that modernization is the process of becoming modernized.

During this era there was a very strong tendency to conceive of modernization chiefly in economic terms. For example, Levy (1966:11) stated, "A society will be considered more or less modernized to the extent that its members use inanimate sources of power and/or use tools to multiply the effects of their efforts." Such writers equated modernization with economic development, and for those intent upon the progress of underdeveloped areas, a critical point in the process was attained when these areas achieved "self-sustaining growth" (Rostow, 1960). Other writers included a political element in the process and paid attention to such things as detribalization, concentration of political power, emergence of nationalism, development of an articulate public opinion, and extent of citizen participation in government (Eisenstadt, 1971; Lerner, 1958). Some of these elements seem very ethnocentric; they appear to equate modernization with Westernization and implicitly define modernization as "becoming more like us."

A common sociological perspective, reminiscent of Spencer and Durkheim, emphasized institutional differentiation, not only the increasing separation of family, workplace, church, and government but also the development and elaboration of new special-purpose institutions, such as schools, libraries, hospitals, prisons, welfare organizations, and so on (Etzioni and Etzioni, 1964; Coughenour, 1969). Parsons (1964) wrote about modernization in terms of "evolutionary universals," including social stratification beyond kinship bounds, cultural legitimation, bureaucratic organization, money and markets, a universalistic legal system, and democratic association in both government and private life. Others saw modernization primarily in terms of changes in attitudes and values (Waisanen, 1968), and this led to attitude surveys and psychological tests to measure individual modernity (Inkeles and Smith, 1970; Bengtson et al., 1975; Barndt, 1969; Armer and Schnaiberg, 1972; Stephenson, 1968). Perhaps the most eclectic and comprehensive treatment of the concept was that of Eisenstadt (1971). Though he stressed institutional differentiation, he was careful to incorporate more than economic and political institutions in his purview, and he also included psychological and cultural changes accompanying these institutional changes, including changes of value systems.

However, in all this modernization literature, one cannot find a definition of the term that is at once comprehensive enough to catch the complete range of the process and concise enough to qualify under standard rules of definition making. Even Lerner's attempt in the *International Encyclopedia of the Social Sciences* (1968) fails to give one much understanding of the process: "Modernization is the current term for an old process—the process of social change whereby less developed societies acquire characteristics common to more developed societies." In his view it included four interrelated processes: urbanization, increasing literacy, development of mass media, and the extension of political participation. He thought that urbanization came first and that literacy increased in the cities, creating a demand for and use of mass media; rising levels of education and attention to the media then brought about informed opinions on public affairs and created a demand for political participation.

Still lacking a usable definition, I decided to try my hand at it, seeking both to identify and incorporate the essential and universal elements of the process and to omit those aspects still in doubt (Cowgill, 1974:127):

> Modernization is the transformation of a total society from a relatively rural way of life based on animate power, limited technology, relatively undifferentiated institutions, parochial and traditional outlook and values, toward a predominantly urban way of life based on inanimate sources of power, highly developed scientific technology, highly

differentiated institutions matched by segmented individual roles, and a cosmopolitan outlook which emphasizes efficiency and progress.

This is intentionally very comprehensive, including most of the institutional and cultural features identified by the various scholars cited above. I have never been convinced that political participation is an inherent or universal aspect of modernization; the contention that it is appears to be a part of the ethnocentrism that infects some of the modernization literature.

Criticisms of Modernization Theory

There is widespread agreement that some such general process of social change has been underway in certain parts of the world during the past several centuries, that it began in Europe and spread to other parts of the world. I think there is also agreement that whereas in the originating areas it was a relatively slow, endogenous, self-generating process, it has become in later stages something that can be borrowed, imitated, and exported, and it is therefore capable of much more rapid progression. But there is disagreement about some of the ways in which the theory has been formulated. The major criticisms relate to its alleged uniformity and universality (Tipps, 1973). It is sometimes presented as a massive, irresistible, and irreversible process that, once set in motion, like a glacier pushes relentlessly onward, overwhelming rural peasant societies and transforming them into a uniform urban prototype. Such overstatement or oversimplification of the theory is obviously not justified. No one believes that all peasant societies are or were carbon copies of each other; we have hundreds of anthropological studies describing their differences in minute detail. Just as modernization can never start from the same sociocultural base, it will never proceed in a uniform pattern; there will always be lags and leads, starts and stops, perhaps even reversals. Certainly there are wide differences in the speed of social change in different societies, and there are also wide differences within societies, varying by region, by social class, by gender, and often by ethnic identity. It would be simple-minded to predict a uniform outcome of such a volatile and irregular process. As with most generalizations and theories, while acknowledging the general thesis, one must allow for much variation in detail.

It has been charged that modernization theory is ethnocentric

(Tipps, 1973; Williamson, Evans, and Powell, 1982:65). In some versions the criticism is probably justified, particularly when the concept is stretched to include development in the direction of democratic political forms (Lerner, 1968 and 1958). Yet it must be admitted that when one's own society is in the vanguard of a world trend, it is difficult to describe and characterize that trend without giving the appearance of ethnocentrism. I can only say that while the United States is one of the most modernized countries of the world, so too is Japan, and the U.S.S.R. is not far behind.

A more fundamental criticism derives from a Marxist or neo-Marxist perspective. This viewpoint holds that it is naive to think of the process in such impersonal, naturalistic terms, when in fact it is manipulable and is manipulated. Andre Gunder Frank (1969) espouses a dependency theory of economics, which holds that underdeveloped areas don't just happen—they are contrived; they are underdeveloped because they are kept in a state of underdevelopment by the machinations of the powers-that-be in the developed areas. They are in a condition of economic dependency relative to the developed areas of the world, and their dependency is exploited for the benefit of the developed areas. In these circumstances only such development (or modernization) as will benefit the exploiters is permitted. This tends to produce very spotty and uneven development, uneven by region and by social class, with extreme gaps between the rich and the poor, between the few who are permitted to share in the benefits of development and the masses who are exploited and degraded in the process.

Immanuel Wallerstein (1979) has expanded dependency theory into "a world-system perspective," with the most advanced capitalist areas at the "core," the exploited areas on the "periphery," and marginal, "semi-peripheral" areas in between. From this perspective it is not a matter of all areas of the world moving in the same direction in a parallel process of development (or modernization), with some in the vanguard and others lagging behind, having entered the race at a later date. Rather, Wallerstein sees the world as one economic system, with a division of labor in which some parts are underdeveloped because others are developed. The unequal development is not a matter of timing; it is a matter of functional utility to the core.

Some scholars (Hendricks, 1982; Tigges and Cowgill, 1981) have suggested that the world-system perspective might be preferable to the modernization perspective in evaluating the status and condition of the aged in a comparative way. This may prove true in time, but at this writing the idea has not been explored sufficiently to determine its utility or to develop a coherent set of hypotheses. For now I shall adhere to the modernization perspective, assuming for purposes of categorization, that modernized areas are those in Wallerstein's core, and nonmodernized areas will be either in the periphery or semiperiphery. In the long run it may prove true that the types of roles played by peripheral areas—whether as supplier of a mineral product such as oil or an agricultural product such as rubber or coffee—may have quite different implications for the elderly in those societies, but at present the empirical evidence is too scanty to even suggest plausible hypotheses.

The issue at this point is one of general sociological theory, not of gerontological theory. Which is the most accurate and valid view of the contemporary social world and of social change, a functional evolutionary view that takes into account continuing population growth and continuing innovation leading to changes in lifestyles and institutions in coherent directions or a neo-Marxist view that sees all social change as the product of conflict between exploiters and exploited? While not unaware of conflict, including class conflict, I hold that other social processes also play a role in societal development—cooperation, mutual aid, and altruism. I reject the one-sided Hobbesian notion that man is a totally selfish creature bent exclusively upon maximizing his own interests. Though there are exploiters, even they must operate within the social system, and no single interest group can for very long control that system. The system evolves and develops on the basis of both cooperation and conflict. One phase of that evolution is called, somewhat myopically, modernization.

Aging in Relation to Modernization

Modernization theory as applied to aging asserts that there are systematic relations between the extent of modernization of a society and the status and condition of the elderly. In the last chapter of *Aging and Modernization*, Cowgill and Holmes (1972:322–323) summarized the variations they had observed in a comparison of 15 different societies:

1. The concept of old age is relative to the degree of modernization; a person is classified as old at an earlier chronological age in a primitive society than in a modern society.

2. Old age is identified in terms of chronological age chiefly in modern societies; in other societies onset of old age is more commonly linked with events such as succession to eldership or becoming a grandparent.

3. Longevity is directly and significantly related to the degree of modernization.

4. Modernized societies have older populations, that is, higher proportions of old people.

5. Modern societies have higher proportions of women and especially of widows.

6. Modern societies have higher proportions of people who live to be grandparents and even great-grandparents.

7. The status of the aged is high in primitive societies and is lower and more ambiguous in modern societies.

8. In primitive societies, older people tend to hold positions of political and economic power, but in modern societies such power is possessed by only a few.

9. The status of the aged is high in societies in which there is a high reverence for or worship of ancestors.

10. The status of the aged is highest when they constitute a low proportion of the population and tends to decline as their numbers and proportions increase.

11. The status of the aged is inversely proportional to the rate of social change.

12. Stability of residence favors high status of the aged; mobility tends to undermine it.

13. The status of the aged tends to be high in agricultural societies and lower in urbanized societies.

14. The status of the aged tends to be high in preliterate societies and to decline with increasing literacy of the populations.

15. The status of the aged is high in those societies in which they are able to continue to perform useful and valued functions; however, this is contingent upon the values of the society as well as upon the specific activities of the aged.

16. Retirement is a modern invention; it is found chiefly in modern high-productivity societies.

17. The status of the aged is high in societies in which the extended form of the family is prevalent and tends to be lower in societies which favor the nuclear form of the family and neolocal marriage.

18. With modernization the responsibility for the provision of economic security for dependent aged tends to be shifted from the family to the state.

19. The proportion of the aged who are able to maintain leadership roles declines with modernization.

20. In primitive societies the roles of widows tend to be clearly ascribed, but such role ascription declines with modernization; the widow's role in modern societies tends to be flexible and ambiguous.

21. The individualistic value system of Western society tends to reduce the security and status of older people.

22. Disengagement is not characteristic of the aged in primitive or agrarian societies, but an increasing tendency toward disengagement appears to accompany modernization.

However, this was not a theory; it was an itemized list of correlations among pairs of variables, some of which were aspects of modernization itself and others indicators of the status or the condition of the elderly. On reviewing this list, it appears that while modernization, as measured by a combined scale of literacy and per capita gross national product, was the major independent variable, it was actually employed in that way in only 13 of the correlations. These included the first 8, which are straightforward assertions that with modernization there are changes in the concept of old age, the criteria for classifying people as old, longevity, the proportion of aged in the population, the proportion of women and widows, the proportion living to be grandparents, the status of the elderly, and the political and economic power of the elderly. At this point in the list the pattern shifts, and items 9–15, 17, and 21 are assertions of correlations between the status of the aged and societal characteristics that are either subordinate aspects of modernization or correlates thereof—ancestor worship, proportion of elderly, rate of social change, stability of residence, urbanization, literacy, useful functions for the elderly, extended family, and individualism. The other items, 16, 18–20, and 22, revert to the use of modernization itself as the independent variable and point to correlations with retirement, support systems, leadership roles, roles of widows, and disengagement.

Not content with this congeries of propositions, I (Cowgill, 1974) sought to integrate them into a more meaningful and more tightly knit theory. In this version of the theory I kept modernization as the main independent variable but took health technology, economic technology, urbanization, and education as the most salient aspects of modernization and related them to the single dependent variable, status of the aged. This had the virtue of simplicity, but it scarcely did justice to the range of variables with which we have dealt in the present volume. For example, it had little to say about different forms of property and their role in savings and inheritance and the ways in which the elderly of some societies have manipulated them to maintain power and control. It scarcely touched on the exploding technology of communications and the double-edged significance of this for the involvement of the elderly; communications technology has played a major part in depriving the elderly of roles that were formerly of major significance, but it has facilitated continued contact and involvement despite physical limitation or geographic separation. Finally, the theory treated value systems as peripheral variables and dealt very marginally with individualism and egalitarianism.

Criticisms of the Theory of Aging and Modernization

Some criticisms of the use of modernization theory to illuminate the development and variations in the condition and status of the aged are really criticisms of the theory of modernization as a way of conceptualizing contemporary social change, that is, of modernization as general sociologial theory. These criticisms have already been enumerated and discussed. Here I shall treat the criticisms that specifically relate to aging and its linkage with modernization.

Many of the critics either imply or charge that the asserted negative correlation between modernization and the status of the elderly is not real. The modernization theorists are charged with romanticizing a presumed "Golden Age" of the past (Quadagno, 1982; Laslett, 1976; Gubrium, 1973). They are chided for supposing that there was "a world that we have lost," that there was a "before" and an "after" (Laslett, 1976). Whether high status of the aged is "good" or "golden" depends upon one's perspective and certainly involves a value judgment. From my perspective, excessive power that permits exploitation of one group by another is undesirable. Gerontocracy is as lamentable as any other form of tyranny. And if there is to be any kind of change, it follows that there must be a "before" and an "after."

Quadagno (1982:199) asserts that retirement is not new and adduces peasant retirement contracts in England as proof. The criticism derives in part from her failure to acknowledge the distinction between modernization and industrialization, modernization being a much broader concept and commanding a longer historical sweep than the more limited technological change identified as industrialization. Even so she does admit that retirement increased markedly in the last half of the nineteenth century (1982:168) and that pensions, which permitted retirement to become a general and accepted practice, are products of the last century. As for her assertion that the aged have been poor throughout history (1982:201), in terms of modern standards of living that is true, just as most people of all ages have been poor until modern times. The issue is not poverty but relative status, and as we have seen throughout this book, in many premodern societies, especially agrarian ones, older people were held in high esteem and were often accorded more than their share of whatever wealth the societies possessed. On the other hand, the allegation that the "degradation of the aged" in late nineteenth-century England was nothing but political rhetoric certainly does not square with Charles Booth's (1894) extensive research and writing on the subject.

Many critics have charged that the theory does not take account of the variations within societies in the status of the aged, particularly the variations by social class and gender (Dowd, 1980; Williamson, Evans, and Powell, 1982). This criticism is justified and the shortcoming needs to be corrected, but it does not invalidate the theory. Any generalization, by definition, overlooks the variations in detail among the cases being generalized.

The charge that modernization theorists often mistake ideal and normative statements about older people for their real condition (Levy, 1966; Laslett, 1976) may be partially true. This reflects a perennial methodological problem for social scientists, one that is most troublesome for those anthropologists who rely upon key informants and participant observation. For example, it has been suggested (Williamson, Evans, and Powell, 1982:59) that scholars sometimes mistake "ritual deference" for actual esteem (Lipman, 1970). One area in which this type of error has been frequently alleged is in regard to the prevalence of the extended family and the frequency with which older people are cared for within extended families. Levy (1965) points out that even in those societies noted for joint or extended family households, most households actually consist of nuclear families, and Laslett and Wall (1972) have shown that this was true of preindustrial England. Given the death rates of premodern societies, vertically extended families must have been rare even when they were the preferred or ideal form. But this is largely beside the point as far as the living arrangements of the aged are concerned. The issue here is: Of those few people who do survive to old age, what proportions live in multiple-generation households? When the question is posed in this way, even Laslett's data point toward extended family arrangements; for example, in six places in England in 1800, 62 percent of the married males 60 and over and 58 percent of the married females of that age lived with children or grandchildren (1976:108).

It has been charged that the early statements of the relation between aging and modernization actually treated modernization in somewhat truncated form, drawing their samples from predominantly agricultural societies while neglecting collective and hunting and gathering societies (Williamson, Evans, and Powell, 1982:162; Finley, 1981). This criticism is well taken, and it now appears that a straight-line linear relationship is not accurate; a more mature view of the matter, as stated by Williamson, Evans, and Powell (1982), is that the relationship is actually curvilinear, beginning with relatively low status in hunting and gathering societies, rising to a peak in settled agricultural societies, and then declining with industrialization. It further appears that we may now posit another rise with the development of postindustrial society (Palmore and Manton, 1974).

We may also need to watch and test for variations in lag and lead time in the relationship between these two variables. Goldstein and Beall (1981) found that although there was no industrialization or urbanization in the immediate vicinity, the family life of older persons in a remote region of Nepal was being disrupted by employment opportunities in India that had lured their sons away. Although the elders were living comfortably enough economically and there was no immediate loss of status, they felt deserted and were unhappy. Here we see early and remotely penetrating effects of industrialization with the potential of a lag in loss of status. Fischer (1977) reported measurable loss of status long before there was much industrialization or urbanization in the United States, though Achenbaum (1978) finds that the major losses have occurred during the twentieth century. The theory must be flexible enough in the statement of the timing of the relationship to permit considerable lag and lead among the variables. However, it should be pointed out that the theory states that the relationship is between aging and modernization, not industrialization. Perhaps the more general term, encompassing more variables, provides the flexibility in timing that is required. Furthermore, it is assuredly true that modernization itself, being multifaceted, takes place unevenly (Williamson, Evans, and Powell, 1982:54; Tipps, 1973). Though economic technology may be the usual leading edge, at times public health measures or education may precede, when introduced by missionaries, for example. On the other hand, urbanization has often proceeded faster than industrialization, resulting in overurbanization.

Several scholars (Tien, 1977; Cherry and Magnuson-Martinson, 1981) have suggested that a lower status of the aged may result from direct political action, independent from other modernizing forces. Of course the prime example of this is China, where the revolution brought legal action abolishing the previous privileges of the aged and mandating mutual responsibility between generations. This has a leveling but not revolutionary effect on status, lowering that of the elderly and raising that of the young. It does indicate that there may be various pathways toward the same end. Some might argue that this case is an exception to the theory, but others, especially those who include political democratization as a part of modernization, will probably see it as just another variation within the same general trend. It provides another argument for a flexible conception of the theory.

Japan (Palmore, 1975b) and the U.S.S.R. have also been cited as exceptions to the theory, but if we acknowledge that there may be delayed responses and perhaps even countervailing forces, such as the ethic of filial piety, they too may be interpreted as merely variations in the same trend.

A Theory of Aging in Cross-Cultural Perspective

Perhaps the most appropriate way to conclude this volume is to attempt a restatement of the theory of aging in cross-cultural perspective that was first projected in the opening chapter of *Aging and Modernization* (Cowgill and Holmes, 1972). Subsequent research and discussion have focused on the issue of modernization, but the original statement, like the present volume, ranged over a broader field—the status and treatment of the elderly under any and all conditions.

The structure of the population obviously has a bearing on the social treatment of different segments of that population. Societies in which older people are rare appear to hold them in higher esteem than societies in which they are commonplace. This shouldn't be posed as a crass supply and demand determination of value, although there may be an element of supply and demand in it. More important is that demographic aging is correlated with other aspects of modernization, the combined effect of which is a lower value of elderly persons (Cowgill, 1974). There are also some other interrelated demographic matters, such as the fact that modern aging populations are more and more female and a greater proportion of them are widows. In societies in which the major responsibility for economic production has been allotted to males, the presence of a large contingent of economically dependent females may give rise to resentment and jealousy on the part of the still productive males who have no feeling of familial responsibility for them. For the first time in human history, we are beginning to see sizable numbers and proportions of elderly people who are great-grandparents. The numbers are sufficient in modern populations to warrant research on the nature of the relationship between people who are three (or even four) generations removed from each other. Impressionistically, it seems that the relationship is rather formal and distant, mediated and filtered by the attentions and claims of the two (or three) intervening generations.

In the initial phases of urbanization associated with industrialization, there is massive migration of young adults to the cities. This entails a separation of those young migrants from their parents, who are at the time middle aged. It tends to break up the extended family and foster neolocal marriages and nuclear family households. This makes intergenerational support and mutual aid more difficult and renders the lives of all generations more precarious. Urban dwellers live in a mass society among heterogeneous strangers. They cannot maintain intimate, caring relationships with all their neighbors and associates. This would lead to an emotional overload. Relationships therefore tend to become fleeting, segmented, superficial, and formal. Many services must be secured through bureaucracies operating impersonally according to formal rules rather than on the basis of personal concern. Little urban housing is suitable for large extended families, and such housing is exceedingly expensive. Furthermore, urban work is individualized, and income is in the form of wages or salaries to individuals, not to families. This is true even in socialist or communist societies. Money is an essential adjustment to mass urban society, as Georg Simmel pointed out long ago (1907). And money tends to objectify and formalize the relationships among the people involved in exchange. Thus people living in a wage economy are always made aware of the cost of services, including the services to nonproducers. Dependency in such an economy carries a definite price tag. For all these reasons, cities pose problems for older people, especially if they are physically or economically dependent.

Whether associated with urbanism or not, high mobility is unfavorable to the elderly. Indeed most cases of known gerontocide are associated with the difficulty or danger encountered by nomadic people in transporting frail elderly kinfolk with them as they migrate. On the other hand, one reason the elderly fare so well among agriculturalists is undoubtedly the greater stability of residence in such societies.

A fundamental aspect of modernization is the scientific revolution that has taken place and the resultant innumerable technological innovations that in turn have accounted for much of the transformation of human existence in industrial and postindustrial societies. Many of these innovations have contributed to the improvement of health and the prolongation of life. These include sanitary engineering, the purification and protection of water, milk, and food supplies, techniques of immunization, improved knowledge of diet and personal hygiene, as well as the more spectacular discoveries in curative medicine and surgery. All these have permitted more people in the developed societies to elude the hazards of infancy and childhood, to become adults, and eventually to live into old age. When this is combined with the technology of birth control and the motivation to use it, the demographic transition is moving into its final phase, and the population is aging.

The manifold applications of scientific technology and management techniques to production and distribution are at the core of the Industrial Revolution. These create a multitude of new products, services, and occupations. The new occupations and new management systems revolutionize the workplace and thereby change the lives and careers of the workers. Work is individualized, and the workplace is separated from the place of residence. Old occupations become obsolete, and new occupations bring new demands for education and training. Selection for these new occupations favors the young, and continued changes of technology perpetuate this preferment. With increased productivity provided by technological efficiency and with increased proportions of the population made up of adults available for the labor market, eventually there is competition for jobs, and mature industrial societies appear to encounter difficulty in employing all the available, able-bodied workers. One adjustment to this situation that has been adopted by all industrial societies is a system of retirement based on age or tenure (Pampel and Weiss, 1983). Such societies are highly productive. If they were not, they could not afford, nor would they be motivated, to excuse able persons from economic roles. But no society has yet combined retirement with income maintenance at a level equivalent to that of active workers. The problem appears to be more intractable in capitalist than in socialist societies. In any event the problem of poverty among a considerable proportion of the elderly has not yet been solved.

In modernized Western societies older people usually live in separate residential quarters from their adult children and other members of the extended family. However, they are seldom isolated from all of them.

One or more children are usually within commuting distance, and frequent contact is maintained with them. Even when they are separated by distances that prevent daily or weekly face-to-face contact, modern technology makes it possible to bridge those distances, and families do maintain intimacy by means of telephone and the postal service. Furthermore, many of them travel thousands of miles during vacations and holidays, spending much time renewing family ties.

Certainly one of the most salient aspects of modernization relative to the status of the aged is the development of specialized institutions of formal education. These, along with libraries, voluminous printed material, and recent revolutionary techniques for storing and retrieving information, have all but completely abolished a formerly highly significant role of older people—that of repositories and transmitters of vital information to the younger generation. Schools, both general and technical, are always viewed as an essential part of any modernization effort. But the main targets and beneficiaries of mass education efforts are the young. One consequence of such efforts is that very shortly the younger generation has command of more information, especially technical information, than the elderly. Certainly the elderly no longer have a monopoly on such information, as they may have in nonliterate societies, and with the loss of that monopoly, they lose a vital status-according role (Silverman and Maxwell, 1983; Maxwell and Silverman, 1970). Furthermore, with the development of electronic means of recording, storing, and retrieving even such marginally valuable information as they may possess, their transient value as possessors of such information is sacrificed as soon as it is recorded.

An elaborate division of labor is not inherently detrimental to the elderly; only when there is a youthful bias in the allocation of valued roles do the elderly suffer relative deprivation. But the cult of youth has to a considerable degree characterized most highly modernized societies, particularly Western societies. Time will tell whether it is an inherent aspect of modernization itself.

Vertically extended family systems appear to be favorable to the maintenance of extensive influence and privilege on the part of the elder generation, while neolocal marriage and the nuclear family system undermine such prerogatives. Likewise, communal sharing of risks in large groups, such as large families, supplies a kind of insurance for all, including insurance against lack of economic support and physical care in old age. Even in modernized societies the "modified extended family" continues to provide most of the home health care and home chore services required by its elderly members. It does this despite separation of residence of its several nuclear family components and despite competing obligations on the part of its individual members. But the strain becomes insupportable for some people in such societies, and societies that adhere to the nuclear family system find it necessary to house and care for a significant minority of their incapacitated elderly in institutional settings.

Undoubtedly there is much truth in the aphorism that property is power. We have seen in Chapter 5 that the greater ability of older people to accumulate property in agricultural societies gives them greater leverage over younger generations, both in the control of such property and its usufruct during their lives and in the disposition of it at their demise. The accumulation of nonperishable property is more feasible in pastoral and agricultural societies than in hunting and gathering societies. Therefore we generally find that older people fare better in pastoral and agricultural societies. A few people can still accumulate property rights in land and cattle in modern capitalistic societies, but this no longer has the same implications, both because it affects a much smaller segment of the population and because the younger generations and potential heirs have other options. They need no longer wait around to see how the old folks will allocate their inheritance; they can develop careers apart from the family of orientation and independent of the property it may have accumulated. As the significance of the potential inheritance is diminished by the availability of alternatives to the younger generation, so the potential of the older generation to wield control over the younger one is reduced.

Rapid social change tends to undermine the authority and status of the elderly generation, so we also find that the authority and status of the elderly is lower in societies that are undergoing rapid change than in folk or traditional societies. In fact Cohn (1982), in a study of 30 countries, has shown that the rate of economic development has a separate and differentiable effect from the mere level of economic development. Rapid change tends to depress the status of the elderly by channeling younger workers into higher-status jobs, while a high level of development depresses the status of the elderly through their greater withdrawal from the labor market (retirement).

Among the most subtle but nevertheless important influences on the welfare of older people are those in the realm of philosophical perspective and what we have called value systems. The general way in which people view themselves and their universe is important. A universe populated with a myriad of animistic spirits—some inhabiting objects and others free-floating, each with a will of its own, each with the potential of helping or harming a person—is a quite different universe from one that is believed to be orderly and operating in terms of natural cause and effect and whose operations are observable, in many cases predictable, and in some instances subject to human control. In the first instance one's welfare is at the mercy of the innumerable mysterious forces that he or she must try to explain and control. Many people inhabiting such a universe have developed extensive lore explaining it and magical skills to cope with it. As noted in Chapter 7, the magicians are often elderly people who because of their special skills are in an advantaged position in their societies. On the other hand, a scientist's view of the universe confers no special advantages upon the aged; on the contrary, it probably favors the young because scientific knowledge is ever-changing and because it is developed and transmitted in specialized educational institutions that are targeted toward the young.

We have seen that ancestor worship appears to provide a significant intermediary role for the aged. They are closer to the ones who have departed and have known more of them as living persons. It is plausible that the elderly would know more of the loves and hates entertained by those ancestors while they were alive and thus might better anticipate their potential for helping or harming those who are still alive. The elders would probably also be aware of ways of pleasing or placating those whom they have known.

Another illustration of the potential significance of a particular cosmology for the well-being of the elderly is the belief in reincarnation as found in Hinduism and Buddhism. From the perspective of Theravada Buddhism, life is a continuing cycle; one's present existence is only one interlude in the chain of life. There have been previous lives, and there will subsequent ones. These lives take different forms according to one's moral merit. One may have been an ant in a previous life and one might become one again. This explains the Buddhists' reverence for all forms of life and their extreme efforts to avoid injury to any form, including, for example, stepping on an ant. According to this view, the form in which one will appear in the next life depends directly upon one's moral progress during this life. This is taken by some to explain an apparent increased attention to religious matters and charities in old age. But in such charities the primary concern is not in improving the condition or character of another person—that is his or her responsibility; the concern of the donor is with his or her own moral welfare. All this obviously has profound implications for one's attitude toward death, which is just a transition from one life to the next. If this life has been a good one, death may be an occasion for celebration and anticipation of the better life to come.

In Chapter 3, I discussed six more specific value systems and their relevance to the elderly. We saw that filial piety is a system of values with a built-in cultural bias in favor of the elderly. This system was widely inculcated in the Orient and may be partly responsible for retarding the erosion of the status of the aged in that part of the world. Familism is another value system that favors a secure and honored status for the elderly. We find it in combination with the ethic of filial piety in the Orient, but familism prevails in many other parts of the world as well.

Egalitarianism operates as a leveler, and where the aged have had a privileged position previously, the introduction of an egalitarian ethic, whether in the guise of democracy or communism, tends to reduce that advantage. Heavy emphasis upon individualism works against such communal systems as familism, wiping out any prerogatives the elderly may have had and leaving them in a somewhat exposed and precarious condition. The work ethic, which has been so extensively correlated with the development of Western capitalism, also contributes to their demotion because in modern Western societies retirement has become most thoroughly institutionalized. When one's identity and status are so tied up with one's work role, retirement can be traumatic, and widespread withdrawal of the aged from the labor force is one factor in depressing the status of the elderly in modernized societies (Cohn, 1982). Modern societies also seem to generate an emphasis on youth amounting to what we have called a cult of youth. This too contributes to the devaluation of old age.

The revolutionary change in age structure, which has happened quite recently and very rapidly, caught us unprepared institutionally and culturally. It is not surprising that there should have been temporary dislocations and even a swing to an opposite extreme of overvaluing youth. In a cross-national analysis of 31 countries, Palmore and Manton (1974) found a curvilinear relationship between modernization and the status of the aged; not only was the status lower in general in more modernized societies, most significantly it was somewhat higher in the most modernized countries than in those slightly less developed. They interpreted this to indicate some improvement in the status of the aged in the most advanced countries. Furthermore, Pampel (1981) reports impressive evidence of improvement in several measures of quality of life during recent decades in the United States. These and other measures provide some basis for believing that those societies that were in the vanguard of the Demographic Revolution are now beginning to come to terms with their aged populations and are achieving appropriate cultural and institutional adaptations. We can also hope that when the Demographic Revolution occurs in the Third World, those people will have learned from our experience both what to avoid and which adaptations will serve them well. Some of their value systems, such as filial piety and familism, may help them avoid the extreme devaluations of the aged experienced by the pioneer societies in the field of aging.

Bibliography

Achenbaum, Wilbert Andrew.
    1978. *Old Age in the New Land: The American Experience Since 1790*. Baltimore: Johns Hopkins University Press.

Adams, Bert N.
    1968. *Kinship in an Urban Setting*. Chicago: Markham.

Adams, Frances.
    1972. "The Role of Old People in Santo Tomás Mazaltepec." Pp. 103–26 in D. O. Cowgill and L. D. Holmes (eds.), *Aging and Modernization*. New York: Appleton-Century-Crofts.

Aiken, Lewis R.
    1978. *Later Life*. Philadelphia: Saunders.

Amoss, Pamela T.
    1981a. "Coast Salish Elders." Pp. 227–47 in P. T. Amoss and S. Harrell (eds.), *Other Ways of Growing Old*. Stanford, CA: Stanford University Press.
    1981b. "Cultural Centrality and Prestige for the Elderly: The Coast Salish Case." Pp. 47–63 in C. L. Fry (ed.), *Dimensions: Aging, Culture, and Health*. Brooklyn, NY: Praeger.

Amoss, Pamela T., and Stevan Harrell (eds.).
    1981. *Other Ways of Growing Old: Anthropological Perspectives*. Stanford, CA: Stanford University Press.

Angel, J. L.
    1947. "The Length of Life in Ancient Greece." *Journal of Gerontology* 2:18–24.

Angrosino, Michael V.
    1976. "Anthropology and the Aged: A Preliminary Community Study." *The Gerontologist* 16:174–80.

Apple, Dorrian.
    1956. "The Social Structure of Grandparenthood." *American Anthropologist* 58:656–63.

Archbold, Patricia G.
    1982. "All-Consuming Activity: The Family as Caregiver." *Generations* 7:(No.2, Winter)12–13, 40.

Arensberg, Conrad.
    1937. *The Irish Countryman*. Garden City, NY: Natural History Press.

Arensberg, Conrad, and Solon T. Kimball.
    1968. *Family and Community in Ireland* (2nd ed.). Cambridge, MA: Harvard University Press.

Armer, Michael, and Allan Schnaiberg.
    1972. "Measuring Individual Modernity: A Near Myth." *American Sociological Review* 37:301–16.

Arnhoff, F. N., H. V. Leon, and I. Lorge.
    1964. "Cross-Cultural Acceptance of Stereotypes Toward Aging." *Journal of Social Psychology* 63:(June)41–58.

Arth, Malcolm.
   1976. "A Cross-Cultural Perspective." Pp. 352–63 in D. P. Kent, R. Kastenbaum, and S. Sherwood (eds.), *Research Planning and Action for the Elderly.* New York: Behavioral Publications.
   1969. "Ideals and Behavior: A Comment on Ibo Respect Patterns." *The Gerontologist* 8:(No. 4)42–44.
Atchley, Robert C.
   1976. *The Sociology of Retirement.* Cambridge, MA: Schenkman.
Atchley, Robert C., and Sheila J. Miller.
   1982. "Retirement and Couples." *Generations* 7:(No. 2, Winter)28–29, 36.
Axelrod, Morris.
   1956. "Urban Social Structure and Social Participation." *American Sociological Review* 21:13–18.
Bachofen, Johann Jakob.
   1861. *Das Mutterrecht.* Stuttgart: Krais and Hoffman.
Barker, Roger G., and Louise S. Barker.
   1963. "Sixty-five and Over." Pp. 246–72 in R. H. Williams, C. Tibbitts, and W. Donahue (eds.), *Processes of Aging: Social and Psychological Perspectives,* Vol. I. New York: Atherton Press.
Barndt, Deborah.
   1969. "Changing Time Conceptions." *Summation* 1:17–28.
Beattie, Walter M., Jr.
   1983. "Economic Security for the Elderly: National and International Perspectives." *The Gerontologist* 23:406–10.
Beaubier, Jeff.
   1980. "Biological Factors in Aging." Pp. 21–41 in C. L. Fry (ed.), *Aging in Culture and Society.* Brooklyn, NY: J. F. Bergin.
   1976. *High Life Expectancy on the Island of Paros, Greece.* New York: Philosophical Library.
Bell, Wendell, and Marion D. Boat.
   1958. "Urban Neighborhoods and Informal Social Relationships." *American Journal of Sociology* 62:391–98.
Bendix, Reinhard.
   1968. "Proba Definicji Modernizacji (Towards a Definition of Modernization)." *Studia Socjolgiszno Polityczne* 25:31–43.
Benedict, Ruth.
   1934. *Patterns of Culture.* Boston: Houghton Mifflin.
Benet, Sula.
   1974. *Abkhasians: The Long-Living People of the Caucasus.* New York: Holt, Rinehart and Winston.
Bengtson, V. L., J. J. Dowd, D. H. Smith, and A. Inkeles.
   1975. "Modernization, Modernity and Perceptions of Aging: A Cross-Cultural Study." *Journal of Gerontology* 30:688–95.
Bennett, John, and Leo Despres.
   1960. "Kinship and Instrumental Activities: A Theoretical Inquiry." *American Anthropologist* 62:254–67.
Bever, Edward.
   1982. "Old Age and Witchcraft in Early Modern Europe." Pp. 150–90 in P. Stearns (ed.), *Old Age in Preindustrial Society.* New York and London: Holmes & Meier.

Biesele, Megan, and Nancy Howell.
1981. "The Old People Give You Life: Aging Among !Kung Hunter Gatherers."
Pp. 77–98 in P. Amoss and S. Harrell (eds.), *Other Ways of Growing Old:
Anthropological Perspectives.* Stanford, CA: Stanford University Press.

Birket-Smith, Kaj.
1960. *Primitive Man and His Ways.* New York: World.

Bixby, Lenore E.
1976. "Retirement Patterns in the United States: Research and Policy Interaction."
Social Security Bulletin 39:3–19.

Blanchard, Wendell.
1957. *Thailand: Its People, Its Society, Its Culture.* New Haven, CT: Human Relations Area Files.

Blatchford, Joseph H.
1974. "Federal Volunteer Programs." Pp. 16–30 in J. G. Cull and R. E. Hardy
(eds.), *Volunteerism: An Emerging Profession.* Springfield, IL: Thomas.

Blau, Zena Smith.
1973. *Old Age in a Changing Society.* New York: Franklin Watts.

Blumberg, Rae Lesser, and Robert F. Winch.
1972. "Societal Complexity and Familial Complexity: Evidence for the Curvilinear
Hypothesis." *American Journal of Sociology* 77:898–920.

Booth, Charles.
1894. *The Aged Poor in England and Wales.* London: Macmillan.

Borders, William.
1976. "Old Age, a New Problem Troubles Indian Families." *New York Times,*
March 9, p. 4.

Borthwick, Mark.
1977. *Traditional and Bureaucratic Forms of Old Age Assistance in the Truk District,
U.S. Trust Territory of the Pacific Islands.* Report to the U.S. Social Security
Administration.

Bower, H. M.
1974. "Aged Families and Their Problems." Pp. 118–36 in J. Krupinski and A.
Stoller (eds.), *The Family in Australia.* Rushcutters Bay, NSW: Pergamon
Press Australia.

Boyd, Rosamonde R.
1973. "Preliterate Prologues to Modern Aging Roles." Pp. 35–46 in R. R. Boyd
and C. G. Oakes (eds.), *Foundations of Practical Gerontology* (2nd ed., rev.).
Columbia: University of South Carolina Press.

Briffault, Robert Stephen.
1931. *The Mothers: The Matriarchal Theory of Social Origins.* New York: Macmillan.

Brocklehurst, J. C. (ed.).
1975. *Geriatric Care in Advanced Countries.* Baltimore, MD: University Park Press.

Brody, Elaine M., and Abigail Lang.
1982. "They Can't Do It All: Aging Daughters with Aged Mothers." *Generations*
7:(No. 2, Winter)18–20, 37.

Bultena, Gordon.
1974. "Structural Effects on the Morale of the Aged: A Comparison of Age-Segregated and Age-Integrated Communities." Pp. 18–31 in J. F. Gubrium (ed.),
Late Life: Communities and Environmental Policy. Springfield, IL: Thomas.

Burgess, Ernest W. (ed.).
1960. *Aging in Western Societies.* Chicago: University of Chicago Press.

Burgess, Ernest W., and Harvey J. Locke.
  1945. *The Family.* New York: American Book Company.
Butler, Robert N.
  1975. *Why Survive? Being Old in America.* New York: Harper & Row.
Butler, Robert N., and Myrna I. Lewis.
  1976. *Sex After Sixty.* New York: Harper & Row.
Chanler, W. A.
  1896. *Through Jungle and Desert.* London and New York: Macmillan.
Cheit, Earl F.
  1968. "Aging: Economic Aspects." *International Encyclopedia of the Social Sciences* 1:196–202.
Cherry, Ralph L., and Scott Magnuson-Martinson.
  1981. "Modernization and the Status of the Aged in China: Decline or Equaliza-tion?" *The Sociological Quarterly* 22:253–61.
Clark, Margaret.
  1972a. "Cultural Values and Dependency in Later Life." Pp. 263–74 in D. O. Cow-gill and L. D. Holmes (eds.), *Aging and Modernization.* New York: Appleton-Century-Crofts.
  1972b. "An Anthropological View of Retirement." Pp. 117–55 in F. Carp (ed.), *Retirement.* New York: Human Sciences Press.
Clark, Margaret, and Barbara Gallatin Anderson.
  1967. *Culture and Aging.* Springfield, IL: Thomas.
Clark, Margaret, and M. Mendelson.
  1969. "Mexican-American Aged in San Francisco: A Case Description." *The Ger-ontologist* 9:90–95.
Cohn, Richard M.
  1982. "Economic Development and Status Change of the Aged." *American Journal of Sociology* 87:1150–61.
Collins, June McCormick.
  1974. *Valley of the Spirits: The Upper Skagit Indians of Western Washington.* Seattle and London: University of Washington Press.
Colson, Elizabeth, and Thayer Scudder.
  1981. "Old Age in Gwembe District, Zambia." Pp. 125–54 in P. Amoss and S. Harrell (eds.), *Other Ways of Growing Old: Anthropological Perspectives.* Stan-ford, CA: Stanford University Press.
Cool, Linda Evers.
  1980. "Ethnicity and Aging: Continuity Through Change for Elderly Corsicans." Pp. 149–69 in C. L. Fry (ed.), *Aging in Culture and Society.* Brooklyn, NY: J. F. Bergin.
Cool, Linda Evers, and Justine McCabe.
  1983. "The 'Scheming Hag' and the 'Dear Old Thing': The Anthropology of Aging Women." Pp. 56–68 in J. Sokolovsky (ed.), *Growing Old in Different Cul-tures.* Belmont, CA: Wadsworth.
Copeland, L. S.
  1978. "Worldwide Developments in Social Security." *Social Security Bulletin* 41:3–8.
Cottrell, Fred.
  1960. "The Technological and Societal Basis of Aging." Pp. 92–119 in C. Tib-bitts (ed.), *Handbook of Social Gerontology.* Chicago: University of Chicago Press.
Coughenour, C. Milton.
  1969. "Modernization, Modern Man and Social Change: Issues and Perspectives." Paper presented at meeting of the Rural Sociological Society, San Francisco.

Cowgill, Donald O.
  1977. "The Revolution of Age." *The Humanist* 37:(No. 5, September–October)10–16.
  1974. "Aging and Modernization: A Revision of the Theory." Pp. 123–45 in J. F. Gubrium (ed.), *Late Life*. Springfield, IL: Thomas.
  1972a. "The Role and Status of the Aged in Thailand." Pp. 91–101 in D. O. Cowgill and L. D. Holmes (eds.), *Aging and Modernization*. New York: Appleton-Century-Crofts.
  1972b. "Aging in American Society." Pp. 243–61 in D. O. Cowgill and L. D. Holmes (eds.), *Aging and Modernization*. New York: Appleton-Century-Crofts.
  1968. "The Social Life of the Aged in Thailand." *The Gerontologist* 8:159–63.
  1965. "The Demography of Aging in the Midwest." Pp. 275–310 in A. M. Rose and W. A. Peterson (eds.), *Older People and Their Social World*. Philadelphia: F. A. Davis.
Cowgill, Donald O., and Lowell D. Holmes (eds.).
  1972. *Aging and Modernization*. New York: Appleton-Century-Crofts.
Cumming, Elaine, and William E. Henry.
  1961. *Growing Old: The Process of Disengagement*. New York: Basic Books.
Davies, David.
  1972. *A Dictionary of Anthropology*. New York: Crane, Russak & Company.
Davis, Dona Lee.
  1979. "Women's Status and Experience of Menopause in a Newfoundland Fishing Village." Paper presented at meeting of the American Anthropological Association, Cincinnati, November.
Dawson, Miles Menander.
  1915. *The Ethics of Confucius*. New York: Putnam's.
de Beauvoir, Simone.
  1973. *The Coming of Age*. New York: Warner Paperback Library.
de Young, John.
  1958. *Village Life in Modern Thailand*. Berkeley and Los Angeles: University of California Press.
Doberauer, Walter.
  1981. "The History of Geriatrics in Austria." Pp. 46–48 in *International Federation on Ageing, The U.N. Assembly on the Elderly and the Situation of the Elderly in Austria*. Washington, D.C.: International Federation on Ageing.
Donahue, Wilma, Harold L. Orbach, and Otto Pollak.
  1960. "Retirement: The Emerging Social Pattern." Pp. 330–406 in C. Tibbitts (ed.), *Handbook of Social Gerontology*. Chicago: University of Chicago Press.
Dore, R. P.
  1969. "The Modernizer as a Special Case: Japanese Factory Legislation, 1882–1911." *Comparative Studies in Society and History* 11:(No. 4, October)433–50.
Dowd, James J.
  1980. *Stratification Among the Aged*. Monterey, CA: Brooks/Cole.
Earle, Leon.
  1980. "Housing Relocation of the Aged: Effects on Social Interaction." Ph.D. dissertation, Monash University, Melbourne, Australia.
Eaton, Joseph W.
  1964. "The Art of Living and Dying." *The Gerontologist* 4:(No. 2, Pt. 1)94–100, 103, 112.
Eisenstadt, Shmuel Noah.
  1971. *Social Differentiation and Stratification*. Glenview, IL: Scott, Foresman.
  1966. *Modernization: Protest and Change*. Englewood Cliffs, NJ: Prentice-Hall.

Elliott, H. W.
  1886. *Our Arctic Province: Alaska and the Seal Islands.* New York: Scribner's.
Etzioni, Amitai, and Eva Etzioni.
  1964. *Social Change: Sources, Patterns, Consequences.* New York: Basic Books.
Fandetti, Donald V., and Donald E. Gelfand.
  1976. "Care of the Aged: Attitudes of White Ethnic Families." *The Gerontologist* 16:544–49.
Finley, Gordon E.
  1982. "Modernization and Aging." Pp. 511–23 in T. Field, A. Huston, H. Quay, L. Troll, and G. E. Finley (eds.), *Review of Human Development.* New York: Wiley-Interscience.
  1981. "Aging in Latin America." *Spanish-Language Psychology* 1:223–48.
Firth, Raymond, Jane Hubert, and Anthony Forge.
  1970. *Families and Their Relatives: Kinship in a Middle-Class Sector of London.* New York: Humanities Press.
Fischer, David Hackett.
  1977. *Growing Old in America.* New York: Oxford University Press.
Flint, M.
  1976. "Transcultural Influences in Peri-Menopause." Pp. 41–56 in A. A. Haspels and H. Musaph (eds.), *Psychosomatics in Peri-Menopause.* Lancaster, Boston, The Hague: MTP Press.
Folsom, Joseph Kirk.
  1943. *The Family and Democratic Society.* New York: Wiley.
Foner, Anne, and David Kertzer.
  1978. "Transitions over the Life Course: Lessons from Age-Set Societies." *American Journal of Sociology* 83:1081–1104.
Fowler, David H., Lois Josephs Fowler, and Lois Lamdin.
  1982. "Themes of Old Age in Preindustrial Western Literature." Pp. 19–45 in P. Stearns (ed.), *Old Age in Preindustrial Society.* New York: Holmes & Meier.
Frank, Andre Gunder.
  1969. *Latin America: Underdevelopment or Revolution.* New York: Monthly Review Press.
Freedman, Maurice.
  1958. *Lineage Organization in Southeastern China.* London: The Athlone Press.
Friedmann, Eugene A., and Robert J. Havighurst.
  1954. *The Meaning of Work and Retirement.* Chicago: University of Chicago Press.
Fuller, Charles Edward.
  1972. "Aging Among Southern African Bantu." Pp. 51–72 in D. O. Cowgill and L. D. Holmes (eds.), *Aging and Modernization.* New York: Appleton-Century-Crofts.
Fung, Yu-lon.
  1952. *History of Chinese Philosophy.* Princeton, NJ: Princeton University Press.
Galbraith, John Kenneth.
  1958. *The Affluent Society.* Boston: Houghton Mifflin.
Garkovich, Lorraine.
  1976. "A Pilot Study of the Dispersal and Assimilation of Indochinese Refugees." Ph.D. dissertation, University of Missouri, Columbia.
Giddings, Franklin Henry.
  1900. *Democracy and Empire.* New York: Macmillan.
Glascock, Anthony P., and Susan L. Feinman.
  1981. "Social Asset or Social Burden: Treatment of the Aged in Non-Industrial Societies." Pp. 13–31 in C. L. Fry (ed.), *Dimensions: Aging, Culture, and Health.* Brooklyn, NY: Praeger.

Glick, Paul C.
1977. "Updating the Life Cycle of the Family." *Journal of Marriage and the Family* 39:5–13.
Goldschmidt, Walter.
1954. *Ways of Mankind.* Boston: Beacon Press.
Goldstein, Melvin C., and Cynthia M. Beall.
1982. "Indirect Modernization and the Status of the Elderly in a Rural Third World Setting." *Journal of Gerontology* 37:743–48.
1981. "Modernization and Aging in the Third and Fourth World: Views from the Rural Hinterland in Nepal." *Human Organization* 40:48–55.
Goode, William.
1963. *World Revolution and Family Patterns.* New York: Free Press.
Goodfellow, D. M.
1968. "The Applicability of Economic Theory to So-Called Primitive Communities." Pp. 55–65 in E. E. LeClair and H. K. Schneider (eds.), *Economic Anthropology.* New York: Holt, Rinehart and Winston.
Goody, Jack.
1976. "Aging in Nonindustrial Societies." Pp. 117–29 in R. H. Binstock and E. Shanas (eds.), *Handbook of Aging and the Social Sciences.* New York: Van Nostrand Reinhold.
Gordon, Margaret S.
1963. "Income Security Programs and the Propensity to Retire." Pp. 430–58 in R. H. Williams, C. Tibbitts, and W. Donahue (eds.), *Processes of Aging,* Vol. II. New York: Atherton Press.
Grattan, F. J. H.
1948. *An Introduction to Samoan Custom.* Apia, Western Samoa: Samoa Printing and Publishing Company.
Gruman, Gerald J.
1966. *A History of Ideas About the Prolongation of Life.* Philadelphia: The American Philosophical Society.
Gubrium, Jaber.
1973. *The Myth of the Golden Years: A Socioenvironmental Theory of Aging.* Springfield, IL: Thomas.
Guemple, Lee.
1983. "Growing Old in Inuit Society." Pp. 24–28 in J. Sokolovsky (ed.), *Growing Old in Different Cultures.* Belmont, CA: Wadsworth.
Gutmann, David.
1969. "The Country of Old Men: Cross-Cultural Studies in the Psychology of Later Life." *Occasional Papers in Gerontology,* Number 5. Ann Arbor: University of Michigan.
Haanes-Olsen, L.
1974. "Housing Allowances for Old-Age Pensioners." *Social Security Bulletin* 37:36–41.
Haber, David.
1979. "Impressions of Old Age in China." *Aging* Nos. 301–302(November–December):7–9.
Halley, Edmund.
1963. "An Estimate of the Degrees of Mortality of Mankind." *Philosophical Transactions of the Royal Society of London* 16:596–610.
Hamer, John H.
1972. "Aging in a Gerontocratic Society: The Sidamo of Southwest Ethiopia." Pp. 15–30 in D. O. Cowgill and L. D. Holmes (eds.), *Aging and Modernization.* New York: Appleton-Century-Crofts.

Har-Paz, Hayim.
1978. *Characteristics, Attitudes and Needs of the Old People in Tel-Aviv-Yafo.* Tel-Aviv-Yafo, Israel: Tel-Aviv-Yafo Municipality and Israel Gerontological Society.
Harrell, Stevan.
1981. "Growing Old in Rural Taiwan." Pp. 193–210 in P. Amoss and S. Harrell (eds.), *Other Ways of Growing Old: Anthropological Perspectives*, Stanford, CA: Stanford University Press.
Harris, Louis, and Associates.
1981. *Aging in the Eighties: America in Transition.* Washington, D.C.: National Council on Aging.
1975. *The Myth and Reality of Aging in America.* Washington, D.C.: National Council on Aging.
Havighurst, Robert J.
1978. "Aging in Western Society." Pp. 15–44 in D. Hobman (ed.), *The Social Challenge of Ageing.* New York: St. Martin's Press.
1960. "Life Beyond Family and Work." Pp. 299–353 in E. W. Burgess (ed.), *Aging in Western Societies.* Chicago: University of Chicago Press.
Havighurst, Robert J., and Ruth Albrecht.
1953. *Older People.* New York: Longman.
Hay, D. G.
1975. "Profiles of Three Nursing Homes and a Long-Term Hospital in Scandinavia." *The Gerontologist* 15:297–303.
Hendricks, Jon.
1982. "The Elderly in Society: Beyond Modernization." *Social Science History* 6:321–45.
Herskovits, Melville J.
1968. "Economizing and Rational Behavior." Pp. 41–55 in E. E. LeClair and H. K. Schneider (eds.), *Economic Anthropology.* New York: Holt, Rinehart and Winston.
1952. *Economic Anthropology.* New York: Knopf.
Hiebert, Paul G.
1981. "Old Age in a South Indian Village." Pp. 211–26 in P. Amoss and S. Harrell (eds.), *Other Ways of Growing Old: Anthropological Perspectives.* Stanford, CA: Stanford University Press.
Hill, Reuben.
1970. *Family Development in Three Generations.* Cambridge, MA: Schenkman.
Hilton, James.
1934. *Lost Horizon.* New York: W. Morrow.
Hoebel, E. Adamson.
1972. *Anthropology: The Study of Man* (4th ed.). New York: McGraw-Hill.
Holmes, Lowell D.
1983. *Other Cultures, Elder Years: An Introduction to Cultural Gerontology.* Minneapolis: Burgess.
1980. "Anthropology and Age: An Assessment." Pp. 272–84 in C. L. Fry (ed.), *Aging in Culture and Society.* Brooklyn, NY: J. F. Bergin.
1972. "The Role and Status of the Aged in Changing Samoa." Pp. 73–89 in D. O. Cowgill and L. D. Holmes (eds.), *Aging and Modernization.* New York: Appleton-Century-Crofts.
Holmes, Lowell D., and Ellen C. Rhoads.
1983. "Aging and Change in Modern Samoa." Pp. 119–29 in J. Sokolovsky (ed.), *Growing Old in Different Cultures.* Belmont, CA: Wadsworth.

Honigman, John Joseph.
  1963. *Understanding Culture.* New York: Harper & Row.
Hornum, Barbara.
  1983. "The Elderly in British New Towns: New Roles, New Networks." Pp. 211–24 in J. Sokolovsky (ed.), *Growing Old in Different Cultures.* Belmont, CA: Wadsworth.
Howells, William W.
  1960. "Estimating Population Numbers through Archaeological and Skeletal Remains." Pp. 158–85 in R. F. Heizer and S. F. Cook, *The Application of Quantitative Methods in Archaeology.* Chicago: Quadrangle Books.
Hsu, Francis L. K.
  1961. *Psychological Anthropology: Approaches to Culture and Personality.* Homewood, IL: Dorsey Press.
  1949. "The Family in China." Pp. 73–92 in R. Anshen (ed.), *The Family: Its Function and Destiny.* New York: Harper & Brothers.
Ikels, Charlotte.
  1980. "The Coming of Age in Chinese Society: Traditional Patterns and Contemporary Hong Kong." Pp. 80–100 in C. L. Fry (ed.), *Aging in Culture and Society.* Brooklyn, NY: J. F. Bergin.
Inkeles, Alex, and David H. Smith.
  1970. "The Fate of Personal Adjustment in the Process of Modernization." *International Journal of Comparative Sociology.* 11:81–114.
International Federation on Ageing.
  1978. *Mandatory Retirement: Blessing or Curse?* Washington, D.C.: International Federation on Ageing.
  1976. *The Voluntary Agency as an Instrument of Social Change: Effective Advocacy on Behalf of the Ageing.* Washington, D.C.: International Federation on Ageing.
  1975. *Home Help Services for the Ageing Around the World.* Washington, D.C.: International Federation on Ageing.
International Social Security Association.
  1973. "Women and Social Security—Study of the Situation in Five Countries." *International Social Security Review* 26:73–134.
Johnson, Colleen Leahy.
  1983. "Interdependence and Aging in Italian Families." Pp. 92–103 in J. Sokolovsky (ed.), *Growing Old in Different Cultures.* Belmont, CA: Wadsworth.
Jonas, Karen and Edward Wellin.
  1980. "Dependency and Reciprocity: Home Health Aid in an Elderly Population." Pp. 217–38 in C. L. Fry (ed.), *Aging in Culture and Society.* Brooklyn, NY: J. F. Bergin.
Kagan, Dianne.
  1980. "Activity and Aging in a Colombian Peasant Village." Pp. 65–79 in C. L. Fry (ed.), *Aging in Culture and Society.* Brooklyn, NY: J. F. Bergin.
Kahn, A. J., and S. B. Kamerman.
  1976. *Social Services in International Perspective.* Washington, D.C.: U.S. Government Printing Office.
Kalish, Richard A., and Sam Yuen.
  1971. "Americans of East Asian Ancestry: Aging and the Aged." *The Gerontologist* 11:(No. 1, Pt. 2, Spring) 36–47.
Kamerman, S. B.
  1976. "Community Services for the Aged: The View from Eight Countries." *The Gerontologist* 16:529–37.

Kamnuansilpa, Peerasit.
1975. "The Relation Between Family Structure and Fertility in Thailand." Ph.D. dissertation, University of Missouri, Columbia.
Kane, Robert L., and Rosalie A. Kane.
1977. *Long-Term Care in Six Countries: Implications for the United States.* Washington, D.C.: U.S. Government Printing Office.
Kardiner, Abram.
1945. *The Psychological Frontiers of Society.* New York: Columbia University Press.
Kaufman, Harold Deva.
1960. *Bangkuad: A Community Study in Thailand.* Locust Valley, NY: J. J. Augustin.
Keesing, Felix Maxwell.
1958. *Cultural Anthropology.* New York: Holt, Rinehart and Winston.
Keith, Jennie.
1982. *Old People as People: Social and Cultural Influences on Aging and Old Age.* Boston: Little, Brown.
1980. "The Best Is Yet to Be: Toward an Anthropology of Age." Pp. 339–64 in B. J. Siegel, A. R. Beals, and S. A. Tyler (eds.), *Annual Review of Anthropology.* Palo Alto, CA: Annual Reviews.
Kellogg, Mary Alice, and Andrew Jaffe.
1976. "Old Folks Commune." *Newsweek* (April 19)97–98.
Kennedy, Robert E., Jr.
1973. *The Irish: Emigration, Marriage, and Fertility.* Berkeley/Los Angeles/London: University of California Press.
Kertzer, David, and Oker B. B. Madison.
1981. "Women's Age-Set Systems in Africa: The Latuka of Southern Sudan." Pp. 109–30 in C. L. Fry (ed.), *Dimensions: Aging, Culture, and Health.* Brooklyn, NY: Praeger.
Kiefer, Christie W.
1974a. *Changing Cultures and Changing Lives.* San Francisco: Jossey-Bass.
1974b. "Lessons from the Issei." Pp. 167–97 in J. Gubrium (ed.), *Late Life.* Springfield, IL: Thomas.
Kii, Toshi.
1976. "Aging in Japan: Policy Implications of the Aging Population." Ph.D. dissertation, University of Minnesota, Minneapolis.
Kingshill, Konrad.
1960. *Ku Daeng: The Red Tomb.* Chiengmai, Thailand: The Prince Royal's College.
Kinsey, Alfred C., Wardell B. Pomeroy, and Clyde E. Martin.
1948. *Sexual Behavior in the Human Male.* Philadelphia: Saunders.
Kinsey, Alfred C., Wardell B. Pomeroy, Clyde E. Martin, and Paul H. Gebhard.
1953. *Sexual Behavior in the Human Female.* Philadelphia and London: Saunders.
Kirkpatrick, Clifford.
1955. *The Family as Process and Institution.* New York: Ronald Press.
Kolodrubetz, Walter W.
1974. "Employee-Benefits Plans, 1972." *Social Security Bulletin* 37:15–21.
Koo, Ja-soon.
1977. "Older People in Three-Generation Families in Korea." Master's thesis, University of Missouri, Columbia.
Krige, E. J.
1950. *Social System of the Zulus.* London: Shuter and Shooter.
Kuper, Hilda.
1947. *An African Aristocracy.* London: Oxford University Press.

Laslett, Peter.
  1976. "Societal Development and Aging." Pp. 87–116 in R. H. Binstock and E. Shanas (eds.), *Handbook of Aging and the Social Sciences*. New York: Van Nostrand Reinhold.
Laslett, Peter, and R. Wall.
  1972. *Household and Family in Past Time*. Cambridge: Cambridge University Press.
Leaf, Alexander.
  1975. *Youth in Old Age*. New York: McGraw-Hill.
  1973. "Every Day Is a Gift When You Are Over 100." *National Geographic* 143:(January)93–119.
Lee, Shu-Ching.
  1953. "China's Traditional Family: Its Characteristics and Disintegration." *American Sociological Review* 18:272–80.
Le Play, Frederic.
  1874. *L'Organisation de la Famille*. Paris: Tequi, Bibliothecaire de L'Oeuvre Saint-Michel.
Lerner, Daniel.
  1968. "Modernization: Social Aspects." *International Encyclopedia of the Social Sciences* 10:386–95.
  1958. *The Passing of Traditional Society: Modernizing the Middle East*. New York: Free Press.
LeVine, Robert A.
  1965. "Intergenerational Tensions and Extended Family Structures in Africa." Pp. 188–204 in E. Shanas and G. Streib (eds.), *Social Structure and the Family: Generational Relations*. Englewood Cliffs, NJ: Prentice-Hall.
Levy, Marion J., Jr.
  1966. *Modernization and the Structure of Societies*. Princeton, NJ: Princeton University Press.
  1965. "Aspects of the Analysis of Family Structure." Pp. 1–62 in A. Coale, L. A. Fallers, M. J. Levy, D. M. Schneider, and S. S. Tomkins, *Aspects of the Analysis of Family Structure*. Princeton, NJ: Princeton University Press.
Lewis, Oscar.
  1963. *Life in a Mexican Village: Tepoztlan Restudied*. Urbana: University of Illinois Press.
Lindenmeyr, Adele.
  1982. "Work, Charity, and the Elderly in Late-Nineteenth Century Russia." Pp. 232–47 in P. Stearns (ed.), *Old Age in Preindustrial Society*. New York and London: Holmes & Meier.
Linton, Ralph.
  1942. "Age and Sex Categories." *American Sociological Review* 7:589–603.
Lipman, Aaron.
  1970. "Prestige of the Aged in Portugal: Realistic Appraisal and Ritualistic Deference." *The International Journal of Aging and Human Development* 1:127–36.
  1961. "Role Conceptions and Morale of Couples in Retirement." *Journal of Gerontology* 16:267–71.
Litwak, Eugene.
  1960. "Occupational Mobility and Extended Family Cohesion." *American Sociological Review* 25:9–21.
Lowie, Robert H.
  1947. *Primitive Society*. New York: Liveright.
  1930. "Age Societies." *Encyclopaedia of the Social Sciences* 1:482–83.
MacLeod, W. C.
  1931. "Gerontocracies." *Encyclopaedia of the Social Sciences* 6:637–38.

Maeda, Daisaku.
  1978. "Ageing in Eastern Society." Pp. 45–72 in D. Hobman (ed.), *The Social Challenge of Ageing.* New York: St. Martin's Press.
Manes, Alfred.
  1932. "Insurance: Principles and History." *Encyclopaedia of the Social Sciences* 8:95–98.
Marshall, Lorna.
  1976. "Sharing, Talking and Giving." Pp. 349–71 in R. B. Lee and I. DeVore (eds.), *Kalahari Hunter Gatherers: Studies of !Kung San and Their Neighbors.* Cambridge, MA: Harvard University Press.
Masuda, Kokichi.
  1975. "The Domestic Cycle in Three-Generation Japanese Families." *Konan Daigaku Kiyo* 16:48–67.
Matras, Judah.
  1973. *Populations and Societies.* Englewood Cliffs, NJ: Prentice-Hall.
Maxwell, Robert J., and Philip Silverman.
  1970. "Information and Esteem: Cultural Considerations in the Treatment of the Elderly." *Aging and Human Development* 1:361–92.
Mazess, R. B., and S. H. Forman.
  1979. "Longevity and Age Exaggeration in Vilcabamba, Ecuador." *Journal of Gerontology* 34:94–98.
McConnell, John W.
  1960. "Aging and the Economy." Pp. 489–520 in C. Tibbitts (ed.), *Handbook of Social Gerontology.* Chicago: University of Chicago Press.
McKain, Walter C.
  1972. "The Aged in the USSR." Pp. 151–65 in D. O. Cowgill and L. D. Holmes (eds.), *Aging and Modernization.* New York: Appleton-Century-Crofts.
McLennan, John Ferguson.
  1886. *Studies in Ancient History.* London and New York: Macmillan.
Medvedev, Zhores A.
  1974. "Caucasus and Altay Longevity: A Biological or Social Problem?" *The Gerontologist* 14:381–87.
Mencher, Joan P.
  1965. "The Nayars of South Malabar." Pp. 163–91 in M. F. Nimkoff (ed.), *Comparative Family Systems.* Boston: Houghton Mifflin.
Miller, Delbert C., and William H. Form.
  1951. *Industrial Sociology.* New York: Harper & Row.
Milne, Mary Lewis.
  1924. *The Home of an Eastern Clan: A Study of the Palaungs of the Shan States.* Oxford: Clarendon Press.
Missine, Leo E.
  1982. "Elders Are Educators." *Perspective on Aging* 11:(No. 6, November–December)5–8.
Moore, Frank W.
  1968. "Current Trends in Cross-Cultural Research." Pp. 469–74 in UNESCO, *The Social Sciences: Problems and Orientations.* The Hague: Mouton/UNESCO.
Moore, Sally Falk.
  1978. "Old Age in a Life-Term Social Arena: Some Chagga of Kilimanjaro in 1974." Pp. 23–76 in B. G. Myerhoff and A. Simic (eds.), *Life's Career— Aging: Cultural Variations on Growing Old.* Beverly Hills, CA: Sage.
Moore, Wilbert E.
  1979. *World Modernization: The Limits of Convergence.* New York: Elsevier.

Morgan, Leslie A.
1976. "A Re-Examination of Widowhood and Morale." *Journal of Gerontology* 31:687–95.
Morgan, S. Philip, and Kiyosi Hirosima.
1983. "The Persistence of Extended Family Residence in Japan: Anachronism or Alternative Strategy?" *American Sociological Review* 48:269–81.
Murdock, George P.
1957. "World Ethnographic Sample." *American Anthropologist* 59:664–87.
1949. *Social Structure.* New York: Macmillan.
Myerhoff, Barbara G.
1978. "A Symbol Perfected in Death: Continuity and Ritual in the Life and Death of An Elderly Jew." Pp. 163–206 in B. G. Myerhoff and A. Simic (eds.), *Life's Career—Aging: Cultural Variations on Growing Old.* Beverly Hills, CA: Sage.
Myerhoff, Barbara G., and Andrei Simic.
1978. *Life's Career—Aging: Cultural Variations on Growing Old.* Beverly Hills, CA: Sage.
Nadel, Siegfried Frederick.
1951. *The Foundations of Social Anthropology.* Glencoe, IL: Free Press.
Nahemow, Nina.
1983. "Grandparenthood in Baganda: Role Option in Old Age?" Pp. 104–15 in J. Sokolovsky (ed.), *Growing Old in Different Societies: Cross-Cultural Perspectives.* Belmont, CA: Wadsworth.
1979. "Residence, Kinship and Social Isolation Among the Aged Baganda." *Journal of Marriage and the Family* 41:171–83.
Nahemow, Nina, and Bert N. Adams.
1974. "Old Age Among the Baganda: Continuity and Change." Pp. 147–66 in J. Gubrium (ed.), *Late Life.* Springfield, IL: Thomas.
Nash, Manning.
1968. "Economic Anthropology." *International Encyclopedia of the Social Sciences* 4:359–65.
Nason, James D.
1981. "Respected Elder or Old Person: Aging in a Micronesian Community." Pp. 155–74 in P. Amoss and S. Harrell (eds.), *Other Ways of Growing Old: Anthropological Perspectives.* Stanford, CA: Stanford University Press.
National Statistical Office.
1970. *Population and Housing Census, 1970.* Bangkok, Thailand: National Statistical Office.
Nelson, Gary, and Nguyen Dang Liem.
1982. *International Conference on Cross-Cultural Sensitivity to the Needs of Asian and Pacific Elderly.* Honolulu: University of Hawaii School of Social Work.
Nimkoff, Meyer F. (ed.).
1965. *Comparative Family Systems.* Boston: Houghton Mifflin.
Noam, E.
1975. *Homes for the Aged: Supervision and Standards.* Washington, D.C.: U.S. Government Printing Office.
Ogburn, William F., and Clark Tibbitts.
1933. "The Family and Its Functions." Pp. 661–708 in President's Research Committee on Recent Social Trends, *Recent Social Trends in the United States,* Vol. I. New York: McGraw-Hill.
Olson, Philip.
1981. "Institutional Care of the Elderly in the People's Republic of China." Paper

presented at meeting of The Gerontological Society of America, Toronto, November 8–12.

Orbach, Harold.
1962. "Normative Aspects of Retirement." Pp. 53–63 in C. Tibbitts and W. Donahue (eds.), *Social and Psychological Aspects of Aging*. New York: Columbia University Press.

Oriol, William E.
1982. *Aging in All Nations: A Special Report on the United Nations World Assembly on Aging, Vienna, Austria, July 26–August 6, 1982*. Washington, D.C.: National Council on Aging.

Palmore, Erdman.
1975a. "What Can the U.S. Learn from Japan About Aging?" *The Gerontologist* 15:64–67.
1975b. *The Honorable Elders*. Durham, NC: Duke University Press.

Palmore, Erdman, and Kenneth Manton.
1974. "Modernization and Status of the Aged: International Comparisons." *Journal of Gerontology* 29:205–10.

Pampel, Fred C. and Jane A. Weiss.
1983. "Economic Development, Pension Policies, and the Labor Force Participation of Aged Males: A Cross-national, Longitudinal Approach." *American Journal of Sociology* 89:350–72.

Pampel, Fred C.
1981. *Social Change and the Aged*. Lexington, MA, and Toronto: Lexington Books.

Parish, William L., and Mosche Schwartz.
1972. "Household Complexity in Nineteenth Century France." *American Sociological Review* 37:154–73.

Parsons, Talcott.
1964. "Evolutionary Universals in Society." *American Sociological Review* 29:339–57.
1960. "Toward a Healthy Maturity." *Journal of Health and Human Behavior.* 1:163–73.
1954. "The Kinship System of the Contemporary United States." Pp. 89–93 in T. Parsons, *Essays in Sociological Theory*, Vol. II. New York: Free Press.
1942. "Age and Sex in the Social Structure of the United States." *American Sociological Review* 7:604–16.

Peace, Sheila M.
1981. *An International Perspective on the Status of Older Women*. Washington, D.C.: International Federation on Ageing.

Pendrell, Nan.
1979. "Old Age Around the World." Pp. 304–08 in J. Hendricks and C. D. Hendricks (eds.), *Dimensions of Aging: Readings*. Cambridge, MA: Winthrop.

Phillips, Herbert.
1965. *Thai Peasant Personality*. Berkeley and Los Angeles: University of California Press.

Pihlblad, C. Terence, Eva Beverfeld, and Haktor Helland.
1972. "Status and Role of the Aged in Norwegian Society." Pp. 227–42 in D. O. Cowgill and L. D. Holmes (eds.), *Aging and Modernization*. New York: Appleton-Century-Crofts.

Pospisil, L.
1963. *Kapauku Papuan Economy*. New Haven, CT: Yale University Publications in Anthropology.

Presthus, Robert.
1964. *Men at the Top: A Study in Community Power*. New York: Oxford University Press.

Quadagno, Jill.
1982. *Aging in Early Industrial Society: Work, Family, and Social Policy in Nineteenth Century England.* New York: Academic Press.
Queen, Stuart A., and Robert W. Habenstein.
1974. *The Family in Various Cultures* (4th ed.). Philadelphia: Lippincott.
Radcliffe-Brown, Alfred Reginald, and Daryll Forde (eds.).
1950. *African Systems of Kinship and Marriage.* London and New York: Oxford University Press.
Redfield, Robert.
1947. "The Folk Society." *American Journal of Sociology* 52:293–308.
Reichal-Dolmatoff, Gerardo.
1951. *Los Kogi: Una Tribu de la Sierra Nevada de Santa Marta, Colombia.* Bogota: Editorial Iquelma.
Reichard, Suzanne, Florine Livson, and Paul G. Peterson.
1962. *Aging and Personality.* New York: Wiley.
Rhoads, Ellen C.
1982. "The Impact of Modernization on the Aged in American Samoa." Pp. 9–10 in G. Nelson and N. D. Liem (eds.), *International Conference on Cross-Cultural Sensitivity to the Needs of Asian and Pacific Elderly.* Honolulu: University of Hawaii School of Social Work.
Riley, Matilda White, and Anne Foner.
1968. *Aging and Society, Vol. I: An Inventory of Research Findings.* New York: Russell Sage Foundation.
Riley, Matilda White, Marilyn Johnson, and Anne Foner.
1972. *Aging and Society, Vol. III: A Sociology of Age Stratification.* New York: Russell Sage Foundation.
Roheim, Geza.
1926. *Social Anthropology, A Psycho-Analytic Study in Anthropology and a History of Australian Totemism.* New York: Boni and Liveright.
Rosenmayr, Leopold, and Eva Köckeis.
1965. *Umwelt und Familie alter Menschen.* Neuwied am Rhein und Berlin: Hermann Luchterhand Verlag GmbH.
1963. "Propositions for a Sociological Theory of Aging and the Family." *International Social Science Journal* 15:410–26.
Rosow, Irving.
1974. *Socialization to Old Age.* Berkeley: University of California Press.
·Rosset, Edward.
1964. *Aging Process of Population.* New York: Macmillan.
Rostow, W. W.
1960. *The Stages of Economic Growth.* Cambridge: Cambridge University Press.
Roth, Walter E.
1897. *Ethnological Studies Among the North-West-Central Queensland Aborigines.* Brisbane: E. Gregory, Government Printer.
Sanday, Peggy R.
1974. "Female Status in the Public Domain." Pp. 189–206 in M. Z. Rosaldo and L. Lamphere (eds.), *Woman, Culture, and Society.* Stanford, CA: Stanford University Press.
Scheper-Hughes, Nancy.
1983. "Deposed Kings: The Demise of the Rural Irish Gerontocracy." Pp. 130–46 in J. Sokolovsky (ed.), *Growing Old in Different Cultures.* Belmont, CA: Wadsworth.
Schulz, James H.
1980. *The Economics of Aging,* 2d. ed. Belmont, CA: Wadsworth.

1976. "Income Distribution and the Aging." Pp. 561–91 in R. H. Binstock and E. Shanas (eds.), *Handbook of Aging and the Social Sciences*. New York: Van Nostrand Reinhold.

Schweitzer, Marjorie M.
1983. "The Elders: Cultural Dimensions of Aging in Two American Indian Communities." Pp. 168–78 in J. Sokolovsky (ed.), *Growing Old in Different Cultures*. Belmont, CA: Wadsworth.

Selby, Philip, and Mal Schechter.
1982. *Aging 2000: A Challenge for Society*. Lancaster, Boston, The Hague: MTP Press.

Shahrani, M. Nazif.
1981. "Growing in Respect: Aging Among the Kirghiz of Afghanistan." Pp. 175–92 in P. Amoss and S. Harrell (eds.), *Other Ways of Growing Old: Anthropological Perspectives*. Stanford, CA: Stanford University Press.

Shanas, Ethel.
1962. *The Health of Older People: A Social Survey*. Cambridge, MA: Harvard University Press.

Shanas, Ethel, Peter Townsend, Dorothy Wedderburn, Henning Friis, Poul Milhøj, and Jan Stehouwer.
1968. *Old People in Three Industrial Societies*. New York: Atherton Press.

Sharp, Henry S.
1981. "Old Age Among the Chipewyan." Pp. 99–110 in P. Amoss and S. Harrell (eds.), *Other Ways of Growing Old: Anthropological Perspectives*. Stanford, CA: Stanford University Press.

Sheehan, Tom.
1976. "Senior Esteem as a Factor of Societal Economic Complexity." *The Gerontologist* 16:433–40.

Shelton, Austin J.
1972. "The Aged and Eldership Among the Igbo." Pp. 31–50 in D. O. Cowgill and L. D. Holmes (eds.), *Aging and Modernization*. New York: Appleton-Century-Crofts.
1968. "Igbo Child-raising, Eldership, and Dependence: Further Notes for Gerontologists and Others." *The Gerontologist* 8:236–41.
1965. "Ibo Aging and Eldership: Notes for Gerontologists and Others." *The Gerontologist* 5:(No. 1, Pt. 1, March)20–23, 48.

Siegel, Jacob S.
1976. "Demographic Aspects of Aging and the Older Population in the United States." *Current Population Reports*, Series P-23, No. 59, U.S. Bureau of the Census.

Silverman, Philip, and Robert J. Maxwell.
1983. "The Role and Treatment of the Elderly in 95 Societies." Pp. 43–55 in J. Sokolovsky (ed.), *Growing Old in Different Cultures*. Belmont, CA: Wadsworth.

Simic, Andrei.
1978. "Winners and Losers: Aging Yugoslavs in a Changing World." Pp. 77–106 in B. G. Myerhoff and A. Simic (eds.), *Life's Career—Aging: Cultural Variations on Growing Old*. Beverly Hills, CA: Sage.
1977. "Aging in the United States and Yugoslavia: Contrasting Models of Intergenerational Relationships." *Anthropological Quarterly* 50:53–64.

Simmel, Georg.
1907. *Philosophie des Geldes*. Leipzig: Duncker & Humblot.

Simmons, Leo.

    1960. "Aging in Preindustrial Societies." Pp. 62–91 in C. Tibbitts (ed.), *Handbook of Social Gerontology*. Chicago: University of Chicago Press.

    1959. "Aging in Modern Society." Pp. 1–8 in *Toward Better Understanding of the Aging*. Seminar on Aging, Aspen, Colorado, September 8–13, 1958. New York: Council on Social Work Education.

    1945. *The Role of the Aged in Primitive Society*. London: Oxford University Press.

Smith, Rockwell.

    1942. "Hebrew, Greco-Roman, and Early Christian Family Patterns." Pp. 59–71 in H. Becker and R. Hill (eds.), *Marriage and the Family*. Boston: Heath.

Sokolovsky, Jay, and Carl Cohen.

    1983. "The Cultural Meaning of Being a 'Loner' Among the Inner-City Elderly." Pp. 189–201 in J. Sokolovsky (ed.), *Growing Old in Different Cultures*. Belmont, CA: Wadsworth.

    1981. "Being Old in the Inner-City: Support Systems of the SRO Aged." Pp. 163–84 in C. L. Fry (ed.), *Dimensions: Aging, Culture, and Health*. Brooklyn, NY: Praeger.

Sokolovsky, Jay (ed.)

    1983. *Growing Old in Different Cultures*. Belmont, CA: Wadsworth.

Spencer, Paul.

    1965. *The Samburu: A Study of Gerontocracy in a Nomadic Tribe*. Berkeley and Los Angeles: University of California Press.

Stehouwer, Jan.

    1970. "Relations Between Generations and the Three-Generation Household in Denmark." Pp. 337–66 in C. C. Harris (ed.), *Readings in Kinship in Urban Society*. Oxford: Pergamon Press.

    1968. "The Household and Family Relations of Old People." Pp. 177–226 in E. Shanas et al., *Old People in Three Industrial Societies*. New York: Atherton Press.

    1965. "Relations Between Generations and the Three-Generation Household in Denmark." Pp. 142–62 in E. Shanas and G. Streib (eds.), *Social Structure and the Family: Generational Relations*. Englewood Cliffs, NJ: Prentice-Hall.

Stephens, Joyce.

    1976. *Loners, Losers and Lovers: A Sociological Study of the Aged Tenants of a Slum Hotel*. Seattle: University of Washington Press.

Stephenson, John B.

    1968. "Is Everyone Going Modern? A Critique and a Suggestion for Measuring Modernism." *American Journal of Sociology* 74:265–75.

Stolnitz, George J.

    1968. "A Century of International Mortality Trends." Pp. 124–51 in C. B. Nam (ed.), *Population and Society*. Boston: Houghton Mifflin.

Streib, Gordon F.

    1972. "Old Age in Ireland: Demographic and Sociological Aspects." Pp. 167–81 in D. O. Cowgill and L. D. Holmes (eds.), *Aging and Modernization*. New York: Appleton-Century-Crofts.

    1965. "Intergenerational Relations: Perspectives of the Two Generations on the Older Parent." *Journal of Marriage and the Family* 27:469–76.

Streib, Gordon F., and Clement J. Schneider.

    1971. *Retirement in American Society: Impact and Process*. Ithaca, NY: Cornell University Press.

Streib, Gordon F., and Wayne E. Thompson.
  1960. "The Older Person in a Family Context." Pp. 447–88 in C. Tibbitts (ed.), *Handbook of Social Gerontology*. Chicago: University of Chicago Press.
Sussman, Marvin B.
  1976. "The Family Life of Old People." Pp. 218–43 in R. H. Binstock and E. Shanas (eds.), *Handbook of Aging and the Social Sciences*. New York: Van Nostrand Reinhold.
  1959. "The Isolated Nuclear Family: Fact or Fiction." *Social Problems* 6:333–40.
  1953. "The Help Pattern of the Middle Class Family." *American Sociological Review* 18:22–28.
Sussman, Marvin B., and Lee Burchinal.
  1964. "Kin, Family Network: Unheralded Structure in Current Conceptualizations of Family Functioning." *Marriage and Family Living* 24:231–40.
Swanson, Guy E.
  1968. "Frameworks for Comparative Research: Structural Anthropology and the Theory of Action." Pp. 141–202 in I. Vallier (ed.), *Comparative Methods in Sociology*. Berkeley: University of California Press.
Taietz, P.
  1970. "The Extended Family in Transition: A Study of the Family Life of Old People in the Netherlands." Pp. 321–35 in C. C. Harris (ed.), *Readings in Kinship in Urban Society*. Oxford: Pergamon Press.
Thomas, Elizabeth Marshall.
  1959. *The Harmless People*. New York: Knopf.
Tien, H. Y.
  1977. "How China Treats Its Old People." *Asian Profile* 5:1–7.
Tigges, Leann, and Donald O. Cowgill.
  1981. "Aging from the World System Perspective: An Alternative to Modernization Theory." Paper presented at meeting of The Gerontological Society of America, Toronto, November 8–12.
Tipps, Dean C.
  1973. "Modernization Theory and the Comparative Study of Societies: A Critical Perspective." *Comparative Studies in Society and History* 15:199–226.
Tomashevich, George Vid.
  1981. "Aging and the Aged in Various Cultures." Pp. 17–41 in G. Falk, U. Falk, and G. V. Tomashevich (eds.), *Aging in America and Other Cultures*. Saratoga, CA: Century Twenty One Publishing.
Townsend, Peter.
  1968. "The Structure of the Family." Pp. 132–76 in E. Shanas et al., *Old People in Three Industrial Societies*. New York: Atherton Press.
  1957. *The Family Life of Old People*. London: Routledge & Kegan Paul.
Townsend, Peter, and Dorothy Wedderburn.
  1966. *The Aged in the Welfare State*. London: G. Bell.
Treas, Judith.
  1979. "Social Organization and Economic Development in China: Latent Consequences for the Aged." *The Gerontologist* 19:34–43.
Troll, Lillian E.
  1971. "The Family of Later Life: A Decade Review." *Journal of Marriage and the Family* 33:263–90.
Turnbull, Colin M.
  1983. *The Human Cycle*. New York: Simon & Schuster.
  1972. *The Mountain People*. New York: Simon & Schuster.
  1965. *Wayward Servants*. Garden City, NY: Natural History Press.

Uchendu, Victor C.
1965. *The Igbo of Southeast Nigeria.* New York: Holt, Rinehart and Winston.
United Nations.
1982. *Demographic Yearbook, 1980.* New York: United Nations.
1975. *The Aging: Trends and Policies.* New York: UN Department of Economic and Social Affairs.
1970. *Social Security in the Context of National Development.* New York: UN Commission for Social Development.
1962. "Demographic Aspects of Manpower." *Population Studies,* No. 33.
1956. "The Aging of Populations and Its Economic and Social Implications." *Population Studies,* No. 26.
United States Bureau of the Census.
1983. "Marital Status and Living Arrangements: March, 1982." *Current Population Reports,* Series P-20, No. 380.
United States Social Security Administration.
1977. *Social Security Programs Throughout the World.* Office of Research and Statistics, Research Report No. 50. Washington, D.C.: Government Printing Office.
Valaoris, Vasilios G.
1950. "Patterns of Aging of Human Populations." Pp. 67–85 in *Proceedings of the Eastern States Health Education Conference, March 31–April 1, 1949, The Social and Biological Challenge of Our Aging Populations.* New York: Columbia University Press.
Valle, Ramon, and Lydia Mendoza.
1978. *The Elder Latino.* San Diego: The Campanile Press.
Van Arsdale, Peter W.
1981a. "Disintegration of the Ritual Support Network Among Aged Asmat Hunter-Gatherers of New Guinea." Pp. 33–45 in C. L. Fry (ed.), *Dimensions: Aging, Culture, and Health.* Brooklyn, NY: Praeger.
1981b. "The Elderly Asmat of New Guinea." Pp. 111–23 in P. T. Amoss and S. Harrell (eds.), *Other Ways of Growing Old: Anthropological Perspectives.* Stanford, CA: Stanford University Press.
Vatuk, Sylvia.
1982. "Old Age in India." Pp. 70–103 in P. Stearns (ed.), *Old Age in Preindustrial Society.* New York: Holmes and Meier.
1980. "Withdrawal and Disengagement as a Cultural Response to Aging in India." Pp. 126–48 in C. L. Fry (ed.), *Aging in Culture and Society.* Brooklyn, NY: J. F. Bergin.
Velez, Carlos G.
1978. "Youth and Aging in Central Mexico: One Day in the Life of Four Families of Migrants." Pp. 107–62 in B. G. Myerhoff and A. Simic (eds.), *Life's Career—Aging: Cultural Variations on Growing Old.* Beverly Hills, CA: Sage.
Vinick, Barbara.
1977. "Remarriage in Old Age." Ph.D. dissertation, Boston University.
Waisanen, Frederick B.
1968. "Actors, Social Systems, and the Modernization Process." Paper presented at Carnegie Seminar, Indiana University.
Wallerstein, Immanuel.
1979. *The Capitalist World-Economy.* Cambridge: Cambridge University Press.
Warner, W. Lloyd, and J. O. Low.
1946. "The Factory in the Community." Pp. 21–45 in W. F. Whyte (ed.), *Industry and Society.* New York and London: McGraw-Hill.

Warner, W. Lloyd, Marchia Meeker, and Kenneth Eells.
  1960. *Social Class in America*. New York: Harper & Row.
Watson, Wilbur H., and Robert J. Maxwell (eds.).
  1977. *Human Aging and Dying: A Study in Sociocultural Gerontology*. New York: St. Martin's Press.
Weatherford, J. M.
  1981. "Labor and Domestic Life Cycles in a German Community." Pp. 145–61 in C. L. Fry (ed.), *Dimensions: Aging, Culture, and Health*. Brooklyn, NY: Praeger.
Weber, Max.
  1958. *The Protestant Ethic and the Spirit of Capitalism*. New York: Scribner's.
  1920. *Gesammelte Aufsätze zur Religionssoziologie*. Vol. 1. Tübingen: J. C. B. Mohr (Paul Siebeck).
Weihl, Hannah.
  1972. "Selected Aspects of Aging in Israel, 1969." Pp. 197–209 in D. O. Cowgill and L. D. Holmes (eds.), *Aging and Modernization*. New York: Appleton-Century-Crofts.
Werner, D.
  1981. "Gerontocracy Among the Mekranoti of Central Brazil." *Anthropological Quarterly* 54:15–27.
Westermarck, Edward.
  1922. *The History of Human Marriage*. Vol. 2. New York: Allerton.
Whyte, William Foote (ed.).
  1946. *Industry and Society*. New York and London: McGraw-Hill.
Wild, R. A.
  1978. *Social Stratification in Australia*. Sydney: George Allen & Unwin.
Williams, Gerry C.
  1980. "Warriors No More: A Study of the American Indian Elderly." Pp. 101–11 in C. L. Fry (ed.), *Aging in Culture and Society*. Brooklyn, NY: J. F. Bergin.
Williamson, John B., Linda Evans, and Lawrence A. Powell.
  1982. *The Politics of Aging: Power and Policy*. Springfield, IL: Thomas.
Wirth, Louis.
  1938. "Urbanism as a Way of Life." *American Journal of Sociology* 44:1–24.
Wolfbein, Seymour L.
  1963. *Changing Patterns of Working Life*. Washington, D.C.: U.S. Government Printing Office.
Wood, Vivian.
  1982. "Grandparenthood: An Ambiguous Role." *Generations* 7:(No. 2, Winter)22–23, 35.
Yang, C. K.
  1959. *Chinese Communist Society: The Family and the Village*. Cambridge, MA: M.I.T. Press.
Yin, Peter, and Kwok Hung Lai.
  1983. "A Reconceptualization of Age Stratification in China." *Journal of Gerontology* 38:608–13.
Youmans, E. Grant.
  1962. *Leisure-Time Activities of Older Persons in Selected Rural and Urban Areas of Kentucky*. Lexington, KY: Kentucky Agricultural Experiment Station, Progress Report 115.
Young, Michael, and Hilda Geertz.
  1961. "Old Age in London and San Francisco: Some Families Compared." *British Journal of Sociology* 12:124–41.
Young, Michael, and Peter Willmott.
  1957. *Family and Kinship in East London*. London: Routledge & Kegan Paul.

Index

221